AF394374

GRASSLANDS

Also by John Wright

A Natural History of the Hedgerow
The Forager's Calendar
A Spotter's Guide to Countryside Mysteries
A Spotter's Guide to the Countryside
The Observant Walker

GRASSLANDS

The Intricate Life of Britain's Hidden Habitats

JOHN WRIGHT

First published in Great Britain in 2026 by
Profile Books Ltd
29 Cloth Fair
London ECIA 7JQ

www.profilebooks.com

1 3 5 7 9 10 8 6 4 2

Designed and typeset by James Alexander

Printed and bound in Great Britain by
CPI Group (UK) Ltd, Croydon, CRO 4YY

A CIP catalogue record for this book is available from the British Library.

Our product safety representative in the EU is BGC Sustainability & Compliance, 7 avenue du Général Leclerc, Paris, 75014, France
https://baldwinglobalconsulting.com

ISBN 978 1 78125 810 1
eISBN 978 1 78283 340 6

For Madeline

Contents

Introduction

GOD gave all men all earth to love,
But since our hearts are small,
Ordained for each one spot should prove
Belovèd over all.

Rudyard Kipling, 'Sussex' (1902)

Being in love often changes us, and sometimes it comes to define us. The object of our devotion could be a person, a dog, a home or, as with Kipling, a landscape. In his poem 'Sussex' he expresses his love for the cliffs and beaches, woods and vales, of what he felt to be *his* county. For your author the beloved area is much smaller – a single area of chalk downland in West Dorset.

Nearly half a century ago I lived there with my wife in a cottage overlooking its green curves. We were there for three and a half years. She liked it; I loved it deeply. Such devotion can come with a price, however. In this instance, my love for this exquisite expanse of grassland, and the billions of tiny lives it harboured, came with a desperate fear at its proposed destruction.

With a little effort on my part, and some truly heroic work by Natural England, my grassland was mercifully left intact. Its name is Hog Cliff, and it continues to thrive today – as we shall see. But while I was lucky, the truth is that across Britain we are still losing important grasslands, one small bite, one small field, at a time.

This book is not a textbook: it is much more personal than that. A love story, perhaps. I write it as someone who has admired grasslands for nearly half a century. I have mourned their loss and, in a small way, sought to protect them.

As a naturalist and forager, and someone who regularly leads walks across the British countryside, my main subject is fungi. It was the fungi that led me to a deep affection for grasslands, as it is in these rich and overlooked areas that many glorious fungi are to be found. Nevertheless, I have not devoted my working life to grasslands. In writing this book, I have sought out experts in many different fields of endeavour, whether by reading their academic works or reports, or by talking to them directly, sometimes during a walk over the hills or through a meadow. Their insight has added to my own understanding of the landscapes I love and deepened my appreciation for the millions of complex lives that play out there. In sharing their work and my own, I hope to do the same for you.

Despite the terrible losses of grasslands that have occurred over the last hundred years, this is a cheerful book. The losses, although great, have seldom been complete – there is life out there still. Just look.

About ten years ago, and only three miles from my home in West Dorset, an area of lowland dry acid grassland suddenly came under threat. For the seventy years it had spent as the site of a radio transmitter for the BBC World Service it had dodged the plough and been continually sheep-grazed. Left undisturbed for centuries, the short grass was species-rich in both grassland plants and fungi. The fabulously colourful waxcap fungi were notably abundant, with nearly enough species found on a single survey to make the site one of European importance. Purple heathers were scattered in patches among the grasses, and plant species such as the Dwarf Thistle, Slender St John's Wort and Heath Bedstraw were there to delight. Skylarks hovered frantically above, marking out their territory with sound.[1]

Lowland dry acid grassland is rare in the south of England, being mostly confined to the New Forest, so it was quite exceptional. It was not doomed to follow the common fate of other threatened species-rich grasslands – the plough or the attentions of inorganic fertiliser. Instead it was to become a solar farm. I have always been a solar panel enthusiast but believe they *must* be situated in the right place. This location could not have been more wrong.

Moves by conservation bodies, local and national, sought to prevent the development. It was at this point that the views taken by some conservationists and members of the general public were exposed. Few expressed concern, and one person whom I knew to be at least fairly interested in natural history told me that it was worth the sacrifice, even though the area was surrounded by species-poor leys (seeded grasslands for pasture or silage) and species-free arable, neither of which would have suffered ecological loss from such an imposition.

The most shocking response to the prospective loss of this splendid area of grassland, however, was from a member of a conservation body who is reported to have wondered what all the fuss was about: it was 'just a patch of grass', they said. This phrase is so telling that I once considered it as an ironic title for this book.

It was a close-run thing, but after a very great deal of fuss the proposal was dropped by the developer and effectively moved to one of those areas of arable land nearby. The uncomfortable truth is that many people, including even those who are knowledgeable about natural history, do indeed dismiss grasslands. When they are viewed as *just a patch of grass*, then there is no reason for anyone to care about them.

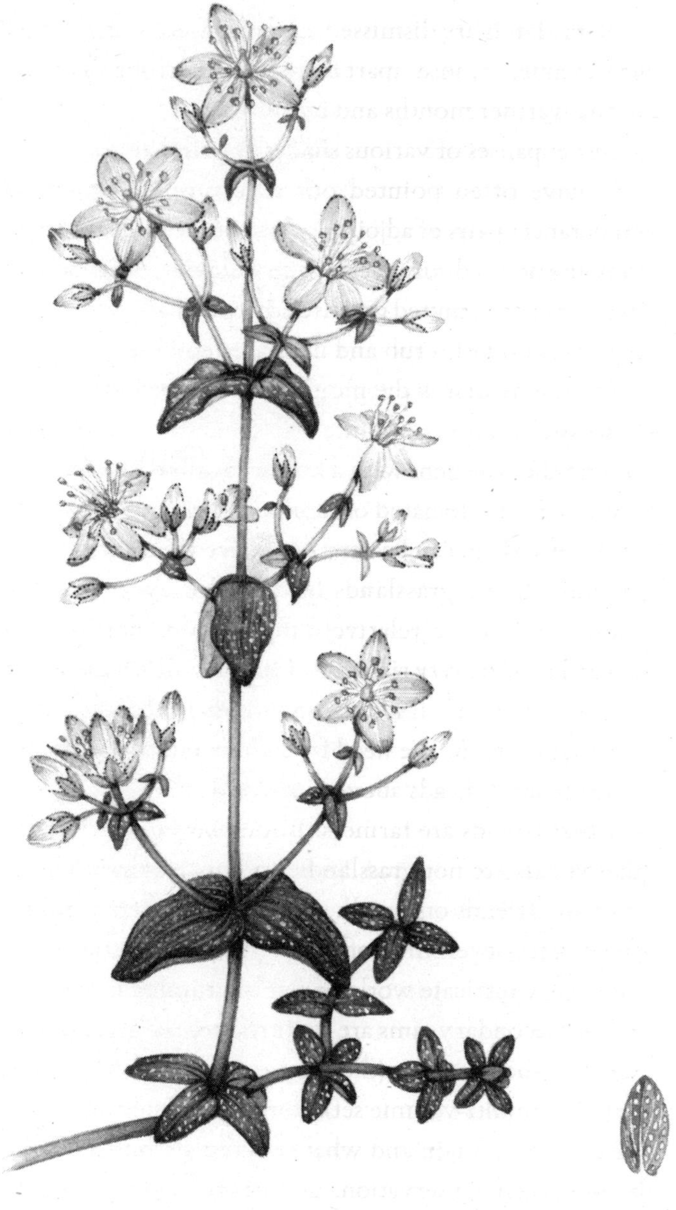

Slender St John's Wort

Grasslands are dismissed as communities of great biodiversity, great value, because, apart from when they are adorned by flowers in the warmer months and by fungi in the autumn, they are seen as just expanses of various shades of green.

I have often pointed out to unsuspecting friends and acquaintances pairs of adjoining fields. One will be a bright emerald, glowing at its admirer across the valley. Its neighbour will be dull in comparison: muted greens and browns all over, patchy, with the occasional bit of scrub and maybe a few flowers at the right time of year. The first is the monocultured, fertilised dud containing Perennial Ryegrass, White Clover and a few weed species, the second the true gem with a hundred or more species of plants and thousands of associated organisms – animal, fungal and more.

Looks, then, can be very deceptive when judging a mere patch of grass. Some grasslands have fooled even grassland experts: those that have a relatively poor representation of plants can nevertheless be *very* rich in fungi. We will see some of these later.

This is not at all a dismissal of agricultural land, even if it is a brilliant green. We need it, and the farmers work hard to keep their financial heads above water and us fed. As they say, some of my best friends are farmers. But however grassy they may look, these fields are not grasslands, and my aim in this book – as it is with my friends on a walk – is to draw your attention away from the surface-level shine of monoculture and introduce you to the gloriously intricate world of semi-natural grasslands.

My secondary aims are to introduce these grasslands in at least some of their variety (though not *all* their variety, which would require a multi-volume set), to relate the story of their loss, what threats still remain and what survives despite it all. We will also explore their conservation, and the entrancing possibility of establishing new ones. Most of all, I hope to show you why we should care.

As I have indicated, areas of 'good' grassland contain more species of plant, fungus, animal and other organisms than can easily be imagined – they buzz and heave with life. This book, then, is an exaltation of complex wonders that demand our appreciation and protection. Species-rich grasslands are, indeed, *not* just patches of grass.

For example, many of the so-called 'microfungi' grow on only one plant (are 'host-specific') or perhaps on only one grouping of plants, such as the trefoils. The more plant species there are in an area, the more fungi there will be, and even a single specimen of a plant may host half a dozen microfungi – something I have seen.

Similarly, an area of rich and varied flora will potentially host (up to) twenty invertebrate species for every plant species found there. So a field where you find twelve different types of plant could be home to many more invertebrates: a veritable world of bees, butterflies, crickets, flies, moths, spiders and so very much more. Invertebrates in general can form upwards of 85 per cent of the number of above-ground species in any one field. Undisturbed by the plough, the soil will also teem with life.

Beyond this, each plant, animal, fungus and other organism will have its own stories to tell, not least about its interactions with others.* There are the parasites such as the many ichneumonid wasps that lay their eggs inside or upon the living bodies of their host, and the hyperparasites that parasitise the parasites; the solitary bees that cut discs from leaves to build their nests; the spider that forms its vertical orb-web low in the grass so that it might catch grasshoppers. There are the plants that depend on

---

* There are organisms found in grasslands that are not animals, plants or fungi: slime moulds, for example.

fungi for their livelihood, while the fungi depend on them. In some long-unploughed grasslands (and regardless of their value in flowering plants) many fungi produce stunning rings that can be many metres across. Then there is the group of fungi on which nearly all grassland plants, indeed most terrestrial plants, depend – a group of microscopic fungi that form an intimate and beneficial relationship with plants: the 'arbuscular mycorrhizal fungi'.

There are puzzles too. Why are plants where they are? How is it that many different species of plant can exist shoulder to shoulder with others when a single vigorous plant could seemingly take over the shop?

It is these marvels and puzzles that make grasslands infinitely fascinating. We should appreciate them in all their glory and seek to protect them.

BEFORE WE BEGIN: A NOTE ON SIZEISM …

While small may, indeed, be beautiful, sizeism is a regrettable affliction of humankind. We are a species that admires organisms that are within a narrow size-range either side of its own, with the upper range for preference. We will ignore small animals unless they are buzzing around our ears, and even when they fall to the fly-spray, we fail to admire the details of their antennae or the complexity of their legs and wings. The same can be said for the details of plants, where the hairiness of stem or leaf, or the sublime intricacies of their flowers, such as pistils, anthers and carpals, are lost in a generalised admiration.

If we were 3 cm tall, we would treasure every plant in a field and write to the council if a Primrose were due for the (mini-) chainsaw. We would have photographs and paintings on our walls of ants, 'forests' of moss and Uncle Sid recklessly climbing the treacherous stem of an Oxeye Daisy or riding an earthworm in the fashion of Paul Atreides. The ecologically disinclined might have their walls adorned with the mounted heads of nematode worms or fungus gnats.

I often hand someone my loupe while leading a walk.* After a considerable amount of trouble getting something in focus (and even in view) the inevitable 'Ooh!' is heard when the intricate details of an ornamented mushroom gill-edge or the florets of a grass come into view. We tend to value only what we can see. Anyone who has looked at pond life under a microscope is likely to have hesitated before throwing the slide with its wonderful creatures into the bin after examination, even though just yesterday they had cheerfully thrown buckets-full of pond water onto their failing potato patch.

Sizeist as we are, large organisms will always be recorded more often than small organisms. An example from mycology makes the situation clear. The Giant Puffball, *Langermania gigantea*, is indeed a giant at 40+ cm in diameter and conspicuously grows in fields where its white skin shines like a beacon. I have seen it in Dorset in perhaps ten locations over the years. It is generally considered to be common, with very many records of its occurrence. However, if one takes, say, a small plant-litter species of 'mushroom', *Hemimycena epichloë*, there are only eight records. The compendious *Fungi of Temperate Europe* describes this species, noting that it is 'Probably rather common, but barely reported'.[2] This regrettably inevitable phenomenon devalues the various databases on which species are recorded, with species under-reported or (arguably) over-reported.

Most organisms are tiny or microscopic and, with some very welcome exceptions, the broadcast media have not helped the understanding of nature as a whole by producing articles and television programmes that tell the stories of predominantly

* A small, high-powered magnifying glass which one holds very near to the eye. Buy one! – ×20 magnification will do nicely.

large organisms: birds, mammals, reptiles and the occasional fish. I love these programmes too, but they do us a great disservice in dealing only with large and charismatic animals. I am still waiting patiently for a BBC epic series entitled 'The Microfungi of Land Plants' or 'Nematode Worms: The True Story'. For now, they merely 'panda' to our prejudices.

My hope, as we take a bug's-eye look at life and descend to the level of grass in these pages, is that you too, dear reader, will begin to see the fascination and wonder of the world beneath our feet and the small creatures and organisms that dwell there.

... AND SOME IMPORTANT HOUSEKEEPING

There is a glossary at the end of the book, but a few terms are worth defining here.

Since **semi-natural grasslands** are the subjects of this book, a definition is in order: semi-natural grasslands are those which consist of unsown vegetation and are maintained by some form of human intervention, for example grazing by livestock or mowing for hay, but have not been substantially modified by intensive agriculture; fertiliser, where it is applied, is usually provided by organic manure; drainage is avoided or consists of shallow surface drains; herbicides are not routinely used.[3] In the UK, the 'official' minimum number of plant species required for a grassland to be counted as 'species-rich' is fifteen in a square metre.[4]

Improved grassland, as the term is used in this book, means 'agriculturally improved', and thus the opposite of conservation, though one can, of course, improve a nature reserve by increasing, say, the percentage of the more valued plants and invertebrates that occur there. Usually, the context makes it clear which sense is being used, but read it as an agricultural improvement if in doubt.

Dividing the flowering plants into those that are neither grasses nor trees has proved difficult. 'Flowering plant' does not distinguish them from grasses as grasses are flowering plants too. The word 'forb' might have been useful for non-grass/non-woody plants but is often restricted to agricultural, with the hint that they are weeds. I have not used this unappealing word here.

For a flowering plant that is not a grass and has no woody parts, I use the familiar **'flower'** or **'wild flower'**.

For those instances where the text refers to *both* grasses and wild flowers, I have used the standard term **'herbaceous'**. While this brings parsley, sage, rosemary and thyme to the mind of many, it does include grasses, though not woody plants.

I have not held back from using technical terms where they might be useful. These are helpful short cuts that make understanding easier and avoid repeated long descriptions. Most are defined on their first mention and again in the glossary.

It is helpful, essential even, to know how organisms are related. Without this understanding, the natural world becomes nothing but 'lots of stuff'. Therefore I will often mention which Genus, Family, Order etc. an organism belongs to and sometimes relate their phylogeny (family tree).

Common names of species have been used where possible. They will be in bold type when the species concerned is first noted as having been found in the *specific location* under discussion. The first time a species is mentioned it will be followed by its Latinised scientific name. For example, in the section describing Horseshoe Bottom in the New Forest I note the occurrence of one of the species found there as **'Black Medick**, *Medicago lupulina*'. Subsequent mentions within that chapter are rendered as 'Black Medick'.

Common names of species will be capitalised to avoid the 'clash of qualifiers' that otherwise occasionally ensues with the lower-case: for example, 'a large small scabious', the 'uncommon common dodder' or 'the pink red campion'. Common names for groups of organisms such as 'trefoils' or 'fescues' will remain lower-case.

I have gone against convention by capitalising the hierarchical names used in taxonomy. So, for example, 'Family' for 'family' and 'Order' for 'order'. This makes their meaning and importance clear, as they have common meanings that can confuse.

I have played fast and loose with the titles 'United Kingdom' and 'Britain'. In fact, this book is applicable to most of north-western Europe, with the United Kingdom being just an example.

Part One

A NATURAL HISTORY OF GRASSLANDS

A Short History of Grass and Grasslands

Quite when grasses first appeared has been a long-standing question, with the date being pushed backwards and backwards again. The notion that they first evolved 50 million years ago gave rise to the idea that no dinosaur was ever troubled (or delighted) by grass. More recently, coprolites (fossilised dung) of dinosaurs have been found containing fossilised grasses.[1] As these had travelled through the gut of a dinosaur, there was little to go on, but the microscopic silica structures that were found suggest that there were already at least five grass species in existence. Some authorities suggest that the history of grasses goes back 100 million years.

All 'true' grasses are in the sub-Family Pooideae, in the Family Poaceae. It is the fifth largest botanical Family in the world, with 'only' around 12,000 species (the Daisy Family boasts twice that number). However, it beats all other Families in the sheer number of plants produced – tall and thin, grasses can pack themselves very tightly. They are the most important of all the plants for human beings as grasses supply 75 per cent of our food – either directly, as with wheat or barley or rice, or indirectly from the grazing of livestock.

In an early novel of the post-apocalyptic genre, *The Death of Grass* (1956), the author, John Christopher, explores what might happen should all of Earth's grasses be lost to a virus. With wheat, barley, oats and pasture all receding into history, nothing good, it seems. Sugar cane and bamboo would disappear, and many would mourn the loss of lemongrass in their curries, but then there would no rice to accompany the dish either. For your author, the loss of barley would be a disaster.

So important were grasses to man, once agriculture was established, that they appear repeatedly in ancient texts, encouraged no doubt by the fact that they were a matter of day-to-day life for agrarian communities. Grass is the first plant to warrant a mention in the Bible – in the first chapter of Genesis, no less. In the King James Version it is rendered as: 'And God said, Let the earth bring forth grass, the herb yielding seed, and the fruit tree yielding fruit after his kind, whose seed is in itself, upon the earth: and it was so.'[2]

In the First Epistle of Peter, the writer reflects on the fragility of life, both life in general and ours in particular: 'For all flesh is grass, and all the glory of man as the flower of grass. The grass withereth, and the flower thereof falleth away.' The author continues, contrasting our fleeting lives with the eternal nature of God.

The word 'grass' has a long heritage from the not easily printed Proto-Indo-European word meaning 'grow' or 'becoming green'. The Latinised word 'poa' and its related nouns are Greek in origin, from *póa*, meaning 'fodder'. A student of, or specialist in, grasses is called an 'agrostologist', deriving via Latin from the Greek for 'pasture', *ágrōstis*. This word reappears in the generic name for the 'bents' or 'bent-grasses', *Agrostis*, which reflects how commonly bents are found in pasture.

GRASSLANDS WORLDWIDE

Grassland, where grasses dominate the landscape in vast swathes, appears to be a relatively recent phenomenon. Huge areas of grasslands only began appearing during the Neocene, a period that ran from 23 million to 2½ million years ago. One reason for this shift in grasslands' fortunes was the change to a cooler and drier climate, itself caused by the creation of enormous dry areas during a period of heroic mountain-building that caused 'rain-shadows' where moisture-laden air did not reach the far sides, leaving only enough rain to support grasslands. Trees were lost, and grasses made a land-grab. There is, of course, a very great deal more to it than this – but we are whizzing through this early history!

The takeover was a tremendous success. The total of world-wide improved arable, natural and semi-natural grasslands now amounts to around 40 per cent of the area of land that is not under permanent ice.[3] Some natural grasslands are (or were) simply enormous. The North American Great Plains, for example, once occupied an area five times that of France. There are hundreds of smaller grasslands that have nevertheless acquired recognition: the Arnhem Land tropical savanna in Australia, the Texas Blackland Prairies, the Middle Eastern steppe that stretches across Jordan, Syria, Iraq and the edge of Iran. There are even aquatic instances such as the large areas of 'floating grassland' of South America and elsewhere.

All of these natural grasslands have their problems. The Texas Blackland Prairies, for example, are a mere remnant of what they once were, with 99 per cent having been lost to farming. Invasion by pernicious weed grasses has also devasted native grasslands: the most troublesome of these is Cheat Grass, *Bromus tectorum*. An alternative name is the less judgemental (to the point of cosy) 'Downy Brome'. It establishes itself in bare patches of soil and quickly spreads, replacing all the resident flowers. It is found in a few locations in Britain but has not proved invasive here.

Grasses, as generally understood, come in two types: 'cool-season grasses' and 'warm-season grasses'. The first are found in temperate climates, the second wherever it is hot and dry. All of the UK's native grasses are cool-season grasses, though many warm-season grasses are to be found in gardens and sometimes on arable farms. Wheat, barley and rye are all cool-season grasses, though maize and sorghum are warm-season grasses.

The family tree of grasses is complex, but this differentiation into two groups of grasses (in fact, it is three) reflects a particularly heroic change within their lineages – that of how they photosynthesise. This is a fascinating subject because precisely *how* so dramatic a change occurred – one mutation or horizontal gene transfer at a time without everything falling to pieces – is difficult to imagine.[4]

THE HISTORY OF BRITISH GRASSLANDS

THE ANCIENT WILDWOOD

The 'green and pleasant land' that is Britain is largely down to its possession of so much grassland, species-rich or not. This amounts to 40 per cent of the land area, forming a patchwork of fields in the lowlands and grand vistas in the uplands.

Quite unlike the grasslands of the savannas, prairies and steppes mentioned above, British grasslands are almost entirely the creation of humans. In a way we should be proud of this as there is no doubt that the diversity of ecological niches in the UK has been increased dramatically over the millennia. But what did grasslands replace?

It has long been thought (and for the most part still is) that once Britain had thawed from the last glacial period, the pioneering grasses, wild flowers and scrub were gradually replaced by dense forest. This is the coast-to-coast 'wildwood' of old. Grasslands would mostly have formed in the resultant clearings when trees fell or were destroyed by fire, and along pathways created by the large mammals that existed for a while after the last ice age. They could also be found on cliff-tops and other extreme places where trees failed to grow.

However, in the year 2000 the eminent Dutch ecologist Frans Vera published a highly controversial book entitled *Grazing Ecology and Forest History*. This challenged the consensus by suggesting that the wildwood that followed the retreat of the ice across temperate Europe was an open one, with large areas of grassland between well-spaced woodlands.

Such a landscape was partially re-created in the 'wood-pasture' system which accounted for a large proportion of the woodland and permanent grassland during the Middle Ages.[5] Here, widely spaced trees were planted and subsequently pollarded at about head-height to provide a 'cut and come again' source of timber. This was used for fires, tool-handles, building and other essentials; in addition, the leaves of cut branches were used for animal fodder. In between the trees there was grassland in the form of permanent pasture. Some wood pastures still exist, and they have an echo in urban parklands.

Vera's hypothesis was based on several observations, the most convincing of which was the challenge faced by the dominant trees of the time – mostly species of oak and hazel: how did they grow on the dark floor of a close canopy woodland? Even when one falls, the established trees will spread their branches to fill the space. Should they grow nevertheless, the hopeful young shoots would quickly be consumed by herbivores.

There were a large number of herbivores in Britain during the Mesolithic period. The number of grazing species was impressive: Aurochsen, Tarpan bison and several different species of deer.* Aurochsen are extinct, and partial ancestors of the cow; the Tarpan is an extinct wild horse. These, Vera argues, would, by both trampling and grazing, have kept any open area free of trees – for a while, at least – allowing for the establishment of grasslands. The

---

* 'Aurochsen' is a plural form: cf. 'oxen'. The alternative is 'aurochs', which is both singular and plural.

result would have been a slowly moving patchwork of grassland and woodland. How, though, do woodlands establish if every sapling, every seedling, is eaten?

Vera's idea was the still observable fact that scrubby areas containing spiny plants that are too troublesome to eat become nurseries for new trees. I have seen this myself, and the phenomenon is described on p. 43. Where herbivores fear to tread (or nibble) among gorse, bramble and briar, saplings can grow unmolested until they are too big to be threatened. I have also seen how quickly trees disappear from open grassland. Most grasslands will host numerous tree seedlings, but I have never known one to grow any higher than 15 cm.

It is a matter of opinion, of course, but I find the idea of great herds of Aurochsen wandering across the open grasslands of Surrey enchanting.

Such a patchwork of grassland, woodland and heath has made the New Forest one of the great jewels in the crown of British species diversity. Indeed this forest was an inspiration for Vera.

I mentioned that Vera's idea was controversial, and indeed arguments for and against have continued for twenty-five years. The arguments against are not, as one might cynically expect, a matter of a refusal to take on new ideas, but are cogent analyses of data, of such things as the palynological records of the time: that is, the distribution and abundance of pollen from involved plant species and the distribution of invertebrates. Beetles, for example, whose tough carapaces can persist for millennia, feature strongly because some live with trees, some with grasses. The dissenters argue that these records are not compatible with Vera's proposal, and that woodlands controlled the number of grazing animals, not the other way round.

Despite its dismissal by most professional ecologists, the siren appeal of Vera's idea has won the hearts of rewilders, and *some* professional ecologists and conservation organisations. What might be created by adopting Vera's evident ideas of 'leaving it to nature' in rewilding efforts could be good or bad – either a thriving, balanced ecosystem with many interacting species or a mess of tangled weeds and starving animals. Proof one way or another would require a reproduction of all or most of the conditions and biota prevailing at the time and on a large scale. This is, frankly, neither possible nor desirable. We will, however, see one such 'experiment' later.

THE HISTORY OF AGRICULTURE IN THE UK

Grasslands, even the most species-rich and beautiful, are almost always artificial, a product of mankind's interference with or destruction of established communities. So many books have been written about the history of British agriculture (most of which appear to be on my shelves), and the matter is so complex, that I feel at liberty to provide only the faintest of sketches. With Vera's ideas gaining only mild support among academics, this sketch assumes the existence of a virtually coast-to-coast wildwood.

Land clearance began with the Mesolithic (10,000 BCE to 4,300 BCE) peoples who arrived soon after the ice retreated. The generally accepted view is that Mesolithic people did create clearings, though these were not agricultural in the sense we understand but part of an enhanced hunting strategy. An area in the woodland would be cleared and the resulting growth of herbaceous plants and tree saplings would entice grazing animals in. Here they could be more easily hunted. The clearings also allowed the growth of plants rarely seen in woodlands, and it is possible that some of these plants were introduced intentionally. Animals would soon have become wary of such clearings and moved on, meaning that new clearings had to be made. This resulted in a patchwork within woodlands, though abandoned clearings would most likely revert to woodland.

Agriculture as we *do* know it was introduced by new arrivals of people in the Neolithic period (4,300 BCE to 2,000 BCE), who cleared large areas of forest. With agriculture come pasture and cornfields, with crop rotation between the two. By the end of the following Bronze Age and through much of the Iron Age, arrays of so-called 'Celtic' fields patchily covered much of Britain that was suitable for agriculture.* Their fields are known from aerial photographs, LiDAR (Light Detection and Ranging) images and archaeological digs, and many still exist or are conspicuously evident from embankments and ditches.

The subsequent millennia saw a waxing and waning of grassland as the climate changed back and forth. A great deal of the waning occurred in cold periods, when formerly wooded upland grasslands were abandoned because of their loss of agricultural value, resulting in wet heath, blanket bog and scrub. ('Blanket bog' is a type of wet moorland underlaid with peat.) Several periods with warm climatic conditions produced resurgences in agriculture, with permanent or rotational pasture alongside arable. When the climate became cold, there was famine, the last major famine being in the early fourteenth century CE, the same century that later saw the arrival of the Black Death. During this time, attempts were made to increase yields by ploughing pastured hillsides, resulting in the terraces known as 'strip lynchets' that are still a striking feature of our landscape today. The Black Death saw a dramatic reduction in agriculture as there was insufficient manpower to tend the land. This resulted in a great deal of abandonment with permanent grasslands turning to scrublands. Suffice to say that, as a climate varies, its people, just like their

---

* The word 'Celtic' is now seriously out of date as many such field systems pre-date the Celts.

grasslands, either suffer or thrive.

Climate is not the only consideration: there is also economics. The feudal 'open field system' was the primary agricultural model in central England and parts of Wales from Saxon times until the mid-nineteenth century. Most of the farmed land was held in common: that is, certain people would have rights to farm certain areas and amounts within a manor. The land would be divided into two, three or four fields that were farmed in rotation. There would also be the grasslands of meadow and perhaps some permanent pasture. There was also the 'waste', where there was some grazing and also woodland and coppice. Grass and grassland flowers also grew between the strips, known as 'selions', and at the 'head', where the plough was turned. These would be grazed along with the stubble. A similar arrangement within the feudal system was made for much of the rest of the countryside, the so-called 'wooded countryside', such as in Devon, much of it being pasture – hence its famous cream.

It is difficult to quantify the comings and goings of semi-natural grasslands over this extended period. There were certainly gains when the open field system was (very slowly) abandoned. The feudal system of farming began its long decline almost as soon as it was born, falling slowly to the notorious practice of 'inclosure'.*

Chiefly in the Tudor period, but also long before that, inclosure was invoked to turn the land over to sheep farming. Many fortunes (and our cathedrals) were made on the back of this bounty, with the peasantry losing out. With the open fields removed from arable, permanent grassland increased in extent. Many such grasslands were later lost when corn prices rose in the

---

* 'Inclosure' is a legal term referring to the removal of the rights of the farm workers to use the land previously held in common – in this way, they were dispossessed. 'Enclosure' is a fence or hedge that encloses land, though it is often used instead of 'inclosure'.

early nineteenth century and sheep walks fell again to the plough.

The vast areas of upland grasslands that are in the west of Britain and in the north were largely, but by no means entirely, intractable wastelands as far as arable farming was concerned; they were too wet, too exposed and impossible to plough. Many were areas of rough grazing of varying quality, interspersed with bog and heath. These changed but little over the centuries, only recently suffering major ecological problems from sheep over-grazing, cattle under-grazing, aerial pollution, unhelpful drainage and poor management.

Many of us set our 'baseline' dates to a glorious age when every field buzzed with life, every cornfield and meadow shone like a rainbow and the springy turf of chalk downland sprang. William Cobbett set his Golden Age around the time of his birth, 1763, giving him a head start when later complaining that things were not what they used to be. Tempted as I am to suggest 1951 for my own Golden Age, I know that this is too recent and subject to something known as 'baseline syndrome'. In the context of biodiversity, this is the pernicious misapprehension of when matters were at their best, so that we know what to aim for. However, and as we will see shortly, my 1951 date does more or less mark the beginning of most of the losses suffered over the last two hundred years.

Types of Species-Rich Grassland

The number of different types of grassland in the UK is enormous. The National Vegetation Classification (NVC) system (of which much more later) covers most of the plant communities in Britain, and one of its five constituent books describes the thirty-seven grassland communities.[6] Many of these embrace variations in the form of sub-communities, so the number could easily be trebled.

Which grassland type occurs in any particular place depends primarily on climate, soil and geological substratum, hydrology (drainage or lack thereof) and management. Some of these variables are reflected in the familiar categories of grassland: lowland meadow and pasture, lowland calcareous (limestones, but mostly chalk), upland calcareous, upland hay meadow, rush pasture, lowland acid grassland, upland acid grassland and floodplain grazing marsh. These encompass most of the primary grassland types, with multiple variations within each category.

Not all grasslands are interesting, with 'improved grassland' (intensively cultivated grassland) not being interesting at all. The concept of 'priority habitats' is useful here. Upland acid grassland is *not* generally designated as being a priority habitat, while chalk downland, meadows and wetlands etc. certainly are. The issue with upland acid grassland is mostly that it is what one is left with when species-rich mires are drained and heathland burned or heavily grazed. Also, it is relatively plant-species-poor. This, however, does not necessarily indicate that a site is of no or little interest. One or two of the grasslands described here fail to meet the target of a rich flora but are of high value in the number of associated organisms, most particularly the fungi they may host.

The Loss of Species-Rich Grasslands

It was a most lamentable thing that the paper-money price of corn tempted so many men to break up these fine pastures; that the turf thus destroyed cannot be restored in a whole century.

William Cobbett, *Rural Rides* (1833)

William Cobbett wrote the above words in 1833, so grassland loss can hardly be considered an entirely modern phenomenon. However, this was just one of the many swings to and fro between pasture and arable throughout history. This can happen short-term, through crop rotation or simply ploughing pasture or meadow, or long-term, as has occurred with the chalk downlands of southern England. In Cobbett's case it was Salisbury Plain, a large, flat area of chalk grassland that would have been very rich in species (much of it, in fact, still is). Relatively few of our semi-natural grasslands are truly ancient, with chalk downlands being one that certainly is. The fate of Salisbury Plain was not an isolated event but one suffered by pasture all over the country. Why were the sheep evicted, and why was so much ploughed? It was a matter of money and simple practicality – though mostly money.

In 1833 the issue was the high price of corn, which in this context refers to any cereal crop – wheat, barley, oats, rye or maize. Prices had rocketed because of protectionist tariffs imposed by the highly unpopular Corn Laws, which were in force between 1815 and 1846. Those who were protected were not the working classes of town and country, of course, but the landowners. In the wake of the Napoleonic Wars, cheap corn had flooded in from abroad, depressing domestic prices. The Corn Laws had been introduced to deal with this problem by blocking, or imposing high tariffs on, imports – but their effect was to artificially raise corn prices to an extraordinary degree.

The poor suffered greatly. In the late eighteenth century and the first half of the nineteenth, the working classes in general spent around 75 per cent of their total income on food. Of this, over 60 per cent was for the purchase of bread, amounting to nearly half their total spend.[7] A modern household on, say, £40,000 per year net would not appreciate spending £18,000 on bread! It is interesting to note that William Cobbett's grandfather left only a riphook as a legacy. One can see why.

HOW MUCH LOSS?

The most common answer is that we have lost 97 per cent of all priority grasslands over the past hundred years – an astonishing amount. This much-quoted figure originally came from a paper published in 1987 by R. M. Fuller, which was based on data gathered between 1930 and 1984.[8] So catastrophic a figure makes one wonder if it is true, but unfortunately it appears to be broadly correct, though there are some caveats. The most important of these is that Fuller's study involved only lowland England and Wales, missing out all upland grasslands, priority or not, and all of Scotland. Nevertheless, the 97 per cent figure still stands.

The more hopeful corollary of 'What has been lost?' is 'What still remains?' Sadly, there is no simple answer: this is a contentious issue with different definitions and methodologies producing wildly different figures. In the UK as a whole, around 137,000 ha of priority grasslands still exist, according to a recent report by Plantlife.[9] Those 137,000 ha amount to 1 per cent of the area of the UK – a little less than that of Greater London. In contrast, the government assessment of semi-natural grasslands tells us that they form 10 per cent of the area of the UK: that is, 2.5 million ha. But this includes the vast areas of upland acid grassland plus some that are species-poor.[10] Statistics should be considered with care.

And so we return to the question of loss. Fuller's paper was published in 1984, so one must ask if there are any more recent reports. Happily, there is a remarkable one from 2019 by Lucy Ridding and co-authors that relates the degree, rates and causes of loss, encompassing the eighty-five years from 1930 to 2015.[11] Like Fuller's work, it deals with lowland semi-natural grasslands, with the difference being that it covers only Dorset in southern England. The authors nevertheless suggest that the results are indicative of the situation in many parts of Europe. Certainly, the technical innovations and farming policies have been similar throughout the EU. Dorset has, in fact, been used as a model by several academics over the years, and we will see it used again later.

To produce their paper, Ridding and her co-authors needed data points. Most particularly, a baseline was needed. And this was provided by an astonishing collection of records made by a certain Ronald Good in 1930. When I discovered the reference, I immediately turned to my bookshelves to find his *Geographical Handbook of the Dorset Flora*. I see that it cost me £2 in a second-hand bookshop. Based on a remarkable collection of annotated maps of Dorset, it is the public face of many years of fieldwork.

Each map shows the locations of plant species recorded by the author. In total, Good visited 7,575 sites evenly spread over the rural parts of Dorset. He collected records of 600 of a total of the 1,300 plant species found in the county. Unimproved grasslands were not the only habitats considered: broad-leaved woodlands, fens, marshes and swamps were also surveyed. Each site, incidentally, is charmingly and appropriately known as a 'Good site'. During two and a half years of survey work he collected 285,864 records of these plants.[12]

Together with four more sets of records from 1950, 1980, 1990 and 2015 Good's survey gives an excellent overview of what there once was, how species and communities have fared and at what rates the changes progressed. To put matters into context, the authors of the 2019 paper looked at the other side of the coin by including arable, improved grassland, coniferous plantation and urban development – those things that most of the Good sites had become.

Much had already been lost in the years since mechanisation took serious hold in the 1940s, owing to the need to grow a great deal more food. However, it was from 1950 that most of the losses occurred. Good's book engenders a great sense of sadness in that most of his sites are lost to us, especially when one considers that rural Dorset has fared comparatively well. In those days all of Dorset buzzed with life.

The Ridding study used (most of) the sites of ecological inter-est recorded by Good, classifying them as: acid grassland, calcare-ous grassland, neutral grassland, heathland, fen plus marsh and swamp, and broad-leaved woodland. Small fields of 0.5 ha or less were not included. As these are often vulnerable to improvement, it may be that the losses reported are underestimates.

The only type of ecologically friendly land-use to do well in the Ridding study was broad-leaved woodland, follow-ing a nationwide trend away from coniferous plantations. There is only bad news after this. The sites of acid grassland dropped by more than 50 per cent, and the number of sites of calcareous grassland (on chalk and harder limestones) from nearly 700 to just 200, with the study more precisely reporting a 62 per cent loss. Fen, marsh and swamp fell from 300 sites to a little over 100, and neutral grasslands fell off a cliff, going from over 400 to a mere 12, with the 97 per cent loss rearing its ugly head again. Neutral grasslands are mostly traditional hay meadows and easy pickings for 'improvement' to arable or monoculture grass.

With all but the fens etc. there was a long decline that steadily levelled out, which is just what one would expect for a limited resource. There were other influences that tended to flatten the curves, such as the introduction of Sites of Special Scientific Interest (SSSIs) and similar habitat/species conservation efforts.

Even the merest of glances at the graphs for arable, coniferous woodland, improved grassland and urban tells us the fate of Good's sites: most show more or less the same general shape of curve as what they replaced, except that they are inverted. The most conspicuous is arable, where 400 of the 500 sites known to Good have been ploughed for corn.

The change from semi-natural grasslands (good) to improved grasslands (bad) showed a steady trend upwards throughout. This greatly increased the yields for pasture, or in leys that can be grazed, used for silage or for hay. All this has been achieved either by ploughing, reseeding and fertilising the land or by more subtle management, mostly by the application of fertilisers. This results in grasslands where the existing flora are outperformed by vigorous grasses, leading to a massive loss of the more welcome plants. It is interesting to note how many of Good's sites suffered in this way: from none to nearly one thousand. To put this in a broader context, 13 million ha of improved grassland now exist in England and only 100,000 ha of unimproved semi-natural grasslands, which is less than 1 per cent. The steepest decline occurred between 1930 and 1980, with the greatest overall losses between 1950 and 1980. A mere 38 per cent of the sites studied by Good still remain.

The only encouraging message in the Ridding paper described

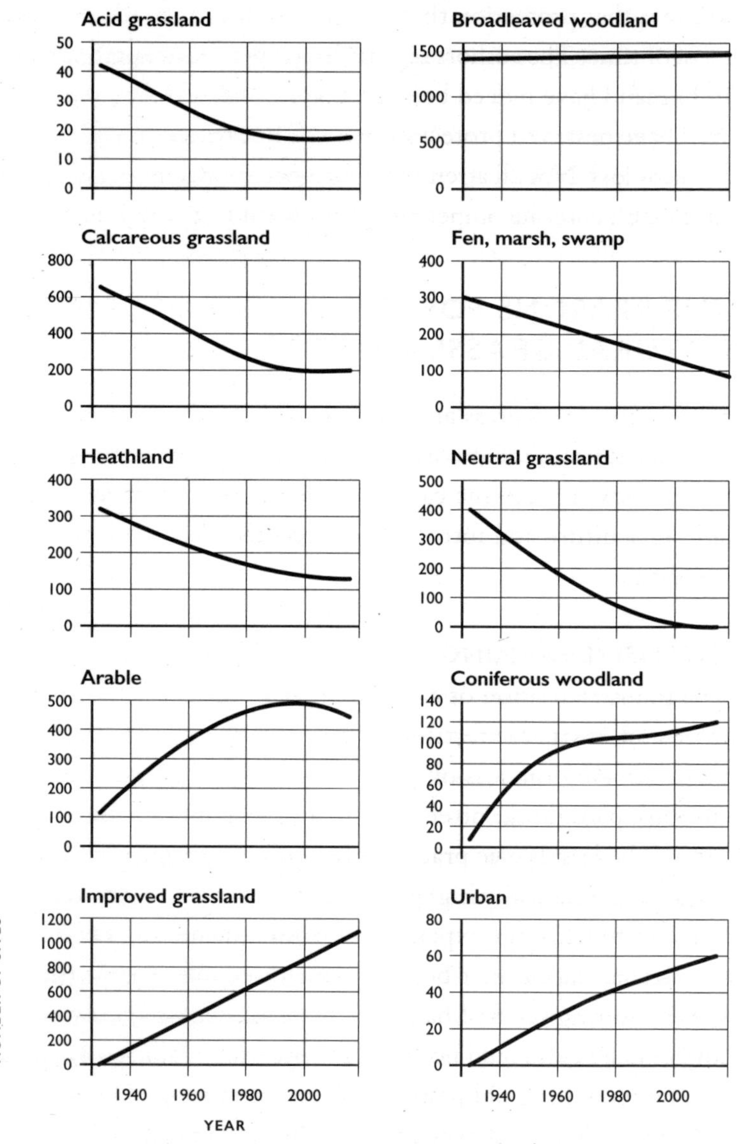

The number of sites for each semi-natural habitat (acid grassland, broadleaved woodland, calcareous grassland, fen, marsh and swamp, heathland, neutral grassland) and intensive land use type (arable, coniferous woodland, improved grassland, urban) across Dorset (confidence estimates omitted for clarity).

above is that protection through the establishing of SSSIs works most of time. The authors report that 91 per cent of protected sites in England have indeed been protected, whereas sites that might well have deserved protection but did not receive it suffered a 73 per cent loss. Not all attempts to protect important grasslands are successful: enter incompetent government intervention.

THE REASONS FOR THE DEMISE OF SEMI-NATURAL GRASSLANDS

If the history of grasslands in the twentieth century is one of decline, a decline that continues into the twenty-first, then it is worth looking into the causes. Here I revisit the issue of intensive agriculture and introduce the regrettably long list of other culprits.

INTENSIVE FARMING

The industrialisation of agriculture, and with it the wide availability of inorganic fertilisers, has been the primary economic factor driving the loss of grasslands. Most losses have occurred through ploughing, often preceded by the application of herbicides. The less drastic practice of simply fertilising a field would produce dramatically higher yields of grass for fodder or grazing, but very much at the expense of the finer grasses and flowers.

Mechanisation first became a major problem for wildlife in general during the first half of the twentieth century. Previously intractable fields could now be ploughed with relative ease, and a ban on ploughing old pasture was removed in 1939.[13] Such practices have continued ever since, with some very serious kit now available to the farmer.

Technology is not the only major driver of farming practice: government policy has had a massive hand in directing agriculture. During the Second World War ploughing for corn, and indeed other crops, came at the legal insistence of the British government in what was termed the 'Great Harvest' or 'plough up'. Britain *needed* to grow its own food.

In 1947 the Agricultural Act introduced subsidies, and price guarantees to encourage expansion have continued ever since, though most have now gone and they will be discontinued completely by 2027. In the 1950s my erstwhile landlord at Hog Cliff, the subject of Part Three, was told by a man from the ministry to 'Take your plough around the farm, Commander Eyre'. The results of this are still evident seventy years later in the form of areas with tall grasses and low numbers of flowers.

In 1973 Britain joined the European Economic Community (EEC), now the European Union (EU). Britain had already lost a very great deal of its semi-natural grasslands by this time, and the Common Agricultural Policy of first the EEC and later the EU continued this pattern by heavily subsidising farming in the late 1970s and well beyond.[14] The geniuses who devised the system did such a good job with their financial incentives that food mountains and wine and milk lakes became a matter of considerable public concern and indeed mockery. As suggested by the milk lakes, it was not just a move of agriculture towards intensive arable farming but also the wholesale establishment of the leys that enabled a vast increase in pasture, hay and silage.

In the late 1980s in West Dorset there was a 2 ha field of good-quality chalk downland that I visited every now and then. There was a financial incentive at the time to grow flax under a CAP scheme, and the field was duly ploughed (probably for the first time in a couple of thousand years) and sowed. However, the payment was made for the *sowing*, not the harvest. Once sowed, the crop was left to grow and subsequently rot in the field. Thirty years later the field is still a scrubby shadow of its former species-rich glory. This is just one tiny example of the casual loss of important grasslands, albeit an exceptionally telling example.

Efforts to draw back from this excess were first introduced in the UK in 1987 with the idea of Environmentally Sensitive Areas (ESAs). This was after the egregious débâcles under the (now) EU's food policy of heavy farming subsidies. However, only very high-quality biologically diverse land had any sort of protection under the ESA scheme, leaving only 10 per cent of the land protected. This approach was by no means a failure, but it was also not the greatest of successes.

Government interventions very often have unanticipated and unwelcome consequences. They also suffer from contradictory rules and different premises between the relevant departments or quangos. In a passage in a 2010 report commissioned by the European Forum on Nature Conservation and Pastoralism, the author and grassland specialist Miles King said most of what we need to know about such matters. There is no requirement to know who the players are or precisely what the issues were to see what a mess the system was in:

> The EIA [Environmental Impact Assessment] Directive definitions of semi-natural bear no relationship to the Natura 2000 Directives; CAP definitions of permanent pasture do not coincide with EIA and the relationship to the Natura 2000 Directives is more apparent through Pillar II than Pillar I of the CAP. The concept of 'highly biodiverse grasslands' introduced by the Renewable Energy Directive does not coincide with the terminology and definitions of the EIA Directive, of Natura 2000 or of the CAP.[15]

The result of the bodies involved having different and often contradictory aims, and of countries within the EU applying the rules governing support payments and protections in different ways, was that semi-natural grasslands suffered. The Good Agricultural Environment Conditions rules, for example, could have the effect of disallowing payments on semi-natural grasslands to the point of encouraging their clearance. In some countries, large areas of biologically interesting permanent pastures were under threat or lost because they were not registered under CAP.

POLLUTION

We are all familiar with the idea of pollution in the air – if not, a few deep breaths beside a dual carriageway will allow you to instantly appreciate its reality. Aerial pollution from motor vehicles, industrial processes and farming itself has caused serious problems in general, and to species-rich grasslands in particular.

Pollution occurs chiefly in the forms of sulphur compounds and nitrogen compounds (the oxides of nitrogen, and ammonia). The most damaging sulphur compound is sulphur dioxide, a noxious gas that acidifies soils.[16] This can be detrimental to plants that require neutral or alkaline soils, and also to acid grasslands where the highly sensitive lichens and bryophytes (mosses and liverworts) are badly affected to the point of local extinction. Such acidification leads to the dominance of acidophiles over less acid-tolerant plants, almost invariably causing loss of plant diversity.

Nitrogen increases the fertility of the soil, something that is anathema to semi-natural grasslands as it leads to the dominance of vigorous, nutrient-loving species that overwhelm the established populations very quickly. Nitrogen also acidifies soils and with severe contamination can destroy a grassland completely.

One further pollutant is relevant here: ammonia, another nitrogen compound. This is most generally produced by petrol and diesel engines, and more locally from the breakdown of ammonium nitrate fertiliser in the soil and from over-aromatic slurry pits. The effect is to increase the fertility of the soil by the nitrates that are formed from dissolved ammonia. This will cause the preferential growth of over-vigorous weed species of wild flowers and grasses. The total output of ammonia from vehicles alone is equivalent to ten units of nitrogen fertiliser per hectare, which is very approximately equivalent to one-fifteenth of that required for a grass ley. Combined with nitrogen from other sources, this is a sufficient quantity to tip the nutrient-poor soil demanded by species-rich grassland into unwelcome fertility.[17]

The good news here is that the situation is considerably better than it once was in the UK. Various governments have legislated against pollution, something made easier by the dramatic loss of industrial manufacturing in the UK, the closing of coal mines and a reduction in such pollution from gas-fired power stations. Mercifully, sulphur dioxide pollution has dropped by an astonishing 96 per cent, mostly since the 1990s.[18] Over the period from 2007 to 2019, soil pH has risen slightly (i.e. it has become more alkaline). This is a positive change, though the rise is more pronounced in intensively farmed grasslands than in semi-natural grasslands. Nitrogen oxide levels have also dropped very considerably, except those created by agriculture. Ammonia pollution has dropped a little and is still a problem for the countryside.

Another form of pollution is quick and very dramatic – run-off from intensively farmed agricultural land onto semi-natural grasslands. This is where artificial fertiliser simply washes down a hill onto a semi-natural grassland. There is also the problem of 'fresh' dung from 'eco-friendly' pig farms. This is arguably OK if the farmer wants some free fertiliser, but on species-rich land it is catastrophic. I have seen this a few times, with pig manure running from the top of the hill on to chalk downland and, in a similar place a few years later, run-off of inorganic fertiliser. The effect is almost instantaneous, with the short, species-rich turf disappearing under a vigorous growth of weed species within two weeks.

Maize grown for biofuels or feed for stock animals has proved to be a problem.[19] With its harvest being so late in the year, fields are sometimes left barren over winter, and the resultant unanchored soil simply washes down the hill, taking any nutrients with it. In my West Dorset parish, some of this run-off is actually channelled from the steep footpath onto a steeper slope of chalk downland to one side. Most of the pollution ends up in Poole Harbour, unless there is heavy rain, when it spreads into the floodplains.

The final form of pollution I will mention is *relatively* trivial, but knowledgeable friends who express an opinion on the matter would have me believe it to be major. It is dog's mess. This is unpleasant, and it releases unwanted nutrients into the soil. Enough careless dog walkers can have a serious, if patchy, effect. Birds, especially those that are ground-nesting, suffer badly from the presence of unruly dogs, with one estimate of a 40 per cent reduction in bird numbers on nature reserves in general owing to the disturbance these four-legged friends can cause.[20] Finally there are the diseases of grazing animals that can sometimes occur where dogs are free to roam. The most prominent are two protozoan parasites found in dog faeces that cause disease in stock: Neosporosis and Sarcocystosis. The first can cause abortion in cows and the latter a potentially fatal neurological disease in sheep.

ABANDONMENT

The abandonment of agricultural land is as old as agriculture itself. In prehistory an area was often cultivated until the soil became depleted in nutrients, forcing people to cultivate elsewhere. Between the wars there was an agricultural decline, and land was abandoned and became 'rough pasture'. This was of little value to agriculture or to biodiversity as they just encouraged weeds and scrub.

Abandonment of grassland has continued irregularly up until the present. Factors that cause this include the cripplingly poor returns from agriculture, the housing of cattle fed on silage and other artificial foods in factories rather than allowing them to graze in open fields, and the isolation of thousands of small areas of grassland. The first two of these explain themselves, but the third, which I will return to shortly, requires a brief explanation.

With so much of the countryside now under the plough, areas of species-rich grassland have become isolated in seas of arable land and too troublesome to bother with. Why would an arable farmer trouble him- or herself with a few difficult-to-move sheep just to graze a small, steep slope of downland? Sheep grazing is now much reduced in lowland UK, and even in Dorset one can look across the hills and valleys in vain for a sheep.

With no grazing, vegetative succession proceeds unhindered by the hand of man. First, tall grasses and vigorous weeds take over the abandoned land, then scrub, then trees, leading to a species-rich grassland becoming nothing more than a fading memory. All too frequently another type of succession occurs – species-rich grassland becomes near-intractable swathes of Bracken. It is a plant that will rapidly take over an area and is nearly impossible to re-move. I have seen just this on a nature reserve I frequent in Dorset.

Restoration of abandoned grasslands is not impossible. A naturalist friend was working on an ancient woodland that 'had been trashed by the Forestry Commission' (it is better now). He looked at some nineteenth-century maps and found that part of it had once been a woodland meadow. He cleared it, and many species of plants reappeared from the old seedbank. It is now grazed.

It is, of course, possible that some abandonment occurs not for reasons of impracticality or economy, but from the best of intentions (see p. 43). This is the overly romantic idea of leaving it to nature — the idea that the field will 'rewild' itself. This is generally impracticable, and always so in grasslands if grazing is not introduced. More on this shortly.

ISOLATION

Two or more thousand years of biological history can be destroyed in an hour or two by the plough, but there can also be a relatively slow destruction.

Britain was once covered in thousands of small farms, many of which followed the familiar children's picture-book rendition of a mixed farm consisting of cornfield or two, a meadow, a chicken run, a few pigs in the sty, cattle in the field and a large flock of sheep on the hill in the distance, accompanied by the obligatory sheepdog. While some still exist in the many smallholdings that are scattered over the countryside, most farming is now a matter of large fields, with arable crops and fields for silage. Any grazing will, for the most part, be on improved grasslands (species-poor).

With this old system of many adjoining mixed farms, there was very little distance between any species-rich areas of grassland that might be present. Small distances between plant communities allow the ingress of species from one to another by means of seed dispersal for plants and flying or even crawling for invertebrates.

The isolation of species-rich habitats almost literally causes a slow evaporation, not of everything, but of some of the resident species that make them so interesting. The term used for extinctions owing to isolation and other slow processes that cause a gradual loss is 'delayed extinction', and another term for isolation is 'connectivity loss'. With small areas of grasslands of biological interest scattered here and there, it is inevitable that many will be isolated. The problem here is that, if a species of plant or animal dies out on an isolated site, it faces local extinction as there is nowhere nearby from where it may repopulate.

An illuminating paper published in 2015 quantified the losses.[21] As with the paper described on p. 29, it uses Dorset as the example and also Ronald Good's extensive survey. It considers only the still extant sites, taking a subset of eighty-two plant species. These consisted of twelve rare plants and seventy that are known as 'Dorset notables', meaning that they are at least uncommon and usually restricted to species-rich habitats. In addition to grasslands, the study included other habitats such as woodland and heath. The authors considered other possible drivers of extinction, such as general deterioration owing to poor management, but isolation was found to be the primary source of the losses.

Very few of the plant species maintained historic populations, and for the rest there was a great deal of variation. Two examples given are the heather known as 'Dorset Heath', which suffered an extinction rate of only 10 per cent, while Ivy-leaved Crowfoot suffered an over 90 per cent extinction rate. The median rate (the middle figure in an ascending list of the percentages) was 31 per cent. These are the headline results, but a few more are of interest.

Of the grasslands, calcareous (chalk and harder limestones) suffered the least, while neutral and acid grasslands suffered the most. Small sites were troubled only slightly less than large sites, and short-lived plants suffered more than long-lived plants. Genetic variation may also play a part in that isolation causes inbreeding, as does self-pollination.

The authors did not include animals or fungi but, since both depend entirely on plants, they would have declined too. A single plant species may have many dependent associated organisms that may well be specific to one plant species or a small number of related plants. Lose the plants, lose its dependants.

CLIMATE CHANGE

It is difficult to write about climate change and its effect on UK grasslands without appearing dismissive – which I do not at all intend to be. It is an area of study where few predictions are established, as these depend on firm evidence that, crucially, excludes confounding factors, the above-described isolation of communities being one such. With the future climate *in any one place* being beyond the reach of science, there is no way to judge what will happen to grasslands, with the UK climate particularly difficult to predict because of its highly irregular temperate climate. This may be a bonus, however, because most of our plants have adapted to an unreliable climate. All that can be done is to set out the scenarios for various possible climates. The factors involved are obvious – they include temperature, precipitation and whether any change will be higher, lower or less consistent than now or stay much the same.

A useful paper on the subject, one that is worth reading if you have the time, makes a few points of interest.[22] The authors note that there is 'medium' evidence that climate change has already affected vegetation and their communities, but agree that any future effects from climate change are unpredictable. They say that there is a natural resilience to warming in plants that enables them to survive owing to genetic variability, but that plants already at the edge of their climatic range could easily be lost through warming.

This latter problem has been seen in Scotland, where the cold-adapted plants have been observed to occur higher up mountains than they once did.[23] Mountains, of course, are only so high, and they are running out of height. Snowy Pearlwort has lost two-thirds of its population, and Drooping Saxifrage and Mountain Sandwort have declined by 50 per cent.

BEST INTENTIONS

It was in 1982 that I first became interested in (though 'distressed by' is more accurate) the loss of species-rich grassland, and I dreamed of owning a large area of intensively farmed land that I might turn into a nature reserve. It seems that I was not the only dreamer, and some of the others have been in a better position than I ever was to realise their dream. The Knepp Estate rewilding project in Sussex is the best-known in Britain. It began this century and has been a very impressive success. Such success is not guaranteed in such matters, but the project has evidently been managed by people who know what they are doing. This is not always the case.

It is very poignant when people with the very best of intentions make matters worse. It happens on a small scale every day – mowing a verge sporting orchids, for example. One relatively benign story of failure is that of a large field where I have taken many fungus walks over the years. In 2020 the owner harrowed it and sowed it with wild-flower seeds of unknown provenance. This was in an effort to 'cheer it up a bit'. I was upset by this folly, but not too much because grasslands will often survive light harrowing or slot-drilling, and it was an example of lowland acid grassland in which the type of plants promised from wild-flower mixes would not fare well. They did not fare at all, and there was no long-lasting damage done to the sward.* This time.

The perfect example of a *catastrophe*, one that has suffered numerous unwelcome headlines, is that of the experimental Oostvaardersplassen project (OVP) in the Netherlands. In 1968 around 56 km² of land was reclaimed from the sea just north of Amsterdam. It was to be used for industry, but this idea was soon abandoned and the reclaimed site was left to its own devices. By

---

* An area covered by grass.

1989 what was now an area of wetlands and grassland had become sufficiently replete with birds to earn Ramsar status – that is, it became a protected area of wetlands (see p. 285).

Concerned that it would be overwhelmed by encroaching willow and the subsequent loss of the existing grassy communities, the bright idea of introducing 'wild' grazing animals to control the willow was mooted. The animals chosen were large, and as close as possible to animals that would occur in such a situation during the megafauna epoch, the Pleistocene. Based on the type of function animals performed rather than their similarity to extinct species, among those introduced were Konik horses, Red Deer and Heck cattle, the last of these being similar to the lost Aurochsen.

No Sabre-toothed Cats turned up, and no other top-level predators were introduced. The hoped-for wildlife corridors via which the creatures could escape overcrowding to other reserves never materialised. This left the introduced mammals with no means of population control other than starvation. Starvation and predation are perfectly natural ways to die, and the common lot of most animals, us included, when nature is left to itself – old age is a recent luxury. However, with the corpses mounting up, and with no scavengers beyond birds and foxes, the project became both a PR disaster and, more importantly, a moral disaster.

Thousands of animals either died of starvation or were shot over the years. Pertinent to this book, though hardly the most pressing issue in such a context, is the fact that the vegetation was inevitably grazed too short, and hoof-fall caused damage to the sward.

The project was based largely on the idea that one can leave things to nature. This may or may not be the case, but either way it is likely to be messy. Management is much improved now, with the idea of leaving nature to itself abandoned. It is now a valued site.

Overall, I am very much in favour of rewilding. It does not need to be at the scale of the 1,4000 ha of the Knepp Estate; rewilding a half-hectare of lowland field to a meadow is sufficient if enough people do it.

If there is one problem that would have arisen, had fortune allowed me to rewild a large area of arable land, it is this: apart from the food supplied by any grazing animals it would take the land out of food production. The loss of production would require more imports of corn or other arable crops. Importation obviously means that the food must be produced elsewhere, and Britain would effectively export its biodiversity loss. I call this 'environmental colonialism'. Discuss.

Tree-Planting

People are not very good at planting trees. Way back in the early 1970s, there was an incitement to 'Plant a Tree in 73', which was enthusiastically embraced by many members of the public and various organisations. With everything apparently going to plan, it was repeated the following year. Few of these trees survived, leading to the damning piece of doggerel: 'Plant a tree in 73, Plant one more in 74, Keep them alive in 75, Burn the sticks in 76.'

I was having lunch with some friends a little while ago, and the subject of conservation came up. Our host, in response to my pointing out that sowing packets of 'wild flower' seeds wherever a space for them could be found was not necessarily a good idea, said, 'Yes, OK. But planting trees is always OK, surely?' My answer was that *it depends*. Like doctors, one should do no harm, and planting trees on species-rich grassland is something that causes great harm.

Another friend of mine who was tasked with granting or refusing permission for tree-planting told me that he visited a family who owned a bit of land and wanted to plant trees there.

Evidently it was to help save the planet. It was a splendid area of species-rich chalk downland, and so, to their disbelief, he refused permission.

Many people embark on the planting of trees for carbon capture, the removal of carbon dioxide from the air. This is 'a good thing' if done in the right place, but, despite appearances, semi-natural grasslands harbour vast amounts of carbon, not so much above ground as *below*. In this context it is stored in organic matter and measured by the weight of stored carbon dioxide, not just the carbon component. If one takes samples to a depth of one metre, 90 per cent of the organic matter is held permanently in the roots. My ecologist friends, well aware of this, bemoan the fact that the most widespread practice is to sample only 15 cm into the soil, resulting in a *gross* misrepresentation of its value. In relation to all of this I introduce you to 'Wright's Law', which says: 'Always consider what you already have before you plant the thing you think you want.'

THE END OF GRAZING?

One potential threat to grasslands came to my attention via yet another friend. He is a vegan in his twenties, and proposed, insisted even, that all animal husbandry be abolished, and any land on which animals grazed should be left to nature. I do not agree with him but could certainly understand his point that eating animals, although a natural part of our make-up, is something that we could manage without.

There is no necessity for me to explore the ethics involved here, as they are well understood by most people. My argument was that no grazing animals would inevitably mean the loss of nearly all of our existing semi-natural grasslands. Along with the loss of these grasslands we would lose perhaps 30 per cent of our flora, 20 per cent of our fungi and thousands of invertebrate species.

I thought that my young friend's proposal was a naïve desire, but governments, in Europe at least, have turned against animal husbandry because of the amount of climate-warming methane produced by the industry. Attempts have been made to ban cattle or drastically reduce their numbers, notably in Ireland, Belgium and the Netherlands. At the time of writing, the idea has been mooted by the UK government for these islands. Farmers have fought back elsewhere with protests, and (again at the time of writing) such policies are in the balance.

Fortunately (if that is the word to use about a terrible loss), there is very little high-value grassland left to damage, and it is most likely that only species-poor *improved* grasslands would be dispensed with. These issues present us with value judgements, but since this book is about semi-natural grasslands, I suggest that these, at least, should be exempt from any such bans.

Grazing

Since it is grazing that maintains semi-natural grasslands in their pristine state, it is a subject I am bound to discuss here. Without it such grasslands would follow a progression from grasses and flowers to scrub and finally to woodland. Even meadows are grazed after they are cut in midsummer. Grazing is thus the very key to semi-natural grasslands. Which grazing animal and what differences are there between them, how often and how much, are a few of the questions I address.

There is an old saying that a sheep should never see two consecutive Sundays in the same field. As old sayings go, this is good advice … on the whole. Nevertheless, a very great deal of advice has been handed out (and sometimes taken) on the subject of grazing, and this simple rule covers only one of the very many considerations faced by those who manage stock and pasture.

The list of variables in the matter of grazing is a long one, but first on the list is 'What do you wish to achieve?' For some it will be the maximum financial reward possible from the available land – a not unreasonable desire. For others the answer will be that they want to maximise biodiversity and, perhaps, facilitate carbon sequestration, or perhaps, for the farmer, that he or she wishes to win another rosette at the county show.

Grazing regimes must also consider such matters as the type and breed of the animals, field sizes, size of the holding, the grazing plants available, field productivity, slope, access, climate and, of course, season. Certainly, moving stock to prevent over-grazing is essential, even if it is from one side of a field to the other. Over-grazed land is damaged land.

GRAZERS

With a few outliers such as the alpaca and rabbits, the main grazers that shape the grasslands of Britain are cattle, sheep and horses/ponies. Each of these has diverse needs, tolerations, diet, method of eating and grazing behaviour. They will also all have differing effects on the grasslands they graze. They are not necessarily chosen for these varying effects, but for the suitability of the land and what the farmer wishes to produce. On nature reserves, however, grazing species will be chosen for their positive effect on biodiversity.

Before we explore further, I will describe the grazing behaviour of grazers, including rabbits, an animal that can have a profound effect on the sward.

CATTLE

Cattle are powerful and invaluable grazers, eating both grasses and wild flowers. They are, however, unable to select what they eat with fine accuracy. This is due to their wide mouth, and lips that are less mobile than those of sheep, which are able to manipulate plant material and choose what is consumed. Cattle only have incisors on their bottom jaw, with what is known as a 'dental pad' on the top. The tongue is the most active organ for cropping grass, hooking vegetation into the mouth – it is effectively a prehensile organ like our thumb and forefinger.

Once the grass is inside the mouth cavity, the jaws close against it, trapping it between the flat top of the incisors and the dental pad. The grass, thus gripped and soon partially cut by the sharp front edge of the incisors, is torn away. The molars then grind the grass into a digestible mash. This manner of feeding results in a relatively long sward – typically 6 cm – allowing plants to grow a little taller than they do with sheep or horses.[24]

Cattle will eat the longer vegetation first, as this is easy to scoop up with a tongue. While preferring fresh, palatable and nutritious grasses, they will eat grass that is tussocky and nutrient-poor (coarse) and standing or fallen dead grasses.

Cattle breeds, of which there are very many, are chosen for their productivity but also their suitability to the land and climate they are destined for.

Overall, cattle are the best animals to tackle difficult, over-grown sites. Their weight, however, can be a disadvantage in that their hooves make deep impressions in soft soil which can form bare and often muddy patches ('poaching') that will allow the ingress of ruderal species. Heavy-footedness can also be an advantage in that it can control some weeds through trampling – the control of unruly populations of Bracken coming to mind.

SHEEP

Sheep are more choosy and subtle eaters. They have a similar arrangement of teeth to cattle and nip away at vegetation by grasping it between the lower jaw incisors and the upper jaw dental pad, with a forward and upward movement that allows the sharp edge of the teeth to do the severing.

Sheep are highly selective in what they graze, eating flowering plants or palatable and new-growth grasses for preference. Winter-grazed sheep are masters at clearing a sward of dead vegetation by eating it. Their bite is close to the ground – between 3.5 and 6 cm. They are accomplished controllers of Common Ragwort, as they will consume the low young growth.

As with all agricultural grazers, the breed must match the environment. There are ninety or so breeds of sheep in the UK, all with different characteristics, though the differences can be minor. But there are some that are frequently chosen for harsh conditions, such as Rough Fell and Hebridean, their hardiness implicit in their names. Even such hardy sheep may not survive, and a farmer friend of mine once commented that sheep in general 'drop dead for a pastime'.

HORSES AND PONIES

Horses and ponies are the same species, just varieties based mostly on size, with ponies measuring under 14.2 hands at the withers. As far as grazing is concerned, there are differences between horses and ponies and even between breeds of ponies.[25] Unlike cattle and sheep, horses and ponies are not ruminants, having a quite different digestive system. They have a full complement of incisors and simply bite off vegetation with their forward-pointing teeth. They prefer grasses above all, and will consume them when dead, be it as hay, standing in a field or as a fallen thatch. Their bite is the closest of all except rabbits, at as low as 2 or even 1 cm.

Horses will usually set aside an area for dunging. This can create areas of high fertility, which will be a problem for semi-natural grasslands, where low fertility is a prerequisite, the corollary being that it does at least reduce the fertility of the un-dunged grassland.

Feral ponies have long been a feature of the British countryside, most often in open sites such as the New Forest, Exmoor and Dartmoor. Each area will have its own breed, usually named after its place of origin, as in the 'Shetland Pony'. There are also introduced species, the most notable of which is the Konik Pony from Poland. We saw this earlier in reference to Oostvaardersplassen, where it was used as a close cousin of ancestral horses, most particularly the recently extinct Tarpan. The reason for choosing ancient breeds is to mimic the wild grazing of ponies in the distant past. This, by the way, excludes domestic ponies.

The use of ponies for grassland conservation is very common now, even for small areas of land. Different breeds are used according to characteristics such as weight, hardiness and the ability to consume certain tough weed species. Horses for courses. Those that are very light of foot can be used to graze fragile grasslands such as those of cliff-tops. One writer noted that feral ponies will eat Soft Rush – a plant that can dominate wet areas – and Purple Moor-grass, *Molinia caerulea*, a plant that has wreaked havoc in upland acid grasslands.[26]

RABBITS

I write in detail about rabbits on p. 208, so for now I will say that they have had a great deal of influence on semi-natural grasslands, most particularly chalk downland, as anyone who has read Richard Adams's *Watership Down* will know. Populations wax and wane owing to a succession of viral diseases, but where they can still be found they produce an extremely fine sward.

COUNTING SHEEP: THE KNOTTY PROBLEM OF 'STOCKING DENSITY'

Depending on the productivity of the location, which animals are to be grazed, the amount of extra feed likely to be supplied, whether or not conservation is an issue and how long the animals are likely to be there, the number of grazers on any particular patch of grass will vary widely.

While minute calculations can be made for particular circumstances, based on the above factors and more, there is a likely range of stocking densities. The typical range for sheep is from six to ten animals per hectare, though in very poor areas such as heathland, this number can drop to just two.[27] Cattle obviously need more land to graze, and so the standard density is one cow per hectare (though in high-productivity land it can be two).

This 'one cow per hectare' notion is what gives us the baseline measurement for the rather unromantic concept of LSUs – 'Livestock Units' – which is what farmers use to decide how many animals to graze on any given area. The LSU is a calculation based on the area necessary for the grazing of an imaginary cow that produces 3,000 kilos(!) of milk in a year on one hectare of land. The calculations involved are impenetrable, and I will not trouble you with them.

Farmers, knowing their land and their stock intimately, will seldom bother about the mathematics of it all – they will always know what is best. They will visit their stock, check the pasture and may decide it is time to move the stock to a new enclosure. I asked another of my farmer friends how he knows what stock levels to use and when stock needed moving. He looked at me blankly and said, 'Well, I just know.'

In addition to 'how much' grazing there is 'when to graze'. In some cases, particularly chalk downland, grazing animals are removed completely from May to late August to allow flowering and the production of seed. With meadows, grazing is confined to the autumn and winter. Failure to graze at the right time is seen in some upland grasslands where cessation of winter grazing has allowed a thatch to form, preventing the regrowth of desired plants.

Part Two

THE DENIZENS OF THE FIELD

Grasses and Grass-Like Plants

And so, after looking at British grasslands in a broader context – still, as it were, standing on the side of a hill and looking out at those two fields in the distance – it is time to descend to the level of grass itself and get our knees muddy as we look at the plants, animals, fungi and more that make their home in our fields. This is the point where, on a public walk, I would get out my loupe and invite you to take a closer look at something tiny, magnified ×20. We will begin, of course, by examining grass itself.

WHAT IS GRASS?

I have a plant called 'Black Mondo Grass' in my garden. It is a ground-cover plant that has now been consigned to a single flowerpot because of its overenthusiasm. For a few years I assumed it was a grass – it most certainly looks like one, if tending to deep purple – and it was only when it began flowering that I saw how wrong I had been. In fact, it is not even remotely a grass but a member of the Order Asparagales. Looking like grass is simply not enough.

Taxonomy is everything here: to be placed within a natural group an organism must have a known heritage. To put this another way, a natural group must be a branch on the tree of life that falls *intact* with a single cut.

To be counted as a true grass the plant in question must be a member of the Family Poaceae. This Family includes all the wild grasses in the UK, all of which are cool-season grasses (see

p. 17), but it also includes imported grasses such as Pampas Grass and Zoysia Grass (both warm-season grasses). All of the grasses of interest here are in the sub-Family of the Poaceae known as the Pooideae (sensitive souls will be reassured to hear that this is pronounced 'poh-**oy**-dee-eye' or, less formally, '**poy**-dee-ee').

Grasses, along with many other groups, fall within a higher taxonomic class: the Order Poales. The Order Poales as a whole is an inevitably eclectic grouping with sixteen Families, of which the Poaceae is one. For example, among them is the Bromeliaceae, a Family that includes the pineapple! Most of the remaining Families are no longer recognised or are obscure, with few species and fewer genera, though the Typhaceae will be familiar as it contains the wetland/lake-edge grass-like plant, the Common Bulrush, *Typha latifolia*. (Common names can be treacherous – it is not a type of rush!)

Sedges (the Cyperaceae) and rushes (Juncaceae) – distinct Families within the Poales – appear in many semi-natural grasslands in Britain. Thus they gain a great deal of attention in this book. Taking the triplet of the Poaceae, Cyperaceae and Juncaceae together, we have all of the grass and grass-like species that help define grasslands in the UK.

Every species in the Poales is an angiosperm: that is to say, they are all flowering plants. Grasses most certainly produce flowers, though since they are wind-pollinated, they lack petals as they have no need to attract pollinators. They forgo the immediate beauty of petalled plants, but they are exquisitely beautiful when seen close up. Take a look at Plates 3 and 4.

THE GROWTH AND STRUCTURE OF GRASSES

When a seed germinates, it begins its growth by producing roots and the primary stages of upward growth. Roots are more complicated than most will imagine, coming in a number of varieties, each with its particular purpose and time of appearance. In grasses, the first roots to appear from the germinated seed are the seminal roots and the radicle. More precisely they grow from the base of a stem-like structure called the 'mesocotyl', of which more shortly. Radicles persist, but the seminal roots support the plant during development and generally do not survive beyond the first year of growth.

Once the roots are capable of supporting them, two structures grow upwards to form the shoot. The lowest, emerging from the seed, is a separate, stem-like mesocotyl upon which the first leaf and its protective sheath, the 'coleoptile', develop. The coleoptile protects the first leaf as it breaks through the soil, growing with the leaf until splitting to allow the emergent leaf to continue its development. The length of the mesocotyl is dependent on the depth of soil at which the seed germinated. If the seed is too far down, the mesocotyl and shoot will die from lack of sustenance.

Subsequent to the growth of the first roots, new roots are formed higher up at the base of the mesocotyl. This base is known as the 'crown' and is a permanent structure. These new roots are known as 'adventitious roots' and will form the primary permanent root system of the plant. This forms a simple grass plant, straight up and down, and some annual grasses will not develop further, producing flowers on a single stem. Perennial grasses cannot rely on such a simple and vulnerable arrangement, so they have developed strategies to make them more robust by spreading sideways.

The 'tiller' is very nearly a defining characteristic of grasses – even annuals will sometimes produce them. Briefly, they are clones that grow from the crown of the primary plant or the crown of a previously established tiller. They acquire their own

Flowering spike, Inflorescence or Panicle
The arrangement of flowers, a flowering cluster.
A panicle refers to a much-branched inflorescence

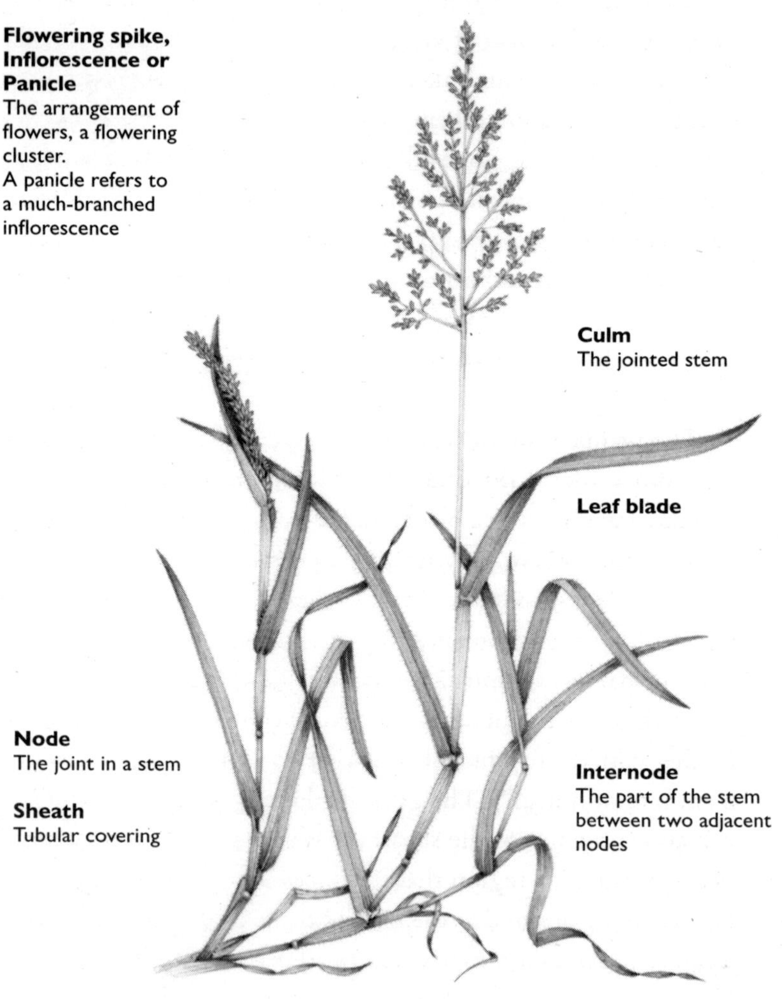

Grass anatomy

roots and can live independently, and can be either (or both) vegetatively and sexually reproductive.

Tillering enables a grass plant to spread laterally, and tillering is thus (arguably) a form of vegetative reproduction. The 'arguably' is because they remain linked by a common vascular system. This vascular system allows them to share nutrients and water between them. Nevertheless, each tiller could survive alone if it became separated. The opposite possibility is that a patch of joined and genetically identical grass plants will form that is metres across.

There are two other, more adventurous methods that some grasses employ to spread themselves laterally: stolons and rhizomes. In short, stolons are just above the ground, rhizomes just below.

The primary shoot from a new plant, or a new shoot growing from a tiller, a rhizome or a stolon, will consist of concentric sheaths, each bearing a blade. There is no central culm (a hollow stem), as these occur only when grass plants bear flowers.

Grass blades, and other grass vegetative structures, grow from the bottom up. A moment's thought will show why this is — any plant or part of a plant that faces a life of being grazed and that grows from the tips of its leaves would be prevented from growing further with the first bite of animal or lawnmower (remember that 2 cm bite of horses?). The grass blades conspicuously arise from just above the top of the sheath. It is here that the all-important 'leaf meristem' (a region that produces new growth) is clearly to be seen as a pale band at the base of the leaf. It is also known as a (type of) 'intercalary meristem'. In addition to lengthening, grass blades must also widen. Here the meristem runs down the centre of the blade. When a grass plant is ready to flower, the culm arises from the crown.

Grass inflorescences (the complete flower-head of each plant) are complex entities that come in three general forms. All bear many individual florets, each one producing a single seed. The forms are a 'spike', a 'raceme' and a 'panicle'.

With a spike, the florets grow directly on the axis (stem) of the inflorescence. On a 'raceme' the florets do the same except that they are on the end of their own small stem – a 'pedicle'. Panicles are the most complex, forming multiple branches, and look like tiny trees. The branches terminate with a single floret, or with a 'spikelet' bearing several florets. All these types vary a great deal between the species.

The florets are complex and consist of many parts. The leaf-like enclosing structures are four in number and will open out to reveal the reproductive parts. At the bottom there are two 'glumes' (upper and lower), then nesting in them are the 'lemma' and its partner, the 'palea', just above it. The palea, and sometimes a glume, may bear an 'awn' (a spike) from their tip or from their outer surface.

Inside these four structures are the female and male parts. Principally they are the 'ovary' and its attached 'stigma' – the former eventually producing the seed and the latter collecting pollen. Stigma are graceful structures – feathery and translucent, and with a surface to which pollen will stick. The pollen is dispersed from the 'anthers' that are perched precariously on the end of individual filaments.

SEDGES

Sedges are usually associated with wet grasslands, wetlands, wet woodlands, riversides, bogs, fens, lakes and the upper seashore. However, a quick scan through Francis Rose's highly recommended *Colour Identification Guide to the Grasses, Sedges, Rushes and Ferns of the British Isles and North-Western Europe* (1989) finds that while 62 per cent prefer wet or very wet areas, 27 per

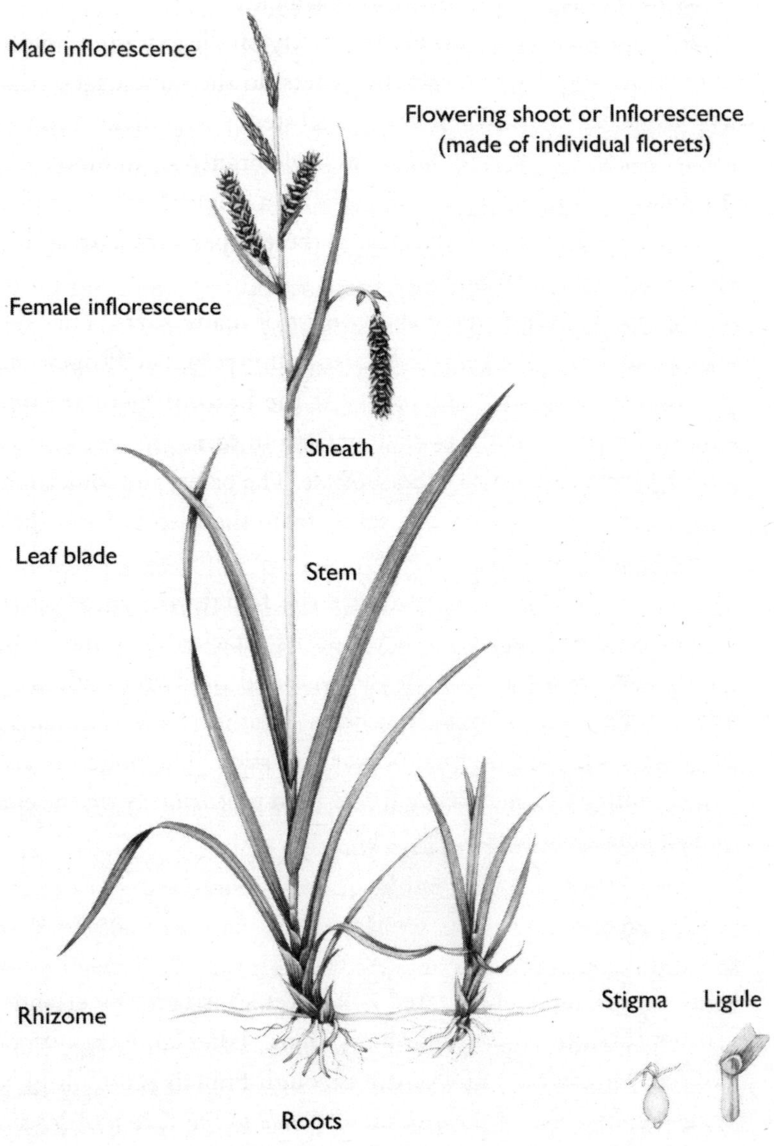

Sedge anatomy

cent are content with drier conditions and the rest can be found in maritime locations. A handful, such as the ubiquitous Hairy Sedge, *Carex hirta*, seem to tolerate both wet and dry situations, but these make little difference to my back-of-the-envelope proportions. Many sedges are intimately associated with grasslands and are often critical members of designated grassland communities under the National Vegetation Classification system.

Carex species within the Family Cyperaceae are considered to be the 'true sedges'. However, there are others, almost invariably plants of bogs, pond and stream sides, and maritime habitats. The cotton-grasses, *Eriophorum*, for example, are in the Cyperaceae, plus several other grass-like plants with the word 'grass' in their name that are not in fact grasses. To add to the confusion there are also the spike-rushes and bog-rushes, which are nevertheless all sedges.

'Sedges have edges, rushes are round' tells us the prominent characteristics of *most* sedges and *most* rushes – it is just a pity about those 'mosts'. 'Triangular' is the most common cross-section shape for *Carex* species and *some* of the cotton-grasses and spike-rushes. There are a total of thirty-five British species in several genera of sedges that are *not Carex*, making a total of 111 species, plus many additional sub-species and hybrids that add a large dash of superfluous excitement to identification efforts.

Sedge stems are solid, unlike grasses, which are hollow except at the nodes. Sedge stems are also tough. The leaves (blades) are flat and can be broad to fine. As with grasses, the colour of the leaves runs from bright green to a dull blue-green. The latter is called 'glaucous', typified by the common Glaucous Sedge, *Carex flacca*. Unlike grasses, where they are arranged in alternate pairs, the leaves of sedges are arranged in threes in a spiral up the stem. As with grasses, each leaf will originate from a sheath.

The flowers are on spikelets, and frequently come in separated male and female flowers, usually with the male above the female on the same stem. Some sedges, by contrast, bear clustered male and female flowers, and maturity for male and female flowers is usually reached at slightly different times, to avoid self-pollination. Other sedges produce their flowers and fruits at the tip. The fruits (utricles) of sedges come in tightly packed clusters. Individual fruits terminate in 'beaks' that will reward close attention when attempting to identify a specimen.

RUSHES

These often large plants can form dense tussocks with their graceful beauty. With most preferring wet conditions, they can frequently be found within grasslands, perhaps as a single patch in a meadow. Again, these are not grasses but grass-like species, but within the Family Juncaceae.

They fall into just two British genera, *Juncus* and *Luzula*. The Juncaceae include another six genera, none of them found in Britain. For Britain, Clive Stace lists thirty-two species of *Juncus* and ten of *Luzula*, not including hybrids and sub-species.[1] Worldwide there are around 460 rushes.

Juncus species demand damp through to submerged conditions and, for the purposes of this book, are the eponymous species that largely define rush pastures (though grasses occur there as well). *Luzula* species are sometimes referred to as 'woodrushes'. They tend to occur in slightly drier conditions than *Juncus* species, with some found in shady places such as woods, and some to be found in meadows, heaths and some drier grasslands.

The stems of rushes, as we saw earlier, are round or oval (remember: 'sedges have edges, rushes are round'), and though a few are *apparently* round from a distance, in fact the stems are 'channelled': that is, they look like the letter C in cross-section. The surface of the stems is often smooth or nearly smooth, occasionally distinctly grooved, with the number of grooves being an aid to identification. Notable examples of this are the near-ubiquitous *Juncus* species Soft Rush, Hard Rush and Compact Rush. Soft Rush is *nearly* smooth with barely detectable longitudinal ridges, while Hard Rush is clearly ridged, with twelve to eighteen ridges. The latter is also noticeably stiff when handled, while Soft Rush is much (surprise!) softer. The associated Compact Rush is also clearly ridged but easy to tell from Hard Rush because of another striking characteristic: its inflorescence always remains a compact ball, not a 'spray' of florets as with Hard and Soft Rush. All three of this common group of rushes, plus three more, have no leaves except as a brown basal sheath.

One oddity in this group is the positioning of the inflorescence. In some it can *appear* to be on the side of the stem, perhaps two-thirds of the way up, but the 'stem' above the inflorescence is *part* of the inflorescence. *Luzula* species possess a clear distinguishing property – they produce leaves that are hairy, with hairs able to appear almost anywhere on some species. The leaves are generally much broader.

IDENTIFYING GRASSES, SEDGES AND RUSHES

I met a lady a year or two ago who told me of her schooldays' experience of choosing a week-long nature course that was to take place just prior to the summer holidays. The choices were: the identification of wild flowers or the identification of grasses, sedges and rushes. Being somewhat adventurous and not one to follow the crowd, she chose the grasses and was the only pupil to do so. Despite being provided with one-to-one expert tuition, it was, she told me, one of the most frustrating weeks of her life. She said that she wished she had chosen wild flowers as at least there would have been other pupils with whom she might have been miserable. Skip to the next section if you do not wish to follow her regretted path and suffer her agrostophobia.

Identifying grasses is one of the most difficult enterprises the naturalist is likely to undertake. Despite taking a few courses on the subject with an old friend of mine and asking other masters of the subject, 'What's this then?' several hundred times, I still find grass identification very difficult. I am not boasting here, but of the *circa* four thousand or so larger species of fungi in Britain I can identify a thousand at little more than a glance. If I cannot identify a species that is not one of that thousand without resorting to books, a battery of chemical tests and my microscope, I can usually place it within a genus. But with the grasses, of which there are *only 220* species in the UK, I am too often frustrated. Having said this, I can identify a couple of dozen of the more common species.

No one reading this book will need the skills to identify grasses in order to understand or appreciate its content, but in order to immerse yourself in the subject of grasslands the ability to identify a few of the commonest and most relevant species is a worthwhile skill. You will, at least, begin to understand the structure of grasses and how they live. I suggest learning some of the relatively small number grasses that appear in grasslands and which are required to understand the flora of grassland communities as used in the National Vegetation Classification system, which I describe on p. 74.

You will need a dedicated book for this and maybe three. There are also many online sources that will help, including 'keys'.★

I suggest the following to begin with, as most of them are fairly easy to identify: Cock's Foot, Crested Dog's-tail, Perennial

★ A question-and-answer system which gradually narrows down to the name of the species under consideration.

Ryegrass, Quaking Grass, Sweet Vernal Grass, Timothy, Meadow Foxtail, Red Fescue, Yorkshire Fog, False Oat-grass, Annual Meadow Grass, Rough Meadow Grass and Wall Barley. The last of these you will almost certainly know – it is the roadside grass that makes an amusing barbed dart to throw at your friends.

Not Just Grass: Other Plants in Grasslands

But of course, grass is not the only type of plant to grow in grasslands. As I have already mentioned, in the UK the 'official' minimum number of plant species required for a grassland to be counted as 'species-rich' is fifteen in a square metre (including grasses).[2] Chalk downland will routinely have twenty-five, and on occasion it can boast forty plant species, all squeezing into the space occupied by my single rhubarb plant.

A. G. Tansley, in his seminal two-volume *The British Islands and Their Vegetation* (first published in 1939 and still a treasure), has two schematic drawings depicting the distribution of plants in a 25 cm square on chalk downland, arguably the most species-rich of all the grasslands.[3] One shows an area that has long been grazed to 4 or 5 cm high by sheep and rabbits, and in this schematic '441 shoots' encompassing twenty-one species are marked as being present.

WHY SO MANY SPECIES?

Such large numbers of different plant species in one area invites the question, 'Why are there so many species when one or a few particularly vigorous species could dominate?' Domination does, indeed, happen sometimes. Rhododendrons and Himalayan Balsam come to mind, both introductions to the British countryside that have little competition or enemies in their adopted habitats. Upland acid grasslands can be dominated by Mat-grass and Purple Moor-grass if the land has been grazed too vigorously, and Bracken if it has not been grazed (or trampled by cows) enough. One way or another, all of these and others like them become boorish in their nature through exceptional circumstances brought about by the hand of man.

The question above is a lively one in ecological circles, with much discussion and opposite sides taken. First of all, the species that occur in a certain area are there because the conditions are right for them: the climate, the consistency and pH of the soil, light levels available on that particular area of land and whether or not there are nearby sources of seed. This is the board on which the game is played. But how is it that so many can win?

One answer, or partial answer, is the Neutral Theory of Species Diversity. This proposes the unlikely notion (but useful as a premise in the context of the theory) that all plants in a particular community have equal fitness. When a patch of soil becomes available for a new plant – perhaps a badger has been scratching around – all the species of plant in, say, a field have a chance to grow there. Yes, the more seeds a plant species produces and the better its seed dispersal method happens to be, the more likely it will be to set seed. But, as noted, *all* the plants are in with a chance, so all will (theoretically) be able to set seed somewhere. First come, first served. This stochastic (random) take on the problem matches well with observations of actual plant communities. However, it does not explain everything.[4] Enter 'niches'.

While all the plants in a community are clearly adapted to it, there will also be niches within it. Such things as the qualities of soil, the shadow of a nearby plant, the presence or absence of the soil fungi on which plants depend, and more, will vary considerably from one part of the community to another, often on a scale of mere centimetres. Particular species of plant will preferentially flourish in these niches. Diversity is thus maintained.

Plants can also fine-tune their behaviour through genetic diversity. There is no intentionality here: it is merely the preferential survival of perhaps a small percentage of the genotypes of any particular species, and it may well vary over a single site. Such tinkering could be a matter of a better toleration of soil toxins or invertebrate attack, growing shorter or taller, producing shorter or longer roots and more.

There is also the game of 'rock-paper-scissors', much more technically known in this context as 'intransitive competitive hierarchies'. Plant A beats plant B, plant B beats plant C, and plant C beats plant A. The two functions here are known as 'equalising mechanisms', which ensure that the component species have minor difference in fitness, and 'stabilising mechanisms', which allow rare species to survive.[5]

Another encouragement that plant communities may enjoy is commensalism: that is, plants, as well as competing for territory, will help their neighbour species in some way. This has a human dimension in the practice of 'companion planting'. In this way, palatable species may survive grazing when growing close to unpalatable species – thistles, perhaps, or bitter or otherwise unpleasant-tasting plants such as ragworts and buttercups.[6]

Further potential interactions occur in the form of what light levels are suitable for a plant, as when a plant is helpfully shaded by another. Or a plant may be next to a member of the Pea Family, a group that creates usable nitrogen compounds. It could be next to a plant with a strong mycorrhizal partner, or two plants that share pollinating insects could benefit from close proximity. Quite what this amounts to in determining which plant grows where is difficult to say, but such associations have been proven to exist.

PLANT COMMUNITIES

Another question that must be addressed is how grasslands remain reasonably stable in their composition of plants and become recognisable communities. The answer is relatively simple: it is a matter of which plants are suited to the local conditions and management.

In meadows, plant communities occur on neutral soils of moderate fertility and are cut once a year, typically in early July, then grazed. In the case of species-rich chalk grassland it is a combination of (relatively) high soil alkalinity, very low nutrient levels, a mild and relatively dry climate, and grazing by sheep and sometimes cattle and rabbits.

With the meadow, no plants that require acid or alkaline soil can thrive, nor those that require high fertility or that flower late in the year. For chalk grassland, circumstances ensure that no acidophilic or water-loving plant would do well there, nor any that require high nutrient levels. Such considerations apply to all semi-natural grasslands.

With most grasslands grazing, or cutting then grazing, as in meadows, is the universal factor. Grassland remains species-rich and is a type of 'plagioclimax' community: that is, a stable habitat made so by human intervention.

But how is it that some plants can tolerate grazing while others cannot? An ecological classification known as the 'Raunkiær plant life form' is of considerable assistance here. Christen Raunkiær, a Danish ecologist and botanist, proposed the scheme in 1907. His idea was to investigate how plants adopt varying physical forms and use varying survival strategies to maximise their reproductive success.

A typical 'life form' is that of a 'phanerophyte', literally 'visible plant' (none of these concepts comes with a user-friendly name). A phanerophyte is a plant that produces its 'perennating buds' at least half a metre above ground level. Perennating buds are those that survive the winter (or any period when growth is not possible) ready to grow again. They are also known as 'resting' or 'renewal' buds. Trees and tall shrubs are clear examples of phanerophytes. An ecologist would describe a woodland as being 'phanerophytic'.

Most plants in grazed fields are 'hemicryptophytes' (literally, 'half-hidden leaves'), the commonest of all the various plant life forms on Earth and particularly common in Britain, where there is relatively little tree cover. This makes most grasslands 'hemicryptophytic', or predominantly so. Hemicryptophytes produce their perennating buds at ground level, below the reach of grazing animals. Most particularly, grasses are hemicryptophytes. As with most categories within Raunkiær's system, this life form comes in more than one flavour: those that form a rosette directly on the ground (rosette form), those that complement their rosette with foliage on stems (partial rosette form) and those that perennate from any rhizomes (protohemicryptophyte – sorry).

All grassland hemicryptophytes are able to tolerate grazing as they can always regrow from the very base, with uprooting being the only grazing risk, and a rare one at that. The familiar Dandelion and Daisy have a rosette form, some grasses have a partial rosette form and the Common Harebell is a protohemicryptophyte. The hemicryptophytic lifestyle protects the plant almost completely from grazing, but also from unfavourable circumstances such as a prolonged drought where the developed leaves have suffered dehydration. Both perennials and biennials can be hemicryptophytes, with the latter less common in grasslands.

There are three more life forms. 'Therophytes' are what are more usually called 'annuals'. The latter name is imprecise, however, as it suggests that the seeds germinate every year. While around 8 per cent of herbaceous plants must do so as they produce only short-lived seeds, most therophytes germinate whenever conditions are suitable, which may simply be next year when a bare patch of land become available, or when conditions of temperature, light and water are suitable. Therophytes in general are rare in grasslands, with Yellow Rattle and closely related species being the most notable. Why are they the most notable, one might ask. It is because they have the advantage over other therophytes in parasitising neighbouring species of plants. They gain free food from their host, while reducing the shade they would otherwise struggle to grow under. This unbalanced relationship also provides relatively more open ground for their (short-lived) seeds to germinate.

'Geophytes' are plants that, when established, grow or regrow from a bulb, corm, tuber or rhizome. Typical examples are Bluebells and Lords and Ladies. Finally, 'chamaephytes' are plants that produce their perennating buds between soil level and 25 cm in height or less. These are generally small shrubs.

All of the above strategies, particularly those of the hemicryptophytes, make survival possible in the seemingly hostile environment of a grazed grassland.

THE NATIONAL VEGETATION CLASSIFICATION SYSTEM

This is a difficult subject to present to the non-specialist: arcane concepts, complex tables, all the names of species given in their Latinised form and so very much detail. If you find this too much or, frankly, too dull, then skip it completely, except for *this*:

1. The National Vegetation Classification (NVC) system names, classifies and describes most of the plant communities of the British Isles.
2. It was published in five volumes, each volume describing and classifying the broad community types – woodlands, grasslands, wetlands and so on.
3. Each 'chapter' is headed with the name of the community: for example, '**MG10** *Holco-Juncetum effusi* rush-pasture'. '**MG10**' alone is enough to distinguish it.

4. There may be sub-communities. **W15**, for example, has four, one of them being '*Calluna vulgaris* sub-community'.
5. The communities are defined by the quantified likelihood of species being found in the community and their abundance.
6. It is not essential to splash out on the books as it is easy enough to find short descriptions of the communities online.
7. I have anglicised the Latin for the purposes of this book: for example, '**W15** Common Heather subcommunity'.
8. I refer to these communities later in the book, using at least such 'names' as CG2 and sometimes the full 'names' such as the two above. This is because there is no other way of referring to them.

Humans are masters of classification: we love to put things in order as an aid to understanding them and where they fit. Heroic efforts have been made over the last 150 years to classify habitats, be they in woodlands, wetland, grassland or seashore. Since the autotrophic and thus fundamental organisms of terrestrial habitats are nearly all plants, it is plant communities that have been classified. There is a vast number of plant communities, very many of which will be grasslands or habitats that may be associated with grasslands.

There have long been loose but easily understandable categories of 'habitats', such as upland hay meadow, dune heath, lowland acid grassland and rush pasture, but each of these can be divided into multiple community types, and many communities had, and still have, no common name at all. So there is no one thing that could pass unqualified as just 'grassland': there are, instead, 'grasslands'. Some way of distinguishing between communities is required, and this has been achieved by some exceptionally talented and determined researchers who collated data and made thousands of site visits.

More formal systems have been attempted over the years, but

the system that is generally (if not always) used today is the NVC system, though a replacement system known as UKHAB (UK Habitat Classification) has entered the stage. Each of the five books that define the NVC system takes one or two broad categories of habitat – wood and heath, grasslands and mires, and so on – and goes into all their minute details.

Each community will be given a name, and not a friendly one. The major community is assigned a name such as '**M21** *Narthecium ossifragum - Sphagnum papillosum* valley mire *Narthecio-Sphagnetum euatlanticum*'. Such names are made up of some of those species that are typical and constant in the community. In fact, this is not entirely true, as some are grammatically changed versions of the names denoting place of origin (*Saphagnetum* instead of *Sphagnum*; *cf.* 'Londoner' and 'London'), which were introduced in earlier ecological classification systems. Sometimes, as with **M21**, there is a reference in plain English to the broad community type: 'valley mire'. The initial letters indicate the very broad habitat, so 'MG' means 'mesotrophic grassland', 'CG' means 'calcareous grassland' and 'M' means 'mire'.

The tables which list the species found are based on: (a) how often each plant was found in a sample quadrat; and (b) the range of how many were found in each quadrat that contained the plant.*

I think that anyone who has encountered these books will agree that they do not make light reading; they are fascinating, essential and hugely daunting for those without a great deal of experience. There are week-long courses that people can attend, with the ability to identify many plants as a prior requirement. Fortunately, most naturalists have little need to read any of these books or to be able to use them in the field – just know

---

* A quadrat is a square area of land for survey: typically around one square metre and marked with a physical square frame.

that they describe real communities and that the classifications are an invaluable aid to understanding. We will encounter many throughout this book, but they are there to help, not daunt, even though they make an excellent stab at the latter.

The system is not perfect, with even the authors agreeing that their attempt to categorise all of the plant communities in Britain is flawed. It does, however, broadly work, as everyone with an interest in ecological matters will always know what you are talking about.

GRASSLAND SOILS

The nature of a soil is at the top of the list of contributing variables that provide a grassland with the ecology it possesses.

Any gardener will be aware of the importance of having the correct type of soil for the garden they desire, so such matters are familiar to a fair proportion of the general public. There are two main factors found in soil that will restrict what grows where — hydrology and pH. There is also 'Eh', a factor that has recently come to the fore in soil chemistry and which I will later discuss briefly.

The hydrology (how wet the grassland is and how variably so) depends largely on bedrock geology and superficial geology. The top of many chalk hills, for example, has a thick overlay of clay (see p. 141) and drains poorly. The slopes, however, bear little or no clay, and water drains quickly through the very thin layer of soil into the absorbent and usually fissured chalk below. At the other extreme, a granite bedrock will absorb no water at all.

Other considerations are the physical properties of the soil: light loams, clay, chalky, sandy and so on. More generally, soils vary in their hydrologies from impenetrable clays and peats to sand that retains water like a sieve, with loams somewhere in the middle. But again, even in penetrable soils, water cannot drain away through impenetrable bedrock, leaving the soil forever wet unless it can drain downhill.

The degree of acidity, the 'pH' (potential hydrogen), appears repeatedly in this book as it is this that rules nearly all. It is sometimes called the 'master soil variable'.[7] The slightly tricky chemistry is beyond the scope of this book, but it is worth mentioning that a low pH (acid) has a relatively high proportion of free hydrogen ions, while a high pH (alkaline) has a preponderance of hydroxyl ions (OH −).

Why does pH matter so much? The effects of soil pH are legion, though we must bear in mind that soil pH is a range and the effects are dialled up and down with the pH, and perhaps only occur at exceptionally high or low values. The best-known is the effect the pH has on the availability of inorganic nutrients such as nitrogen, phosphorus and calcium. But there are other things to consider. Highly acidic soils, for example, are unable to break down organic matter, leaving plant corpses in the form of peat. At a pH less than 5.5 (very acidic) metal plant toxicity can occur where metals such as cadmium and aluminium become available, while required phosphorus and molybdenum nutrients will have very low availability. At high pH figures, phosphorus can be unavailable owing to it being 'captured' by calcium.

At a pH of 7 the soil is neutral, with the hydrogen and hydroxyl ions in balance. With the exception of those adapted to exceedingly high or low pHs, plants have an easy time at this pH, though the 'sweet spot' for most plants is often given on the acidic side: a pH of 6.5. All nutrients are available to acceptably differing degrees at a pH of 6.5 to 7.5. 'Nutrient availability' is the proportion of the accessible mineral nutrient in question. Most elements occur in vastly more than sufficient quantities in any piece of soil, but very little of it is in soluble (ionic) form: that is, *accessible*.

I would have liked to provide the range of pH acceptability of the various inorganic nutrients in a neat diagram. One such was published in 1946 by the eminent American soil academic Emil Truog. It is one of the most reproduced tables in biology, appearing to this day online and in articles and even academic papers. Scientist that he was, Truog realised the limitations of his diagram, but its neat form has led to its wide acceptance. While there is some truth to be found in Truog's diagram, soils, especially those that harbour life, are complex. Ultimately, the availability of nutrients in any one soil of any one pH will depend on other factors, such as rainfall, soil temperatures, soil structure, constituent plants and more.[8] The pH of a soil is also a two-way balancing act, with an established pH modified by biological activity, usually at the level of fungi and bacteria, with or without the involvement of the plant root system. No readily understandable graphic can encompass so many variables, such complexity.

Life in general adapts to fill difficult ecological circumstances, and plants can adapt in the long term to high and low pHs. In so doing they fill niches that would otherwise remain unoccupied. To do this they develop any of several methods, such as an increase in mycorrhizal activity (of which more shortly), that present an increased surface area for collecting nutrients in short supply, or using chemicals known as chelates to quarantine toxic elements.[9]

Grassland types are naturally classed according to the pH of their soil. These classes are simply acid, neutral and alkaline, the last of these terms often being replaced by 'calcareous', reflecting its association with limestones. A handful of grasslands from each of these grassland classes are described in Part Four below.

I promised an explanation of 'Eh', and I may well disappoint. The 'E' stands for 'electron activity' and the 'h' represents hydrogen and is something of a left-over from a previous system. While 'pH' is all about levels of protons, Eh is about levels of electrons, more particularly, a soil's capacity to lose electrons or gain them. The processes involved are known as 'redox', a portmanteau abbreviation of 'reduction' (gaining electrons) and 'oxidation' (loss of electrons). Overall, Eh is a measure of redox potential.

In practical terms, Eh can be placed on one axis of a graph with the other axis being the pH, soil fertility and other factors depending on both. Each plant will have a preferred position on the graph, and, as with pH, Eh has a strong effect on the availability of plant nutrients, explaining to some extent why pH alone is an unreliable indicator.

It seems to be the case that some plants can modify the Eh, as happens with the pH. Since redox reactions are the stuff of all life, micro-organisms will be affected by levels of Eh and can also change them.

For grasslands, Eh is one of the factors that determines which plant grows where and, almost by definition, the Eh and the pH will be right for them. This is not necessarily so in agriculture. One comprehensive and meaty report both helpfully reviews our understanding of Eh and proposes that agronomists take account of Eh as much as they do of pH.[10] Eh has, however, already become important in 'no-dig' horticulture.

There is, of course, vastly more to the subject than this, but the key message is that pH has lost its crown and is now just one of *two* master variables.

THE SOIL ORGANISMS OF GRASSLANDS

THE INVERTEBRATES, PROTOZOANS AND PROKARYOTES

It is often said that the soil beneath one's feet will harbour billions of creatures and perhaps thousands of species. This is not just gee-whiz science: it is true. So it must be with grasslands, the exquisite plants above-ground seemingly no more than the green mask of another world. Most of these soil organisms will be prokaryotes – bacteria and the more elusive archaebacteria, both of which will have their roles in the life of soil – but small animals, protozoans and fungi also exist in this dark environment.

The standard and well-respected work on the subject of soils is *The Nature and Properties of Soils*, at the time of writing in its fifteenth edition." It is comprehensive book, with the 1,100-page large-format paperback weighing in at 2.2 kg. Among the many stories this book tells is one that comes in a remarkable table that provides information on the various groups of organisms that occur in soil.

I should mention that this is soil *in general*, from sparse tundra to tropical rainforest, so where there is a range of values given it is a matter of both sense and modesty to choose the moderately lower ends for British grasslands.

First, I will give the (wet-weight) figures in kilograms per hectare (kg/ha) for the major groups. This is a dense section filled with numbers designed to illuminate and impress you with how very much life exists below an area of grassland. Just remember that a hectare is the area of nearly one and a half football pitches, and that 1,000 kg of compressed organic matter would overfill a cubic metre dumpy bag. We are in the billions of organisms here, and for the bacteria we are talking about trillions.

The Archaea and Bacteria amount by live-weight to between 400 and 5,000 kg/ha, not counting the Actinobacteria, which have precisely the same range. The Fungi are way ahead, with 1,000 to 15,000 kg/ha, the Protozoa 20 to 300, nematodes 10 to 300, mites and Collembola 2 to 500, and earthworms a very healthy 100 to 5,000.

Overall, and including some minor contributors, the range

is from 2,000 kg/ha to 32,600, though either extreme is highly unlikely as it would require all of the component inhabitants to occur in respectively minimum and maximum quantities. Taking a 3,000 lower limit and a 25,000 higher limit, a reasonable guess for species-rich grasslands would be 8 tonnes per hectare. This is close to the 5 tonnes of soil organisms per hectare in agricultural land, and considering that semi-natural grasslands contain much more permanent organic matter, is nearly spot on.[12]

Soil organisms are (very) roughly classified by size: micro-, meso-, macro- and mega-fauna. Sometimes organisms that are not 'fauna' will be dubbed '-flora' instead. This is for algae, protozoans and fungi, but since these are no more flora than they are fauna, I will stick with '-fauna'. The sizes involved are as follows. Microfauna measure up to 100 µm (a tenth of a millimetre), which will include archaea, bacteria, slime moulds, (some!) fungi and protozoans. Mesofauna range from 100 µm to 2 mm. This will include small animals such as springtails, pot worms, some nematodes and tardigrades (water bears). From 2 mm to 20 mm there are many insects, spiders, centipedes etc., and above 20 mm there are the megafauna, which will include anything from earthworms to rabbits. (They burrow!)

Archaea and Bacteria

The most abundant organisms in almost all ecosystems are the Bacteria. But there are also the Archaea. The latter were once thought to be odd bacteria but were recently and dramatically reassessed as being in a separate Domain, one that has been added to the two other Domains (the classification *above* a Kingdom), the Bacteria and the Eucaryotes. The latter of these comprises organisms with a nucleus – plants, animals, seaweeds, amoeba and so on and on. The Bacteria and Archaea are prokaryotes and lack nuclei. The Archaea are, for the most part, extremophiles, which is to say that they have adapted to live in very salty/acid/alkaline/hot/ cold environments, but some lead a more mundane existence in soils. Little research has been done on this, but for grasslands they are believed to provide several functions: the availability of the essential element phosphorus, the production of methane (though this is less welcomed now), the fixing of nitrogen and the enabling of some plants to grow in extreme conditions such as bogs.[13]

The Bacteria are much better known and vastly more common in soil than the Archaea. Their talents are seemingly endless. The breakdown of organic matter and the fixing of nitrogen in root nodules (Rhizobia) are two. They have a hand in the conversion of ammonia to accessible nitrates; they suppress pathogens or *are* pathogens; they release plant growth hormones, improve soil structure, bind iron and make it accessible to plants via the rhizosphere (the volume around the roots). Bacteria also clean up soil pollutants, sequester carbon and actively participate in the operation of mycorrhizal fungi.[14]

The best-known soil bacteria are the 'Actinobacteria'. They are branching filamentous organisms that were thought to be fungi until fairly recently and are also known as the 'Actinomycetota'. They perform several functions in soils, the most noticeable, though hardly the most important, is that they provide us with the familiar and distinctive smell of soil in the form of 'geosmins'. Again briefly, they generally exist in the rhizosphere of plants, where they can protect plants by producing antioxidants, degrade pollutants, produce biofilms (otherwise familiar as the 'scobies' floating around in kombucha and dental plaque!) that stabilise soils, protect plant roots, maintain the desired pH (buffering), in some instances enhance nutrient availability to plants and fix nitrogen. One more notable skill is the ability to digest chitin, a substance found in the crunchy exterior of insects, the structural exterior of fungal hyphae and the shells of some Protozoa.

SEARCHING FOR SOIL ORGANISMS

I have spent hours, days and weeks peering down my budget-busting microscope to see what organisms are to be found in soil samples. Considering the vast number that are reported to be found in soil, my reaction when I first looked many years ago was one of profound disappointment. This is partly because grassland soils are poorer than woodland soils, but mostly because of the dilution caused during the extraction of their organisms into a microscope-friendly volume of water. Added to this is the fact that the drop of sample water viewed will be tiny and spread thinly over the square centimetre of the cover slip. It is still worth a look, even with a relatively cheap microscope, as some of the organisms are very beautiful. Another world.

The commonest, and most commonly found under a high-powered (×1,000) microscope, are the free-living bacteria. Though they are far too small to resolve beyond a dot or a short line without an electron microscope, some are flagellate and can be seen whizzing around the thin film of water. The most conspicuous, however, are the nematodes, many of which are visible with the naked eye, followed by rotifers, the occasional Enchytraeids (tiny, segmented worms) and much more besides.

Protozoa

Taxonomically, what I have termed the Protozoa are a nightmare classification of organisms, many of which may well belong in another Kingdom, such as the Chromista. As an example, at school I learned all about amoeba, a knock-down example of a protist if ever there was one. In truth, however, it is a *form*, rather than an organism or group of organisms on a single branch on the tree of life, as was once thought. More technically, older phylo-genetic ideas classed amoeba as a natural group (monophyletic), when what they had was a very polyphyletic group.* Amoeba, or amoeba life stages, turn up in every major lineage – plants, animals, slime moulds and fungi.

Protozoans are single-celled animals or animal-like organisms. They come in three varieties: rhizopods, ciliates and flagellates. Rhizopods take the form of amoeba, and ciliates are covered in short, motile, super-fine hairs (cilia) that enable them to move, attach themselves, sense things and assist in feeding. The flagellates bear a powered tail that enables them to swim – like sperm. These are all tiny organisms that swim or crawl through the surface film (water) on soil particles and roots.

Mesofauna

Most of these are in the Phylum Arthropoda: that is, insects, centipedes, spiders and many more organisms with a chitinous exoskeleton. Most of the rest are in the Nematoda and the sub-Order Lumbricina (earthworms). The mesofauna are numerous as general groups and in the number of individual species within these groups. Not all are 'beneficial', in that many are parasitic on plants and inside grazing animals, though they only really cause serious problems in monoculture arable. Elsewhere, they provide the checks and balances needed in any ecosystem. A reasonably extensive list of these organisms is in the table overleaf.

Nematodes

Despite the general difficulties and complications of finding soil organisms, there is seldom a problem when it comes to nematodes, sometimes known as 'roundworms'. With between 100,000 and 10 million individuals to be found in a square metre, this comes

* 'Phylogeny' refers to where organisms belong on the tree of life: 'monophyletic' means that an organism or group of organisms is on a branch or branches that will come away intact with a single cut; 'polyphyletic' requires more than one cut, indicating that it is not a natural group.

Common term	Classification	Description
Coneheads	Protura	Long segmented abdomen. Six thoracic legs, blind, front two legs used as sensory organs.
Earthworms	Lumbricina	Large, segmented worms.
Insect Larvae and Pupae	Insecta	Highly variable, but consider crane flies and midges.
Millipedes et al.	Myriapoda	Body segments fused in pairs. Some translucent. Note: Pauropods (above) are included in this group.
Mites and Ticks	Acari	Same Class as spiders. Eight legs when mature. Body unsegmented.
Pauropods	Pauropoda	Like a miniature woodlouse. Nine to eleven segments, each bearing a pair of legs. Short antennae. Able to run!
Potworms et al.	Enchytraeidae	Small, whitish, segmented worms.
Roundworms	Nematoda	Without segments. Four different mouth structures possible in terrestrial species, according to prey.
Spiders	Araneae	Eight legs. Lacking antennae. Note: only very few occur underground or in the leaf litter. Consider the funnel-web spiders.
Springtails	Collembola	Up to six segments. Bears a small structure under the abdomen (a 'collophore') to regulate water, and for excretion.
Water Bears	Tardigrada	Lumbering on fat legs with hand-like structures. Circular mouth with plant and animal-piercing needles.
Woodlice et al.	Isopods	Segmented, with seven pairs of jointed legs.

Table of some of the main types of small animals that occur in soils and soil litter for at least part of their lives.

Size Range Britain	Feeding	British Species
0.2–2.5 mm	Mostly fungi hyphae, but also dead plants and arthropods	12
25–200 mm	Internally digest surface plant litter	27
0.5 mm to 10 cm	N/A	unknown
10–70 mm	Millipedes: dead organic matter. Centipedes: small animals	~200
0.3–12 mm	Microbes, soil, dead plants and animals	363
0.3–1.5 mm	Dead organic matter	24
1–30 mm	Dead plant material, fungi, bacteria	70
<1–7 mm	Bacteria, fungi, other microscopic prey. Some parasitic on animals and plants	~300
2–14 mm incl. legs	Small invertebrates	650
0.25–6 mm	Decomposing organic matter	250
0.1–1.2 mm	Fungi, bacteria and algae. Also prey on nematodes	70
5–30 mm	Decomposing organic matter	35–40

Notes: Many of these species are not, or not solely, found in soils. Many are found in rich woodland/shrub soils. However, these habitats often occur in association with most grasslands. The British species numbers provided are 'best guesses' for some groups. Size-ranges are similarly best guesses.

as no surprise. There can also be anything from ten to a thousand *species* in a square metre, though the top end must represent a rare occurrence.

Nematodes are fascinating to watch as they thrash around in the glare of the microscope's light. They almost tie themselves in knots. When they slow down, it is possible to see their mouth parts. These come in five varieties, depending on their intended food. These are dubbed bacterivore, fungivore, herbivore, predator and omnivore. They are impossible for anyone but a specialist to identify to a particular species. However, since nematodes are generally transparent when viewed in a microscope, their mouths are visible and distinctive for each feeding type, enabling the observer to at least determine which feeding type they are.

Not all are 'beneficial' in that they are parasitic, but beneficial to what? Again this is one of those checks and balances. For example, some juvenile bacteriophagous nematodes find their way into an insect, bringing associated bacteria with them. The bacteria feed on the insect, and the nematodes (bacterivores) feed on the bacteria. This will not necessarily be a good thing if it is a rare butterfly that meets such a gruesome end but, by the numbers game, any insect that becomes pestilentially common will be preferentially destroyed.

The primary benefit gained in grasslands and attendant woody areas by the feeding behaviour of nematodes is the release of nitrogen locked in dead organic matter, chiefly fungal matter but also bacteria, especially in arable land, where fungi are much less common. The conspicuously mobile nematodes also carry bacteria around the soil.[15]

Earthworms

That earthworms are beneficial to soils is something every gardener knows. What few know is that there is more than one

Immature inflorescence of Wild Parsnip

The workers

Cock's Foot inflorescence

Yorkshire Fog

Top: Grass spike up close. Bottom: Yorkshire Fog

Immature inflorescence of a sedge

Joint-leaf rush

Abandoned chalk downland

A common moss close up

Two 4 mm long nematode worms

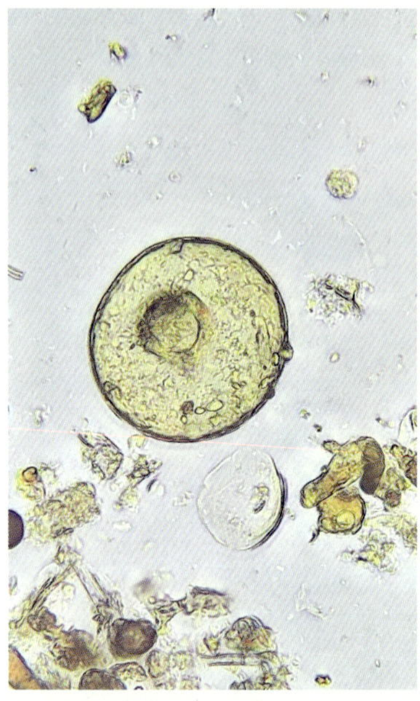

An *Arcella* amoeba

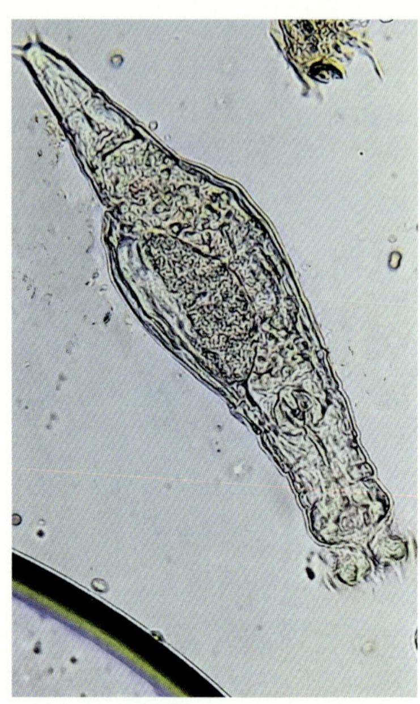

Rotifer and ciliates

A grass rust fungus

The rust fungus *Puccinia betonicae*

Mostly waxcaps collected on a walk at Kingcombe

Blue Edge Pinkgill

Scarlet Caterpillar Fungus

Cowpat Gem

Mosaic Puffball

Slender Parasol

A white club fungus

species in the UK: twenty-seven, in fact. The commonest is *Lumbricus terrestris*, a native of Europe and a serious competitor of native species elsewhere when it has been introduced.

Earthworms come in three functional types: epigeic earthworms, which live only in the litter layer of dead organic material; endogeic earthworms, which form horizontal burrows in the soil, coming to the surface for food; and anecic earthworms, which make deep vertical burrows, the operational mode of our familiar *Lumbricus terrestris*.

Burrows are created by brute force, pushing the soil aside with the hydrostatic pressure caused by longitudinal segmental muscles. Some soil is removed by the worm consuming it and depositing it behind. Anecic worms draw vegetation down from the surface, then retire to digest it. They move by alternately gripping the tunnel sides with extending, multiple, short setae (bristles) on their front half, then drawing forward the back half. The front half is moved by the back half gripping the wall and the front half extending. By reversing this they can go backwards.

I have not found any answer in the literature to one question that has worried me for years: how do worms turn around in their narrow vertical burrows to ensure the appropriate part of their anatomy is in the correct place to produce their famous casts (poop)? Some drawings of burrows show side-tunnels via which, I hypothesise, they perform a three-point-turn. They also produce short, blind tunnels in which they lay their eggs.

Darwin was a great admirer of earthworms, writing: 'It may be doubted whether there are many other animals which have played so important a part in the history of the world, as have these lowly organised creatures.'[16] It is certain that without earthworms soils would be quite different and relatively poor compared with what we now have. The list of earthworm soil functions is short, but they are of significant importance: vastly improved drainage from the deep vertical tunnels; the removal of surface litter; the conversion of this litter into fine particles; its positioning above ground as a cast where seeds can set; general improvement of soil structure and aeration; and the provision of accessible nitrogen and other compounds. They may even be a major distributor of Arbuscular mycorrhizal fungi, whose spores they bring to the surface.

Description	Name
Living on dead organic matter in or just above the soil	Saprotroph
Living on dung	Coprophilous fungi
Form intimate mutualisms with shrubby plants and trees	Ectomycorrhiza
Form intimate mutualisms with herbaceous plants	Arbuscular mycorrhiza
Form intimate mutualisms with plants in the Family Ericaceae	Ericoid mycorrhiza
Parasitic on living plants, invertebrates and other fungi	Pathogens
Form intimate mutualisms with above-ground structures of grasses	
A mutualism where the fungus supplies the physical structure and inorganic nutrients, and an algae or cyanobacterium provides sugars by photosynthesis	Lichens

The functional types of fungi in grassland

THE FUNGI OF GRASSLANDS

The essential role played by grassland fungi has been largely neglected in books dealing with grasslands over the years, only recently gaining much of a mention. George Peterken, in his splendid book *Meadows* (2018), evidently admires them and describes their beauty well and goes into at least some detail.

Groups	Associates	Typical examples
Basidiomycetes Ascomycetes Oomycetes	Any plant, animal or fungus	Field Mushroom Puffballs
Basidiomycetes Ascomycetes	Dung, chiefly of grazers, including rabbits	Inkcap Fungi Cowpat Gem
Basidiomycetes Ascomycetes	Mostly trees. Some shrubs	*Cortinarius epsomiensis* Grisette Summer Truffle
Glomeromycota	Herbaceous plants	(Microscopic)
Basidiomycetes Ascomycetes	Members of the heather Family	*Rhizoscyphus ericae*
Basidiomycetes Ascomycetes	Plants, plus invertebrates	Rust and Smut Fungi Ergot
Ascomycetes	Grasses	*Epichloë* spp. (Choke)
Ascomycetes A few Basidiomycetes		Hound's Tooth

C. J. Smith, in his compendious and otherwise admirable *Ecology of the English Chalk* (1980), writes in intricate and exhaustive detail of the geology, climate, soil and plants of chalk downland, but barely at all of the fungi, and then only where they affect trees. Fungi are major players in the ecology of all types of grasslands, so they deserve a little more here.

So, fungi are not neutral partners 'merely' rotting down dead organic matter but highly active members of grassland communities. It is impossible to provide anything more than an overview of grassland fungi and their ecologies as the finer details are the subjects of many thousands of academic papers. Still, since there are believed to be some 12,500 species of fungi in the UK (including microspecies), it is worth exploring a few of the more interesting species, interactions, mechanisms and ecologies.

Fungi in grasslands come in eight functional types (see pages 90-91): that is, I have classed them here by what they *do* in grasslands. They are: (i) those that break down dead organic matter; (ii) those that live on or in dung; (iii) those that form intimate mutualisms (an uneasy but generally beneficial relationship between two or more organisms) with shrubby plants; (iv) those that form intimate mutualisms with grasses and wild flowers; (v) those that form intimate mutualisms with heathers and related shrubby plants; (vi) those that are parasitic on plants and animals; (vii) those that form an intimate mutualism with the above-ground parts of grasses; and (viii) lichens. The appearance of lichens in this list may come as a surprise to some, but these occur in grasslands too and they are indeed fungi, albeit with an internal photosynthesising algal or an external cyanobacterial partner.*

---

* In several cyanobacterial lichens the two partners are merely connected.

It is difficult to understand these fungi and their relationships without a little knowledge of which type of fungus or fungi engages in which of these processes. So, first, a very brief primer on the taxonomy of Fungi.

The categorising of organisms is a long-term project, and differences in opinion over what fits where on family trees, and at what level, are rife. As they say, 'other phylogenies are available'. All that can be done here is to give groups a name and an idea of more or less where they fit on the fungal 'tree of life'.

The Kingdom Fungi is (arguably) divided into eight groups, traditionally known as 'Divisions'. Only three of these will make an appearance in this book – the Basidiomycota, the Ascomycota and the Glomeromycota. There are also the 'Oomycetes', but these are merely 'FLOs' – 'fungus-like organisms' – despite the name indicating that they *are* fungi. The Basidiomycota and the Ascomycota are known as the 'higher fungi'. This may seem a value judgement, but they are the most recently evolved and, indeed, the most complex.

Members of the Basidiomycota are what you are most likely to see on a walk through the woods or fields: the familiar bracket fungi, jelly fungi, mushrooms and more. Their spores are generally 'dropped' from their fertile surface or surfaces, most typically the 'gills' of mushrooms.[17]

The Ascomycota form the bulk of the remaining higher fungi: that is, those that are readily visible to the naked eye. They form the largest group. They generally shoot their spores from microscopic, sausage-shaped vessels known as 'asci', hundreds of thousands of which cluster together in, for example, cup-shaped structures, such as the Cowpat Gem (see Plate 8). There are many other forms they can take, and they are most often microscopic and single-celled, like the yeasts.

Saprotrophic Fungi

Consuming dead organic matter is the commonest lifestyle choice of most fungi. Indeed, every fungus in the Division Basidiomycota has the ability to follow this path, at least in the early stages of development.[18] It is also the case that some species of mycorrhizal fungi can switch between nutritional pathways and adopt saprotrophism, with some populations of individual species following one pathway in one geographical location and the alternative pathway in another.[19]

Grasslands could not survive without saprotrophic fungi, as without them a thatch would build up quickly and, apart from the contribution of bacteria, nutrient recycling would cease. The primary mechanism is simple enough: the mycelium infiltrates into the soil-litter layers and their constituent hyphae exude a cocktail of enzymes. These break the bonds within complex organic matter, releasing glucose from cellulose, more complex sugars from starch, amino acids from proteins and fatty acids from lipids.[20] In digesting organic matter they release inorganic matter into the soil that will be reused by plants and fungi.

Dung Fungi

These form a specialist group among the saprotrophs and are sufficiently distinct to warrant a separate introduction to other saprotrophs. They are distinguished as the 'coprophilous [dung-loving] fungi'. Grazing animals consume between 43 and 73 per cent by weight of the plant-material growing in pasture.[21] A large proportion of this passes through the grazer as dung, leaving what would be a catastrophic problem for all concerned if it was not disposed of quickly.

The army sent to deal with the mess come in three battalions: invertebrates, fungi and bacteria. I highly recommend bringing a damp (OK, you can collect a dry one and wet it later) and slightly aged sheep-dropping home and placing it in a jar with some muslin on the top. It is quite amazing what eventually crawls out of it. Though for the most part they will be beetles, there will also be fungi. There are many species of fungi that have taken to consuming dung, or sometimes consuming invertebrates that have consumed dung, such as the *Ballocephala* species that parasitise tardigrades.[22]

If you have the stomach for it, you will also be rewarded by bringing home a slightly mature cowpat and placing it in a casserole dish, again covered in muslin and again kept moist. Regrettably, I must recommend obtaining your collection from a farm that either eschews pharmaceuticals or uses them wisely. The reason is that those fungi whose lifestyle involves passing through an animal first may be compromised by certain medicines.

The most likely and visible species you will see is the Cowpat Gem, *Cheilymenia granulata*, a small, bright orange disc fungus in the Ascomycota. There is also the tiny and remarkable Dung Cannon, *Pilobolus crystallinus*. This has a filamentous stipe (stem) on top of which is a 'cannon' complete with a 'cannonball'. The latter is a spherical packet of spores that is fired at high velocity to land outside the 'area of revulsion' (the area around the dung, where cattle will not graze), to be consumed with the fresh grass by unsuspecting cows. Around and around we go. If the cow responsible for the cowpat is infected with lungworm, then the juvenile of the nematode concerned will crawl up the stipe of this fungus and on to the cannonball to receive a free ride.

In similar vein is a species known to appear on cowpats, but which is more common on rotting wood: the Artillery Fungus, *Sphaerobolus stellatus*. I have never seen one, despite its reputation for being common. Its spore mass forms inside a small sphere which is sat in a neatly fitting cup. When the sphere is mature, the cup will invert suddenly, propelling the sphere at a sufficient velocity to lodge in a human eyeball – or so I am told. It is number three on my bucket list.

Various 'Inkcap fungi' can appear on dung of varying origin, such as *Coprinopsis pseudonivea*. The largest dung mushroom you are likely to find (always on horse dung) is the stately Egghead Mottlegill, *Panaeolus semiovatus*.

Most of the other fungal species on dung are microscopic, but help comes in the form of the *Keys to Fungi on Dung* (1971), by a couple of old friends, M. J. Richardson and Roy Watling. They describe sixty-five species in total, most of them requiring a serious microscope and a great deal of patience, not to mention courage. As a postscript, unrelated to fungi but related to dung is a slender book entitled *Insects of the British Cow-Dung Community* (1991). It is out of print and second-hand copies fetch ridiculously high prices, but I did once find the PDF online. Rather wonderfully, the author is Peter Skidmore.

Ectomycorrhizal Fungi (EMF)

Mycorrhizal relationships are where the filamentous mycelium of a fungus within the rhizosphere encompasses and partially penetrates the roots of woody plants. The mycelium will also extend far beyond the rhizosphere, absorbing nutrients clearly inaccessible to the plant.

The hyphae that make up a mycelium are extremely thin: between 1 and 5 µm in diameter, meaning that between a thousand and two hundred may be placed side by side in a line in one millimetre. This forms an enormous surface area for the absorption of accessible nutrients. The mycelium connects with the plant roots via a fungal structure known as a Hartig net, a 'woolly sock' made from hyphae that encompass and partially penetrate the roots.

Via the Hartig net the fungus provides water and inorganic

nutrients to the plant (phosphorus being the most important), and in exchange the plant provides the fungus with sugars. Both the Basidiomycetes and the Ascomycetes can form these relationships, though this ability is not at all ubiquitous within either group, with saprotrophs outnumbering them by a large margin.

This relationship is common in woody plants such as oak, beech and birch, though not all trees form such a relationship, and trees that are, for whatever reason, in a particularly nutrient-rich soil may at least partially renege on any deal they have made with a fungus.

Hedges and woodlands often produce fruiting bodies (mushrooms) of ectomycorrhizal fungi in neighbouring permanent grassland, along with their supporting underground mycelium. Sometimes the fruiting bodies can be found ten metres from the host tree. What, however, might be happening if one of these fungal fruiting bodies is found *one hundred* metres from the nearest suitable tree?

This is precisely the question I asked myself forty years ago at Hog Cliff, the subject of Part Three of this book. It was a Panther Cap, *Amanita pantherina*, sitting in the grassland with no suitable tree in sight. I found several more instances of one species or another being in the 'wrong' place and puzzled over this for years, as none of my then few books on fungi expressed an opinion. So it was only much later that I discovered that an association between some EMF species and the dwarf grassland shrub *Helianthemum nummularium*, the Common Rock-rose, had been recorded during the 1950s but had only become well known in the 1970s, albeit only via academic papers.

This seems to be an almost unique phenomenon, with only one more that I know of in the UK, that of the shrubby plant Mountain Avens, *Dryas octopetala*, which has a similar relationship with a few *Cortinarius* and *Tricholoma* (Webcap and Knight) species, though it is a plant of the rockier parts of calcareous lands, not grasslands.

Arbuscular Mycorrhizal (AM) Fungi

The arbuscular mycorrhizal (AM) fungi are all within the Division of the Kingdom Fungi known as the Glomeromycota. They are invisible to the naked eye, mere waifs, quietly going about their work. They are filamentous soil fungi that form mycorrhizal relationships with between 70 and 80 per cent of vascular plants on the planet, including grasses and wild flowers. Hence they are critical to plant ecologies everywhere.

With the ectomycorrhizal fungi, the mycelium surrounds and partially penetrates the roots; with AM fungi, they only penetrate. Within the roots, 'arbuscules' are formed by the fungus, and it is via these that the transfers take place. Arbuscules look remarkably like microscopic trees, providing their name (think 'arboretum'). These structures are formed *within* plant cells, with their associated plumbing being *between* plant cells. Phosphorus is again the primary nutrient collected by AM fungi, but also nitrogen in the form of nitrates and ammonia. Usually, this is by simple absorption from the soil, but phosphorus is sometimes obtained from organic material using the enzyme phosphatase.

In addition to nutrients, AM provide soils with stability – the mycelium has been likened to a fine 'sticky string bag', which really says it all.[23] AM fungi also protect against disease, and they enable plants to grow in poorer soils than would normally be possible. Here infected plants out-compete plants that lack an AM association, such as members of the Goosefoot and Cabbage families.

Considering that AM fungi are perpetually underground and produce no structures for aerial dispersal of spores such as we see with mushrooms, the question of how they colonise new ground is one that has puzzled researchers. They do produce spores, though they are odd in that some 'spores' can contain thousands of haploid chromosomes (effectively a bag of genetic material) and are correspondingly large – a spore of spores. Sometimes they produce hypogeous (underground) agglomerations of spores that are vaguely like a tiny truffle. The single spores range in size from 40 µm to 800 µm, both extremes enormous for most fungal spores, with the latter extreme just short of a millimetre.

Large spores cannot easily be dispersed by wind, so wind dispersal may be a relatively minor strategy, though water transport may well occur in certain situations. Spores sometimes find themselves congregated as mats on the surface of the soil, from where they may be transported by the feet of birds, in the guts of small mammals or by wind or water. Similarly, spores may simply be brought to the surface by earthworms or other soil invertebrates.[24] There is also 'vegetative' dispersal. This would take two forms – the simple growth of AM through the soil or the dispersal of pieces of mycelia by animal or even wind vectors. More (as they say) research is needed.

As taxonomic Divisions go, the Glomeromycota is minuscule, with only one Class, in which there are four extant Orders.[25] Nearly all of the 230 known species within this Kingdom are believed to form mycorrhizal relationships with plants, with the suspicion that several live independently.[26] As something of an aside, one species, *Geosiphon pyriformis*, is known to have left the pack by forming a symbiosis with a cyanobacterium in the genus *Nostoc*, a group known for producing green/brown 'jelly blobs' on damp footpaths. It and its associated cyanobacterium produce small, black, vaguely pear-shaped nodules known as 'sclerotia' on the roots of trees and shrubs. These are visible to the naked eye – just about.

The identification of individual species of AM fungi is difficult, even for those with an electron microscope and a DNA testing kit. Suffice to say that they are certainly there and would be lost or damaged were the land given over to agriculture.

Ericoid Mycorrhizal Fungi

The Ericoid mycorrhizal fungi are specialists in that they form relationships only with plants in the Family Ericaceae such as heathers and Cowberry. I mention them only because acid grasslands vie with heathland for space and are thus relevant here.

Parasitic Fungi

Nearly forty years ago I attended a talk run by the British Mycological Society. I cannot remember the name of the speaker or the title of the talk, but it could be paraphrased as 'Let's hear it for the bad guys!' It was a well-presented talk on why we should welcome parasitic fungi as much as any other species. They are life, after all, and most live in an evolutionary balance with their host plants, animals and, indeed, fungi.

It is generally human intervention that causes problems, most often in the establishment of monoculture crops where disease is easily spread. Not that monoculture could easily be discarded – we would starve. Another anthropogenic problem is the transfer of a pathogen from one territory where it lives in relative harmony with its host or hosts to another territory where the hosts are not adapted to it. Ash dieback, caused by the fungus *Hymenoscyphus fraxineus*, which is believed to have arrived from East Asia, for example, is a case of the latter. Incidentally, Britain hosts a close relative of this fungus, *H. fructigenus*. It is a tiny orange cup-fungus that grows benignly on dead hazelnut shells, beech mast and acorns.

This is a huge subject, so I am limiting my discussion to the grasses alone. Nearly all terrestrial plants suffer the attentions of parasitic fungi, and the information for those of grasses will apply, for the most part, to other herbaceous plants.

The growing of cereals has allowed fungal parasites to flourish, and the resultant crop failures have been disastrous through to the present day – Black Stem Rust and African Wheat Blight being among the most virulent current offenders. There are around ninety more such diseases of cereals, and many more for grasses in general.

Wild grasses, wild flowers and other denizens of grasslands, although suffering depredation, nevertheless exist in an uneasy harmony with their fungal parasites. Again, they are life. While I enjoy a walk along a hedgerow or across a species-rich field in spring as much as anyone, I prefer nature in its summer and autumn clothing, when thousands of invertebrate and fungal parasites bring these places very much more alive.

The fungi that infect plants will be familiar to the gardener as the blotches, rusty patches, tiny lollipops, cups and multiple other forms. For the mycologist, or anyone with a microscope, they are complex structures of great intricacy and beauty. The microfungi are another world.

The standard British work on this subject is *Microfungi on Land Plants*, by Martin B. Ellis and J. Pamela Ellis.[27] It spends sixty-nine of its weighty eight hundred pages on the parasitic and saprotrophic fungi that are found on grasses. Counting these has proved difficult for your author, most particularly because there is a list for every genus of grass, not one list for them all, and while some species are specific to a particular genus, others are less fussy, parasitising more than one genus – they are 'plurivorous'. Counting which are parasitic and which are saprotrophic is another problem, and a big one as Ellis and Ellis do not say which for each species, though some groups of grass fungi are career parasites such as the

Rusts and Smuts.

Nevertheless, after some extremely tedious analysis I have discovered that there are 120 fungi that are relatively unfussy about which grass or group of grasses they grow upon or infect, and 185 that are specific to a certain group (fescues, bromes, ryes, oats etc.) or an individual species, such as Red Fescue. This provides a total of just over three hundred species of fungi associated with the aerial parts of a grass in the UK.

How many of these are parasites, and how many are saprotrophs? Since I did not have the time to discover the dining preferences of three hundred fungi, I considered only the typical feeding habits of their group. Rust and smut fungi are always parasitic, disc fungi are mostly saprotrophic, other ascomycetes are a mixed bag of preferences and the Hyphomycetes and Coelomycetes are mostly parasitic. Very approximately, there are equal numbers of saprotrophs and parasites.

Now to the fungi themselves. There is no exam for you to pass on the long taxonomic names, so just let them wash over you.

There are five groups of fungi associated with grasses, the Rusts, the Smuts, the Ascomycetes, the Hyphomycetes and the Coelomycetes, with the Ascomycetes divided by Ellis and Ellis into the 'cup fungi', which look like what one might expect, and the 'other Ascomycetes', which can look like anything.

The concept of what something 'looks like' is confounded rather as the life stages of fungi are complex and very often only at the microscopic level. Using plain sight, perhaps augmented with a hand lens, the fungi are evident from what they do to the host plant and what the fruiting body or bodies (they can produce sexual or asexual fruiting bodies and sometimes both) look like.

You will be more familiar with these obscure organisms on grasses than you may think. Every discoloration of a grass, every blotch and imperfection, is likely be to the work of a fungus.

Sometimes this extends to entire patches of grass, most particularly lawns which appear to need watering but have in fact been suffering from a fungal disease.

Rust and smut fungi are the major parasites of grasses and plants; more technically they are 'obligate biotrophic plant pathogens'. They are both Basidiomycetes, respectively in the Classes Pucciniomycetes and Ustilaginomycetes. Smut fungi are also known from the small and related Order, the Tilletiales.

Rust fungi are conspicuous, usually establishing fruiting bodies in the form of pustules that are often bright orange – hence the name. Most are specific to one or more host plants, and relatively easy to name if one knows the name of the host as this dramatically focuses one's search efforts. They invariably grow on leaves and stems.

Smut fungi produce masses of black spores, making their host plant appear in urgent need of a bath. Hence the name. Grasses and various grass-like plants suffer most by far, but one species is frequently to be seen on the flowers of Red Campion, more particularly the anthers on which they develop. It is *Microbotryum violaceum*. Smut fungi are relatively uncommon in semi-natural grasslands, their main hosts being cereals. They can infect any part of a grass but have become specialists in favouring the reproductive organs where they create their spores. They are, in effect, sexually transmitted diseases.

Ascomycetes range from single-cell organisms such as the yeasts all the way to morels – large, vaguely brain-shaped structures on a fissured stem. Many that form on herbaceous plants are cup fungi, named after the cup-like structure of their fruiting bodies. Most of these are saprotrophic and often seen decorating dead grass leaves and stems. The other Ascomycetes of grasses are highly variable in behaviour and morphology. The sexual fruiting body of many of these is not a cup (apothecia) but a flask known as a 'perithecia', both of them containing large clusters of finger-shaped asci from which four or eight spores are shot into the air.

One of these is the fungus mentioned above that does so much damage to lawns – *Ascochyta*. There are over fifty *Ascochyta* species in the UK, seventeen of them on grasses. All is not lost as the fungus infects only the aerial parts of the grass, leaving the roots and perennating buds ready to fight another day. Powdery Mildew is also an Ascomycete.

Hyphomycetes are best known for their preference for aquatic habitats. There are, however, many that can be found on land, including grassland, and they are even to be found covering entire mushroom fruiting bodies with their bright colours. Some form raised black colonies, some branching colonies, and there are many other forms. They are common in grasses.

The Coelomycetes, formerly known as the Fungi Imperfecti, are what is often called a 'waste-basket taxon', meaning that the status of individual taxa (species, genera etc.) is uncertain. The only things they have in common are reproductive structures that are embedded in the surface of their host and which produce only asexual spores. There may or may not be a *sexual* stage of individual species, but often it is unknown, or known but with little chance of linking it to the asexual stage, or the fungus is permanently asexual in its reproduction.

Where asexual and sexual stages are known but unlinked, one species will have two names, a circumstance that is anathema to taxonomy – it is similar to giving different species names to tadpoles and frogs. A great deal of effort has gone into addressing this problem, though it is not going all that well.

The groups of fungi listed above do not quite cover all of the groups that are pathogenic on plants. There are also White Blister-rusts, which are not Rusts at all, and Downy Mildews. Both of these are members of the Oomycetes and enjoy honorary status as fungi here. Downy Mildews produce pale blotches on leaves.

Two particularly interesting grass pathogens are worthy of their own treatment. They are the Ascomycetes known as Choke and Ergot.

Choke

Choke (*Epichloë typhina s.l.*, which I will call *Epichloë* here) is a parasite of grass, though 'hemiparasite' or even 'commensal' might be more accurate. It only makes itself visibly known, without some serious laboratory kit, by its striking reproductive structure. This is a typically 4-cm-long sheath that encompasses grass culms, hence 'choke'. It will be white, then yellow to orange, respectively producing asexual then sexual spores. Close examination will see pustules in the colourful sexual stage, though I once followed the fortunes of a cluster of grasses, each bearing a white stage that did not develop further. The sexual spores have a relationship with fly species in the genus *Botanophila*, in that the fly is attracted to the fungal fruiting body and consumes its spores before spreading them to another grass plant. Their meal of spores apparently includes a laxative, ensuring that they do not hold on to them for too long. When urgency demands release, they smear their excrement in a zigzag pattern to provide a good chance of infection. This behaviour is, remarkably, induced by the fungus.

The fungus itself will live as a mycelium in the thin gruel between the cells of the grass for some time, and when (and if) the reproductive structure grows, it will commandeer extra sustenance by preventing the culm (flower stem) from developing an inflorescence. It also reproduces clonally by the extraordinarily direct method of growing *into* the seeds, continuing their life in a new plant. I know of few fungi that have attracted as much enthusiastic attention from mycologists as *Epichloë*, but this no doubt reflects its difficult taxonomy, complex biology and importance for grasslands, commercially grazed or not.

Since few people have ever seen the white-yellow/orange reproductive sheath of *Epichloë*, and naturalists with an interest in the fungus may only see it once or twice in a good year, it is surprising to hear how very common it is. A study of eighty-seven managed grasslands (pasture, meadow) in Germany found that *Epichloë* was present in an average of 66 per cent of tillers. Where it was present, the proportion of grass plants infected ranged dramatically, from 1 per cent to 99 per cent.[28] The reason *Epichloë* remains almost completely unnoticed is that the fruiting body itself is exceedingly rare. In Europe, around one hundred grass species have an association with *Epichloë*.

Despite its clearly parasitic seconding of plant nutrients, it cannot be said that *Epichloë* is a true parasite as it only seriously interferes with the life of the grass in those individuals where its fruiting prevents flowering. For the rest, *Epichloë* can be highly beneficial. This beneficence comes in the form of alkaloids that deter insect pests and grazing mammals, with different alkaloids employed according to the target in 'mind'. They also provide their host plants with vigour and an ability to survive drought conditions.

The problems with *Epichloë* can arise with pastured animals. Alkaloids are famously bitter and cause grass avoidance in grazing animals. If they still consume infected grasses, they may suffer very serious poisoning that can result in death. This is of small concern in Europe, but still causes problems in New Zealand, Australia and the USA.

Ergot

The close relative of *Epichloë* in the Family Clavicipitaceae, Ergot, *Claviceps purpurea*, is also common and cryptic for most of its life cycle. It is conspicuous only when seen in its resting state as a sclerotium, visible as black structures that look a little like black 'wild rice' grains. It grows on the florets of many grasses at the fruiting stage and in place of the seeds, though usually in just twos and threes. Most frequently it is found on ryegrasses, and with Perennial and Italian Ryegrass being dominant in pasture, it has the potential to be consumed by grazing animals and by humans who consume cultivated Rye, *Secale cereale*.

The problem is its high toxicity. It contains an unpleasant cocktail of alkaloids that can cause a deadly degree of vasoconstriction that can cause gangrene, and also lysergic acid amines, which cause hallucination. The creation of LSD was 'inspired' by this in the middle of the last century.

Ergot has an extensive, colourful and above all grim history, having caused agonising deaths in *at least* the hundreds of thousands over the millennia, and it could thus be the most poisonous of all fungi by body count. Its recorded history goes back to an Assyrian cuneiform tablet dated to 600 BCE. It records Ergot as a 'noxious pustule in the ear of grain'.

Ergot did not arrive in Europe until the Middle Ages, but there it wreaked havoc. Eighty-three epidemics have been recorded. One of the most recent was in France in 1778, when eight thousand people died.[29] The convulsions and hallucinations, not to mention deaths, that result from Ergot poisoning are believed by some to have been central to several ghastly witch trials, notably those of Salem.

For the most part Britain managed to avoid the ravages of Ergot because wheat was and is the staple cereal, not Rye. In Britain it was known as St Anthony's Fire, from the Hospital Brothers of St Anthony, who attempted to treat victims. I find it nearly every year in fields and along hedgerows, with wet summers sometimes providing a bumper 'crop'.

Parasitic fungi are by no means confined to plants – they can infect almost any living thing. Since grasslands house more invertebrate species than any other organisms, their fungus parasites are very much part of the community. They are known as the 'entomopathogenic fungi' (literally, fungi that induce pathologies in insects) and include multiple groups of fungi, most of them within the Ascomycota. The number of UK species is in the hundreds, with a few being well known for their use as a biological control agent: *Beauveria bassiana*, for example, is used to control aphids, and *Hirsutella gregis* parasitises many invertebrates.

The best-known of these, in grasslands, is the attractive bright orange, club-like sexual fruiting body of species around the genus *Cordyceps*, one of which is *Beauveria bassiana*, mentioned above. These are members of the Family Cordycipitaceae, all of which make a living by infecting invertebrates and, sometimes, other fungi, notably 'false truffles'.

Among the handful of UK species in the genus *Cordyceps* is *C. militaris*, the Scarlet Caterpillar Fungus (see Plate 7). It is conspicuously visible as a small *orange* club nestling in grass. Close attention will see this club covered in near-transparent hemispheres housing the surface fertile layer from which the spores are fired. I have exhumed several of these over the years, determined to show people what lies beneath: often the pupa of a moth or butterfly wrapped in a shroud of mycelial threads, its living parts digested by the fungus. I see it very nearly every year, and it is not at all uncommon.

This group of fungi has long been admired by mycologists for its extraordinary behaviour and has gained public notoriety from the book and later film (unusually, the film is better!) called *The Girl with all the Gifts* and a television series called *The Last of Us*.

Some members of the Family can take over the 'brains' of

invertebrates, causing them to behave in a manner that will suit the parasite. The best-known (real) fungus that induces such behaviour is the tropical *Ophiocordyceps unilateralis*, the 'Zombie-ant Fungus'. It infects ants, inducing them to climb high up a plant stem to ensure effective subsequent spore dispersal, and then remain immobile while it dies. A club-like fungal fruiting body grows from its head. Despite the premise of the above fantasies, humans are not and are never likely to be susceptible to such infection.

Lichens

Lichens are fungi that form an obligate relationship with algae: that is, one that is essential to one or both of the partners. The fungus forms the structural part of the lichen, while the associated alga is the photo-synthetic powerhouse. Also, though much less frequently, some lichens are made up of a fungus and a cyanobacterium, the latter generally forming a separate body, one that is 'plumbed into' the fungal structure. Lichens are named after the fungus, so technically there are no Latinised names for lichens as such.

Lichens certainly occur in grasslands; what they do not generally do is form interacting parts of a community with its ecological checks and balances; they just find somewhere to live. The only exception to this was provided by a lichenologist friend who told me that lichens in grasslands can control mosses by simply growing over them.

For lichens to appear in grassland, they require niches such a rocky outcrops, scattered stones or pieces of chalk, or stable scree. Collapsed rabbit burrows on chalk downland, for example, sometimes expose sizeable areas of flint once the thin soil has been washed away. Most lichens are sensitive to the pH of whatever substratum they usually inhabit, so which lichen grows where is highly dependent on the rocks or other substrata available.

In upland areas, lichens are ubiquitous on rocky outcrops. Both lowland and upland acid grassland are a balance between heath and bog, with the lichens of heath often abutting grassland in the patchwork that is often a feature of the landscape known as 'grass heath'. The best-known of these are the pale green, branching lichens in the genus *Cladonia*, known to model railway enthusiasts, who use it to imitate scrub and trees. On these grasslands they sometimes form domed patches half a metre in diameter.

Chalk downland often accommodates lichens because the poor soil results in less competition from plants for light. A small piece of partially embedded chalk can often be a useful habitat for lichens. The British Lichen Society notes that sixty-five species of lichen have been recorded on pieces of chalk and no fewer than seventy-eight on flints, with an exceptional forty-one found at a single site – Porton Down in Wiltshire.

MACROFUNGI OF GRASSLANDS

For the purposes of this book, these are quite simply the mushrooms, toadstools, puffballs, club fungi and other conspicuous fungi that one might find on an October morning stroll through permanent grasslands. Many species are found only, or chiefly, in grasslands, resulting in a quite different mycota from woodlands, where fungi will often be associated with trees through ecto-mycorrhizal relationships or adapted to parasitising trees as rot fungi or consuming the dead organic matter of woodlands, be it leaf litter or woody material. Woodland macrofungi outnumber grassland fungi by about eight to one, but by existing in an open environment the latter tend to be the more striking. On admittedly rare occasions – usually after heavy rainfall after a prolonged drought – there are so many fruiting bodies that one can barely see the grass.

There is almost no crossover between grassland fungi and woodland fungi, except where the fruiting bodies of the ecto-mycorrhizal fungi of trees appear in grassland along wooded edges. The only other striking exception that comes to mind is the occasional waxcap that can be found in the depth of woodlands. Incidentally, in many other countries waxcaps are found *mostly* in woodlands.

Grassland fungi are much fêted and alone can provide areas of very high biodiversity interest *regardless of the quality of the grassland plant community in which they occur.* Indeed, they very often occur in grasslands of otherwise relatively low biodiversity – upland and lowland acid, for example – and a fair proportion of old domestic lawns and cemeteries can often be classed of 'local interest', or even 'national interest', because of their fungi.

FUNGAL COMMUNITIES?

While plant communities have been minutely defined, there seems to be no strong concept of fungal communities. This is partly because fungi are heterotrophs, depending on the plant communities in which they are found. But to some extent certain plant communities host certain 'communities' of fungi.

Are there broader communities? Woodlands with trees that host ectomycorrhizal fungi, plus saprotrophic fungi, could be said to form a different community from a woodland of Sycamore and Ash, neither of which has ectomycorrhizal fungi. However, a woodland with both ecto- and non-ectomycorrhizal trees would be a messy mixture of the two, giving us the concept of intimately overlapping communities.

With grasslands there is one very distinct (or at least well-known) fungal community – waxcap grasslands, of which much more below. It may be thought that this is *the* fungal climax community – what emerges in any suitable grassland if all goes well, and usually after a prolonged period of development. However, there are ancient, rich grassland communities of fungi that boast no waxcaps at all, and often none or few of the associated fungi of waxcap grasslands. These have not been well recognised, if recognised at all, by conservation bodies and are thus vulnerable to loss. I discuss this community more fully later.

FUNGAL SUCCESSION

Like hedgerows and woodlands, grasslands can take an exceedingly long time to become fungus-rich. Fields that were once ploughed, then laid or left for permanent pasture, will be slow to develop a mycota, partly because the soil will spike in its nutrient levels, something that fungal mycelia tolerate poorly or not at all. The early adopters are the small ephemeral saprotrophs: *Paneolus* spp., *Conocybe* spp., *Parasola* spp. and *Bolbitius* spp.; respectively, Mottlegills, Conecaps, Pleated Inkcaps and Yellow Fieldcaps. The Field Mushroom, *Agaricus campestris*, and some others that grow in rings are also early adopters; the odd puffball and the Shaggy Inkcap, *Coprinus comatus*, can also turn up.

Assuming that a grassland and its soil are suitable, more or less neutral grasslands can develop much further, resulting in the above-mentioned waxcap grasslands. Some waxcap grasslands have been recorded as establishing a good mycota from previously arable land in a mere thirty years. Perhaps there were remnant mycelia in the soil — which seems unlikely as there is little evidence of their long-term survival — or there were fungus-rich grasslands nearby that could 'seed' them.

To provide a truly rich mycota it needs to be left in peace for a very long time. One authority maintained that it can take centuries or even a thousand years to establish the richest of sites, an opinion with which I concur completely.[30] Such sites are almost invisible marvels of survival and complexity, so it is a tragedy that they can so easily be destroyed. Now for some more details on these purported communities.

WAXCAP GRASSLANDS

Shallow as we can sometimes be, preferring beauty over all, it is not too surprising that waxcap grasslands have gained so much attention, from those who know of their existence at least. Waxcaps are quite extraordinarily attractive, putting both rainbows and Joseph's technicoloured dreamcoat to shame with their many more colours. White, brown, yellow, orange, grey, scarlet, crimson, green, pink, purple – they are astounding against the green of the sward. Except the green ones, of course. Quite why they sport these colours, indeed why any fungus should sport a colour at all, is one of the mysteries of mycology. No one knows. Maybe here, however, it is to save them from grazing animals, though this still does not explain those green ones.

I have taken over six hundred fungus walks over thirty-four years and am always surprised how very few people have seen a waxcap before. All I can hope for is that they search them out and marvel again.

A rich waxcap grassland appears to be the 'climax' mycota of more or less neutral grassland communities of fungi, though fungi are considerably less particular about pH than most plants. These grasslands tend to be of low fertility and with a moderate composition of plant species: in other words, not the best, but certainly not the worst in plant biodiversity terms. Some waxcaps, however, do prefer extremes: the Heath Waxcap, *Gliophorus laeta* (rare), is adapted to a low pH, and the Limestone Waxcap, *Hygrocybe calciphila* (very rare), to a high pH. Despite my insistence on neutral grasslands, the NVC section on grasslands states that calcareous grasslands will also bear waxcap communities. I cannot confirm this from my own experience of chalk downland. These have thin soils over a chalk bedrock and are highly calcareous – perhaps a little too high for most waxcaps.[31]

Mosses invariably accompany the headline waxcap species, most particularly *Rhytidiadelphus squarrosus*, though whether this indicates a functional link between them or whether it is just that the conditions are those favoured by both is a matter of ongoing discussion. The sites need to be 'damp' rather than wet (with a few exceptions, as in a *Hygrocybe coccineocrenata* that appears in mires), and, above all, they, and all the other fungi likely to appear alongside them, require the grass to be kept reasonably short with grazing or topping, or by a lawnmower if it is a domestic grassland (lawn).

Preferably, this will be from sheep grazing, as cattle can easily damage the sward and mycelia. Short swards are essential for the fruiting of waxcaps, and indeed all macrofungi in grasslands, as they simply refuse to grow if the grass is too long. Any attempt to fruit in long grass would be futile as the spores would fail to be caught by the wind. Ten centimetres or below is a good height for the sward, so grazing must be both light and frequent, especially in the fruiting season, which runs any time from a week or so after rain from mid-July up to the end of November or even December, barring frosts. If the grassland is not grazed, then topping, or application of a lawnmower, must always be followed by a removal of 'clippings'. If left, they will prevent fruiting and damage the sward.

The frequently used measure to assess the quality of waxcap grasslands in terms of its fungi comes in the form of the acronym CHEGD, from Clavarioids, Hygrocybe, Entoloma, Geoglossoids and Dermoloma, all of them groups of fungi. These are in no particular order, just the one that provides at least some hope of a pronounceable acronym. Not all of the species within the various genera concerned can be found in grasslands.

At its heart CHEGD is a head count of these five species groups – the more species found on a site within these five groups, the better the grassland will be, for fungi at least. It ignores numerous other groups that are frequently found in mature grasslands, such as parasols, mushrooms (*Agaricus* spp.), *Paneolus* species and *Lepista* species (Blewits).

Clavarioids are any of the several club fungi within three genera that occur in grasslands. I have found these in the company of other people hundreds of times and none but a tiny few had ever seen one before, presumably because they are somewhat hidden in the grass. This is a great pity as they are miniature beauties and common. Many are a bright yellow, others white or grey-brown. There is one bright purple/pink species, *Clavaria zollingeri*, but it is exceedingly rare. Some form singly or in groups of single clubs, others in dense, branching clusters. Clavarioids are composed of the genera *Clavaria*, *Clavulinopsis* and *Ramariopsis*.

Hygrocybe refers to the waxcaps themselves. When I first took an interest in waxcaps, they were all in the genus *Hygrocybe*. This has now been split into several new genera, with the original name retained by relatively few species. Now we are stuck with *Hygrocybe*, *Gliophorus*, *Cuphophyllus*, *Neohygrocybe*, *Porpolomopsis* and *Gloioxanthomyces*.

Hygrocybe is the most persuasive of the five groups and could easily be used as a reasonable guide without the assistance of its companions; they are, after all, called 'waxcap grasslands'. In fact, CHEGD is a development of the practice of using waxcaps alone to identify mycologically rich grasslands of this type.[32] They are certainly the most eye-catching. Textures run from dry to sticky to slimy. Most are just a few centimetres across, some reaching 12 cm and more.

Entoloma refers to the 'pinkgills', reflecting the salmon-pink of the spores as seen on the gills. *Entoloma* is the sole genus in this group. There are several fairly large grassland species of *Entoloma* (other large *Entoloma* species occur in woodlands), the commonest of which are the tall species, the grey/beige *E. prunuloides*, the brownish *E. porphyrophaeum* and the fairly rare and metallic-blue *E. bloxamii s.l.*, respectively the Mealy, Lilac and Big Blue Pinkgill. Most are easy enough to identify with some experience, but it is difficult to mentally manage the tricky triplet of *Entoloma sericeum*, *sericellum* and *serrulatum*.

Geoglossoids are the 'earthtongues', encompassing five genera, and well named as a group because most look like tongues, mostly black tongues. They are the devil to identify, requiring a microscope. I see very few of these.

Dermoloma encompasses four genera, the Crazed-caps, Fanvaults, Meadow-caps and *Pseudotricholoma metapodium*, the last of these on its own and mercifully missing out on a common name. All are small and unprepossessing agarics, except *P. metapodium*, which is sizeable and fleshy. *Dermoloma* species are characterised by a cracking cap.

Armed with the results of a survey, an ecologist can make that head count and decide which category of 'importance' the grassland should be placed in. The scoring system is tweaked every now and then, but a typical scheme is that three or fewer at a site mean that the site is of 'no importance', four to eight is of local importance, nine to sixteen is of regional importance and above this is of national importance. Beyond this there is 'international importance', which informally means twenty-two and above. A mycologist who finds so many can cheerfully retire to the pub and wax lyrical about his success.

OTHER FUNGAL COMMUNITIES

There appear to be at least two other grassland fungi communities: those of grassland on chalk, the mycorrhizal *Helianthemum* (Common Rock-rose) community, and those in which ring fungi are the most conspicuous.

Helianthemum Communities

These are best shown with an example, so the finer details of these extraordinary communities can be found on p. 172, where I discuss them in the context of Hog Cliff. I also mention them in the introduction to functional types of fungi. For now, they are the fungi mentioned briefly above that have an ectomycorrhizal association with the dwarf shrub the Common Rock-rose, *Helianthemum nummularium*. This is precisely the same as the association between certain woodland fungi and trees, excepting that the fungi tower over their host plant rather than the other way round!

Ring Fungi

One of the most striking features of fungus-rich grasslands is the often enormous rings some species can form. The origin of these rings was once considered a matter of mystery and magic – they were 'fairy rings', where fairies danced in circles, presumably scattering fairy dust as they frolicked. In the past, everything that existed without obvious explanation was put down to magic, magical beings or the gods. With the Enlightenment came naturalistic explanations such as lightning scorching a ring in the soil from which the rings grew, or simply that some animals walk around in circles depositing dung in their perambulation. Both hypotheses are absurd, but at least they did not require hobgoblins and the like. It was down to the great William Withering of digoxin fame (the heart medicine) to discover the true nature of fairy rings in the eighteenth century. He simply dug up a ring and noticed that fungal mycelia were more prolific there than in nearby soils.

When spores of a species prone to such behaviour germinate, they form a mycelium which will combine with another mycelium to form a mycelial mass capable of forming fruiting bodies (mushrooms). Starting from a single spot in a field, as they must inevitably do, they can only grow outwards. At first this forms a disc of mycelium, but as it spreads it dies out in the middle as food resources are consumed. This leaves a ring of mycelium from which the mushrooms may grow once conditions of temperature and soil moisture content are suitable.

Such rings are often visible with no mushrooms present. In fact, there are three types of rings growing in grasslands: named unimaginatively as types 1 to 3. Type 1 is seen in the Fairy Ring Champignon, *Marasmius oreades*, and, to a lesser extent, the Horse Mushroom, *Agaricus arvensis*. These form rings where the grass is greener on the inside of the ring, where nutrients have been released by the feeding mycelia and the turf playing dead on the outside of the ring, where it has been compromised by chemicals released by the fungus, notably cyanide, and the crowding of the mycelia. It must be presumed that this is to allow these short fungi to drop their spores in open air, rather than among (relatively) tall grasses, where dispersal would be impaired.

Type 2 are fungi that merely stimulate the growth of grasses through the release of nitrogen compounds from consumed organic matter in the soil. The effect is that the grass grows lush and green. Type 3 has no visible effect on the grass. Waxcaps, which only grow in rings on occasions, are Type 3 and their mode of feeding has proved elusive to researchers.[33]

There are other ring types, most particularly 'tethered rings', which I have only seen in woodlands. These occur with ecto-mycorrhizal fungi that are, by definition, tethered to their host trees or shrubs. Since ectomycorrhizal fungi occur in grassland on the Common Rock-rose, one might expect to see tethered rings, though I cannot say that I have done so.

Reports of these rings growing to several hundred metres in diameter are commonly found in secondary literature, though these are difficult to confirm. Nevertheless, I am confident that they do occur. Such monsters are not always conspicuous as they often fragment as parts of the ring die out, forming arcs or small patches of the fruiting bodies. The ring-forming Common Funnel, *Infundibulicybe geotropa*, for example, is very often seen in linear troops, raising the question of whether they are fragments of an indefinitely large, ancient and highly fragmented ring.

How fast do ring fungi grow? The standard answer, found in many books and other sources, is up to 20 cm a year. However, the distinguished British mycologist John Ramsbottom wrote in 1926 of 50 cm for some species, and an almost identical rate was described in the *Journal of Ecology* in 1984.[34]

Having casually followed the fortunes of many rings over many years, I have always been doubtful of these values and recently studied a ring of *Lepista panaeolus* (a rare species of blewit), using the ruler function on an online historical series of aerial photographs. I also measured several other rings around West Dorset and found that the rate of growth was approximately 100 cm a year. The thrill of finding so dramatic a speed of growth, one that was so much higher than those reported elsewhere, was short-lived. A year later I discovered a paper that reported a relative of *Lepista panaeolus*, *L. sordida*, growing at precisely the same rate.[35] Younger rings are known to grow faster, so I have consoled myself with the 140cm/year growth rate of a small ring of *Melanoleuca grammopodia*. Both species, incidentally, bear large fruiting bodies, and I counted four hundred on the *L. panaeolus* ring when I last saw it in 2023. So there.

Do such rings affect soil conditions sufficiently to make changes to plant growth other than that in the ring zone? Certainly, ring fungi are known to have a dramatic effect on soil quality such as a change in pH, and also its bacteria.[36] So yes, they do have an effect on plants, favouring some species over others. This is considered by some researchers to be detrimental to the grassland concerned, by reducing the number of species. As I have indicated, the changes are dramatic where a ring is active but fades where it has died out, the soil largely returning to normal in a central expanding disc inside mature rings. This is seen conspicuously in 'rings within rings', which only occur in old rings.

The findings of an academic paper from 2020 that used DNA sequencing of soil samples to study the Type 2 rings in the montane grasslands of the eastern foothills of the Pyrenees, 'highlight[ed] the importance of particular keystone taxa in the structuring of fungal communities and their effect on the overall grassland fungal community', and that fungal diversity inside the ring was greater than outside, possibly owing to the available dead matter or the nutrients released from its breakdown.[37] (The 'keystone taxa' mentioned are the fungi that cause fairy rings.)

Most were microscopic, but there were also macrofungi such as club fungi, puffballs and members of the difficult agaric genus *Psathyrella*. To be honest, I have never noticed much activity inside a fairy ring, perhaps because the fungi either do not fruit or are microscopic. But then the authors note that the locals who were familiar with these rings had never noticed them either.

Ring fungi are seen in many types of grassland, their primary considerations being that the land has not been disturbed for at least twenty years, the grass is kept short and the field is not too wet. What they do not seem to care about is the plants among which they grow and on which they depend. I have seen them on land that hosts twenty-five species of plants to a square metre, and on those that host a mere seven.

This has left them vulnerable to loss as grasslands are judged by their flora, not their mycota. Some of these rings are truly ancient, so we lose much when the plough arrives – something I have witnessed. I plead for their protection.

INVERTEBRATE PARASITES OF MACROFUNGI

Since the object of this book is to reveal that *species-rich* grasslands are exactly that, it would be remiss in this section on the fungi not to mention those organisms that depend on them, often entirely. The main consumers of fungal fruiting bodies, at least from the outside in, are slugs (never snails, to my knowledge). They are more common in woodlands, but a few will nibble holes in grassland fungi. Then there are the fungus gnats, best known in larval form as the much-despised maggots in your *cèpes a la crème*. They depend *entirely* on fungal fruiting bodies for their existence. Fungus gnats are life too, of course, and they are threatened by the loss of fungal fruiting bodies, which in turn comes from loss of habitat and, to a *much* lesser extent, from people picking mushrooms.

There are an impressive 574 species of these gnats in Britain, with only a handful of researchers able, or prepared, to identify them.[38] Identification is extremely difficult, with minute differences in male genitalia providing most of the clues. There is no unlikely prurience here – different groups have key characteristics of key features. With fungi it might be the size and shape of the spores; with trees the first thing to look at is leaf shape. It is simply the case that with fungal gnats it is the male genitalia that stand out.

There are many other groups of invertebrates that rely on

fungal fruiting bodies for their livelihood. Grazing animals ignore them as they would a rock, though I have heard of the odd horse taking a bite. I have noticed 'V-shaped' holes caused by corvids in some specimens of horse and field mushrooms. One might think that crows and their ilk have taken to mycophagy, but the holes are no doubt caused by crows who clearly prefer the maggots to the mushrooms.

THE CONSERVATION OF GRASSLAND FUNGI IN THE UK

With waxcap grasslands not receiving the level of protection afforded to plant-rich grasslands, their communities are under threat throughout northern Europe. This threat is greater still with the two putative grassland fungal communities I described above, as they are barely recognised as possessing any value at all.

Although we British have an unfortunate habit of denigrating ourselves,* we have been exceptionally good at maintaining high-value grassland sites for fungi, albeit inadvertently. Fungi are highly susceptible to aerial pollution, most particularly nitrogen compounds. This suggests the possibility that our success is due at least in part to Britain being upwind of the rest of Europe, most of the time anyway.

Despite this encouraging news, sites of mycological value have been seriously undervalued in the past, and only recently have they begun to receive the attention they deserve, and then not comprehensively. They are still being destroyed, often by people with the very best of intentions who think that planting trees is *always* a jolly good thing (see p. 45 for why this is not the case). Heaven protect us from the well-intentioned.

Some sites are protected, but only a tiny fraction meet the

---

* Sometimes this is well deserved, sometimes not. And of course, it is not usually *themselves* but other Brits of whom they disapprove.

various criteria for protection, usually the number of component plants, or of fungi when a waxcap community is being considered. Even then, the criteria are set too high, with plant-poor fungus-rich grasslands containing ring fungi virtually ignored. Many more simply go unnoticed, unprotected and simply lost: something I have seen happen. While every field with a moderately rare orchid growing in it will attract the attention of a naturalist and possibly the local wildlife trust, twenty species of uncommon fungi will be passed by as of no interest or just 'too difficult to identify'.

Where efforts have been made, the surveys of grasslands that *may* be rich in fungi continue to be fraught with difficulty. Most of the year a piece of pasture can be very dull, with just a few flowering plants brightening the sward from time to time. Then the autumn comes, and it is a blaze of fungal form and colour. *Or not.*

Grassland fungi are very susceptible to drought conditions and flatly refuse to fruit in anything other than moist soils. Woodlands, by contrast, stay wet much longer because of the cover they provide. Sometimes it is *too* wet for fungi, and quite often very few appear for no readily apparent reason, though depletion of the mycelia from which they arose in a previous year of heavy fruiting may reduce fruiting.

There is an old story of a mycologist who watched a 'fairy ring' in his lawn grow by observing the expanding ring of lush grass known to be formed by an unnamed ring fungus. It was thirty years before it produced a fruiting body by which he could identify it. In a similar vein, forty years ago, at Hog Cliff, Dorset, I observed how a diminutive species of puffball grew on very nearly every one of the thousand or so anthills that are found there. I haven't seen it since but suspect it is still there, preparing for its big comeback.

Even when they do appear, a field may produce fruiting bodies for just ten days and they are therefore very easy to miss. On one site I know very well, the number of species visible as fruiting bodies on any one October day can vary from three to fifty. This does not happen with plants – apart from the annuals, they are always visible. This highly unreliable fruiting of fungi means that any site of likely interest will need to be surveyed for several years to determine what is there – ten years being reasonable – though the great British mycologist Peter Orton visited the same place for twenty-five years and found something new every time.

This is exacerbated by the fact that most grassland surveys are made during the summer, when the flowering plants are both more visible and easier to identify. With some exceptions, macrofungi do not appear until late August, with the all-important waxcaps seldom fruiting before late October, though in the north it can be earlier.

Finally, the identification of fungi is a hard-won skill. Most people who collect records are amateurs, which is fine, but they must be *good* amateurs in possession of perhaps fifty (expensive) books to aid identification, plus a chemistry lab of reagents that can sometimes help (colour change), a good microscope and the skills to use it.

Professional mycologists able to identify species are rarer still. Finding professional taxonomists who are able to identify *any* of the 'difficult' groups – in addition to fungi, micro-moths, ichneumonid wasps and fungus gnats come to mind – is increasingly difficult, as they are not replaced when they retire. One wag suggested that such taxonomists deserve 'schedule 8' status.[39]

Apart from the issue of budgets, there is the low status that is generally applied to taxonomists with the skill to differentiate species within a given group, and they are somewhat likened to stamp collectors. If a university or botanic garden was a hospital, the scientist studying, say, calcitonin in chick embryos would be a consultant, while the scientist doing fungus surveys would be a hospital porter or Grade 4 nurse at best. An injustice, I am sure you will agree, but one that discourages young people from adopting 'field taxonomy', and we now need them more than ever.

One final issue is 'observational bias'. This is a nightmare in taxonomy, producing seriously skewed records. A specialist in the taxonomy of, say, parasitoid wasps might intensively record the objects of his or her passion found in nearby nature reserves. When he or she goes on holiday to Cornwall, he or she (much to the ire of their spouse) will record species there. This will inevitably produce two hotspots, with the rest of the country apparently bereft of this interesting group. A more real-world example is the Annual Autumn Foray run for members by the British Mycological Society. These are week-long events, and many hundreds of records will be made on each one. Many of the official records for fungi are from the various sites where these jamborees have taken place. Records age, however, and become useless when one wishes to know what is there *now* – they only show what was there *then*.

Fortunately, or not, the comparatively unromantic practice of taking soil samples and running them through a DNA sequencer has changed matters, though it is prohibitively expensive at the time of writing. Even then, species often occur only once in, say, a 1 ha nature reserve. This would require up to a million samples for it to be noticed. I have heard of an occasion when the most notable fungi on one particular site were missed completely by this method.

My final plea is a reiteration of the point I have made several times: fungi, waxcaps or not, should be recognised as species of value when found in a grassland, regardless of the presence or absence of valued plant species.

PERSONAL RESPONSIBILITY

If you have ever noticed grassland fungi (especially waxcaps) on your land, be it farm, stately home or lawn, then my advice is to leave the management precisely as it is, since it is likely to already be good. If you think matters could be improved, then I suggest the following:

1. If the site is grazed, then graze it lightly and preferably with sheep. The sward should be no more than 10 cm, particularly in the fruiting season, and should never be lank. Similar advice applies if it is topped or mown.
2. Remove all the arisings (cut vegetation) to avoid a thatch and high nutrient levels.
3. Never apply inorganic fertilisers and never apply farmyard manure or any other organic fertiliser.
4. If possible, avoid giving anthelmintic or other fungus-toxic medicine to stock or horses.
5. Never use lime, as this will kill the moss.
6. Never scarify the sward to remove said moss.
7. Keep records if you can.
8. *Tell someone about it*. I suggest Natural England, the local environmental records centre or perhaps your county wildlife trust.

FUNGI AND AGRICULTURE

A fungus-rich field can be lost in a day through agricultural activity such as ploughing or through the application of nitrogen fertiliser – something fungi are unable to tolerate. Slower deaths occur from abandonment, with the grass growing long and lank. If the long grass and resultant thatch persist, fungal mycelia can die. Ultimately the site will be overwhelmed by scrub or Bracken or the coarser herbaceous plants.

With nutrients supplied to crops in the form of inorganic fertilisers, AM fungi reduce in biomass as they become of less importance to their associated plants. A field of wheat or a new ley will require the use of the plough and harrow, causing great disturbance to the delicate AM fungi.[40]

The effect on soil organisms in arable land is a hot topic in ecological studies, especially in comparison to permanent grassland. A recent paper investigated the soil fungi in multiple sites in Europe at different latitudes from Spain to Sweden.[41] Employing DNA, the authors studied the prevalence of fungi in the soil.[42] It is a truism in mycology that many species are very common, but very many more are rare. Comparing soil samples found in both arable land and permanent grassland, they report that fungal diversity was always lower in arable land than in permanent grassland, and that rare fungi were almost invariably absent from the former.

In this part of the book I have explained and examined the many aspects of grasslands that so often pass us by when we go for a walk: the types of grassland, their management, their loss and the grasses, plants, animals and fungi that make semi-natural grasslands what they are.

Having examined these details of grasslands in general, it is now time to turn to the particular. I present, first, a particular site in fine detail, then several instances of grassland types, in less detail than those of Hog Cliff, to show how different grasslands can be. It is feet-on-the-ground time.

Part Three

ONE PATCH OF GRASS

For a moment, the clouds part in the west and a blast of setting sunlight illuminates the damp chalk coombe. The black evening clouds in the east retain their foreboding aspect, and a perfect rainbow forms, arching over the matching downwards curve of the landscape.* This is Hog Cliff at its flamboyant best, grand and dramatic, but it is not for such spectacles that Hog Cliff is valued: it is for what is found there – the life both on and in 'The Chalk', as such grasslands are romantically called.

Having discussed the history of species-rich grassland, their losses and current threats, their component organisms and a little ecology, it is time to put matters in the context of a real patch of grass. We will begin where I began, at Hog Cliff, the place where I learned about grasslands and came to love them for the great joy they gave me and give me still. Here I provide a detailed (though by *no* means exhaustive) account of just one of the many grassland types found in Britain.

Those details include its history, its geology and climate, the effects of human intervention, the fine details of the various grass-land communities it proudly supports and some of the very many plants, fungi and animals that make their home here. These are the details that make it and other good grasslands what they are – intricate havens of *life*.

For the most part I stress the *numbers* of species that exist here – it is these that give us the 'diverse' in 'biodiverse'. But I also tell

* I won't be going on like this, I just wanted to prove that I could do it.

the *stories* of many of the organisms of Hog Cliff – their lives, their friends and enemies, their intricate glory and beauty.

I have chosen this patch for so expansive a description because I know it so very well, having lived at its edge for a few years and visited it hundreds of times during the subsequent decades. It is also a 'good' site, in that it sports a large number of species, and it is varied in the types of grassland that are there and the edge habitats of scrub and woodland that do so much for diversity. It is also one of the best places I know for fungi.

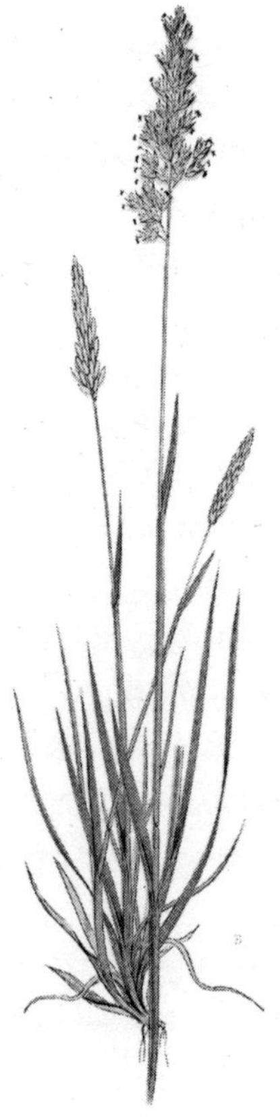

Crested Hair-grass

Hog Cliff – Chalk Downland

Since the Second World War the UK has lost around 80 per cent of its chalk downland. In the South Downs, for example, it now covers just 4 per cent of the National Park's area. Over one-third of the sites are less than 1 ha in size, leading to isolation and abandonment.' Ideally a site of at least 20 ha is needed to remain stable. There are 38,000 ha of chalk downland in England, but in a map of those in Dorset they appear as islands in a sea of arable land.

Hog Cliff, as Plate 11 shows, consists of the above-mentioned coombe which meets a long, dry valley to the west, forming a short, tilted and very curvy T. The coombe and valley sides plunge downwards at perilous angles of up to 27 degrees – equivalent to a one-in-two slope. Above these valley sides a great deal of scrub exists, and there are areas of moderately flat grassland above and below the slopes that have not seen the plough for seventy years.

The name comes from the southerly part of the valley, Hog Cliff Bottom, which is largely within the area of the SSSI (Site of Special Scientific Interest). The 'Hog' part of the name is unlikely to be a reference to pigs. This is sheep country, so it no doubt comes from Hog, Hogg, Hoggerel or Hogget, all words for young sheep.

Such a topography, such a geology and climate, and the various agricultural methods that have been applied over the centuries, have produced a complex patchwork of grassland and other habitats. All the grasslands at Hog Cliff are heaving with life, but it is the steep slopes that are by far its greatest treasures. Chalk downland is exceedingly rare worldwide, with the English chalk being by far the largest in extent, with smaller areas in north-western Europe.

Two of the denizens of Hog Cliff were once myself and my wife, though it is not for me to say if we were among the 'treasures'. We moved there in 1981, not long after we were married, then moved into the village three and a half years later, when the elderly farmer, our landlord, needed to sell up and retire. While I would have stayed there for ever, we were not sorry to leave our damp and freezing little house, perched at the top of the coombe as it was.

Some places affect us deeply, teaching us, changing us and even showing us that profound love can be felt for something other than a person or animal. Not that it was always easy.

For my wife, a Londoner born and bred, Hog Cliff was an enormous shock. Having no neighbours within a mile in any direction was unthinkable for her – as were: treading on a pheasant hiding in long grass (they sound like a hysterical helicopter when they take off), finding (usually, first by smell) the horrific sight of the occasional cow that had died with its calf half born, innumerable rabbits dead or dying horribly from myxomatosis and listening on a still night to the conversation of people who (really) seemed to be camped in our garden but who were actually camping on the far side of the valley, 600 m away. Two incidents that come to mind were plain dangerous: dealing with a couple of local deer poachers who were (obviously) armed, and having .22 rounds whizzing past my ear courtesy of the neighbouring farmer, who was on a reckless rabbit-shooting spree.

Having spent my first five years in a small north Hampshire village, I was marginally more prepared for country life. I considered the firearms incidents to be a bit of excitement, though I never quite got over the sight of those poor dead cows, blown up to twice their size from all the trapped methane. But, as the farmer calmly told me, 'Where there's livestock there's dead stock.'

During those long-ago years, I explored every square metre of the then 210-acre piece of land: the now lost-to-arable large field along Long Ash Lane that sported a hundred rings of Field Mushrooms; the fungi, plants and badgers of the two conjoined coppices on the far valley side; and the new world of the scrub that ran around the brows of the sloping grassland that was nearly a woodland. Every part holds many memories, but the most evocative are of those grassy slopes that characterise the land, for it was these that taught me to treasure all semi-natural grasslands.

The farmer who owned it was Commander 'Snowy' Eyre. He was an extraordinary character: secretary of the Cattistock Hunt, bad-tempered and charming in equal measure and an indefatigable enthusiast for 'the ladies'. I have always felt that he would have been happier still as an eighteenth-century squire, and he did play a bit-part as a hunter in the film of Fielding's *Tom Jones*. He farmed the land almost entirely on his own, arriving in the morning to put out hay and feed, and to check that his breeder herd of cattle was doing well. Apart from that, he visited only for topping grass that threatened to lie lank and wasted over winter, repair the odd fence, help load the sold calves onto the lorry for fattening by another farmer and, once a year, hunt foxes. Such a farming method seems lazy and inefficient, but it worked well enough for several decades. It also came with a major benefit – the land was largely left to its own devices.

A BRIEF HISTORY OF HOG CLIFF

Hog Cliff is near the western extremity of The Chalk. There is a great deal of this in England, though the massive 'Southern Chalk Formation' is by far the largest. It stretches from a mile or two to the west of Hog Cliff, progressing eastward, with a finger stretching past Brighton. A second, more northerly finger runs to Dover, and a third shoots north of London and far into East Anglia. Even where chalk is not visible, it lies hidden deep under the clay of London and the sand of the Hampshire Bowl.

It has long been believed that The Chalk was the first major landscape type to be farmed. The river valleys were permanently wet, so the dry hills held an appeal as fertile land, though settlements were more likely on the sheltered lower slopes. In addition, the primal trees that would have inhabited those hills were likely to be sparse and shallow-rooted and thus relatively easy to clear for both arable and grazing. There is the question of why early peoples would have ploughed the slopes, as such a project is difficult even with today's high-tech machinery. In fact, it is believed that they were cultivated with hand tools such as 'ards' – primitive and sometimes hand-held ploughs.

I used to look westwards out of our first-floor window at the strange ridges in the large, sloping field on the distant lower valley side, wondering who created them. They made no obvious sense as much was missing, and much was overlaid by later work. The modern Lidar images, however, do begin to make sense of matters as they can reveal long-hidden features in the form of shallow banks and ditches.

The most notable thing about what is now visible as an extensive field system is that the fields are all studiously rectilinear when viewed from above, with the rolling topography of the land seemingly ignored. They are also oriented in more or less the same direction. Such ancient fields are known to archaeologists as 'terrain-oblivious coaxial field systems'. The general idea seems to be that just because one diagonal half of a square field was horizontal, while the other half quickly ascended a hill, it did not mean it could not look rectangular from above – which they do. These fields were part of a planned landscape where the plan was everything, though the steep and species-rich hillsides proved exempt and were left for open grazing.

Such a landscape is typical of the time around the Middle Bronze Age, placing them at anything from 1,800 BCE to 1,300 BCE. These field traces and the field system they reveal could be 3,500 years old. The 'could' should be taken seriously as such landscapes are difficult to date. A first-class report by Historic England of a 10 × 10 km square that happens to include Hog Cliff notes that most of the early field systems could be of Iron Age/Roman vintage, but that some could be earlier.[2] Certainly, there are many Bronze Age artefacts and fields in the vicinity, and known Bronze Age field systems are common in parts of West Dorset.

By the time of Domesday (1086 CE), little land in the area around Hog Cliff was arable, and sheep and some cattle dominated.[3] Indeed, sheep have always been the mainstay of The Chalk everywhere.[4] Yes, the top fields and valley bottoms have long been under the plough, with smaller patches of the dry valley bottom preserved for meadow, but the steeper slopes were left for grazing as there was still nothing else worth doing with them.

Much later, the fields defined by parliamentary inclosure were involved in 'sheep corn husbandry', a practice that involved driving the ewes and lambs down from the hilltops every day to feed on the lush vegetation of the water meadows of the Frome, then driving them back up again in the afternoon to spend their night sleeping and dunging within frequently moved hurdle enclosures that were situated on the as yet unseeded cornfields on the hilltops. The point of this, beside producing sheep, was to bring back the nutrients washed from the hills. The rest of the time, while the corn was growing, the sheep lived off the pasture of those slopes and the stubble after the harvest.

I do not know exactly how the land was farmed between the

end of this charming practice in the late nineteenth century and the arrival of Snowy Eyre. He had bought the farm shortly after the Second World War from a Mr Elsworth, whose son Gerald, despite mysteriously missing out on his inheritance, became the farm manager under the new owner. Gerald and his family lived in a wooden house, the seemingly indestructible brick chimney of which still nestles within a square of pine trees a hundred metres from the new house. The new house had been built for him and was the one in which I lived in the early 1980s.

Agricultural improvements were very much the order of the day in the 1950s, Britain having suffered difficulty in growing enough food during the war years and after. This is when Snowy was strongly encouraged to plough some of his land. I have little certain knowledge of what the land was like before Snowy followed this advice, but it is almost certain that some areas of surviving ancient grassland were lost to his plough. Nevertheless, most survived and survives still as it came to the attention of what is now Natural England, which, in 1985, notified it as an SSSI.

THE ESTABLISHMENT OF HOG CLIFF AS A NATIONAL NATURE RESERVE

This short story seems like bragging, but it is interesting to note how these things can happen and that among the losses there are success stories. After three and a half years at Hog Cliff, the entire farm was put up for sale, and my wife and I had to move into the village. Our friend Dave, a worker on another farm for whom conservation was a posh jam, came to tell us it was likely that the steep slopes would be ploughed, presumably after they had been sprayed with herbicide, and that it might end up as turf for lawns. He added that it would be a considerable achievement to plough so steep a slope, and great fun to watch.

I fell into something of a depression about this and had many nightmares about what would happen. However, and without much hope of success, I contacted what is now Natural England to ask if there was anything that might be done. They looked on their maps but thought it not worthwhile because of the species-poor and heavy clay-with-flint cap on the hilltops (of which more later) that was revealed in geological surveys.

Nevertheless, I sent them my list of plant and fungi species, and not long after one of their officers arrived and I took him on a walk around. He loved the place and thought it worth saving. After (for the sake of my sanity) studiously ignoring the fate of Hog Cliff for a year or so, I discovered that the downland and woodland parts had been bought outright by Natural England, with the considerable bonus that a number of similarly rich areas across the road to the east of Hog Cliff were included in the purchase. I was near to tears with relief and joy.

Much more recently something similar happened nearby. Land immediately to the west of Hog Cliff was put up for sale by another farmer, and again I worried about its fate as it contains some under-grazed but historically and biologically interesting grassland and some splendid chalky strip lynchets. Against all my expectations Natural England bought it. I will revisit the establishment of this new nature reserve in detail in Part Five.

Considering the minimal amount of effort required to initiate the salvation of an important site, it was a stunning success. In this I had it *very* easy, and I know not every attempt to save a much-loved patch of land will succeed, but I hope you find it encouraging.

THE GEOLOGY OF HOG CLIFF

The Chalk is a complex of formations laid down in the Late Cretaceous Period, between 100 million and 66 million years ago. These are primarily made up of massive deposits of minute calcium carbonate 'skeletons' that once gave structure to organisms known as the 'Formanifera'. When they died, they sank to the bottom of the sea in which they lived. Most of these were 'heterotrophs', meaning that they lived by consuming other organisms, while some were 'autotrophs' relying on contained chlorophyll, just like plants, or internally hosting algae that could do it for them. There are around 50,000 'skeletons' in a cubic centimetre, so a square kilometre of (level) chalk formation, 300 m thick (it ranges from 200 to 560 m thick[5]) will contain 150 billion trillion. Please excuse my lapse into gee-whiz science: it was too good to resist. Other organisms also make up the chalk such as crustacea and molluscs, and flinty fossils are common there, mostly in the form of the heart-shaped Micraster, a type of sea urchin. For anyone who lives on The Chalk it is odd to think of these vast numbers of corpses beneath our feet.

The most conspicuous characteristic of chalk downlands is their rounded nature: 'the succession of shapely outlines; the vast protuberances and deep divisions between, suggestive of the most prominent and beautiful curves of the human figure', as W. H. Hudson so evocatively puts it while leaving us in no doubt as to which sex those curves belong to.[6] How did they come about?

The famous rounded form of chalk downlands has puzzled geologists in the past, but it is now known that they were caused by relatively gentle glacial meltwater from summer thaws and heavy glacial meltwater during interglacials. Chalk is not so much eroded as dissolved by carbon dioxide in the form of carbonic acid, a process indicated now by hard-water areas where chalk is deposited in pipes and kettles. The dissolution occurs chiefly where the chalk is vertically fissured, something that occurs in some areas but not in others. Where fissures are absent, dissolution is slow, leaving hills; where they are present dissolution is fast, and creates valleys.

It is easy to imagine the vast tract of chalk to be homogeneous, but it is not so. That this is the case has long been known, and even obvious where the layers of chalk are exposed in quarries or on cliff-faces. Until recently, three primary layers were accepted – the Lower Chalk, the Middle Chalk and the Upper Chalk.[7] Now there are around ten. Hog Cliff is on the Upper Chalk and consists of two primary layers (both chalks) and a superficial layer. The upper exposed layer is the Seaford Formation;* the lower exposed layer is the Lewes Nodular Chalk Formation.[8]

Since Hog Cliff is nearly all valley, most of the land is steeply sloping. It is on these slopes that the chalk is very near the surface, mostly less than 10 cm. When a rabbit hole collapses, the depth is clearly to be seen. It is in these thin, calcareous and nutrient-poor soils that the chalkland flora of such sites grow, though many plants will grow into the fissures in the chalk and into the softer chalks.

The tops of the hills are quite different. Here there is a thick layer of what is called a 'clay-with-flints cap'. Fine clay particles naturally accumulated within the chalk while it was being deposited on the sea bed. As the subsequent chalk eroded, the clay was left on top, together with some flints, to form the surface layer. It is worth knowing that the chalk eroded (vertically) a very great deal – a kilometre or two – thus providing an abundance of flints.

The British Geological Survey map of the area shows this clay cap to occupy the tops of the hills, with only a small amount within the circumscription of the National Nature Reserve (NNR). On some of the slopes there are clay deposits from solifluction, a process involving repeated alternate freezing and thawing towards the end of glacial periods. On most of the slopes the deposits have washed away to be deposited in the valley bottom as the 'head', an unsorted mixture of clay, chalk, sand and weathered flint.

---

* 'Exposed' means just below the thin layer of soil and not necessarily visible.

As any gardener knows, clay tends to produce acidic soils and poor drainage, which limits the types of plants that will grow there. Those that need, or at least prefer, a *high* pH (alkaline) soil are known as calcicoles; those that prefer a *low* pH (acidic) soil are called calcifuges. At Hog Cliff the soils at the top and bottom of the hills have a lower pH than most of the slopes. Such seemingly small matters have a profound effect on what grows where.

The most startling characteristic of chalk downland for those familiar with more impenetrable bedrocks is that only the major valleys have running, or even still, water. There is not a trace of either at Hog Cliff except in a couple of (man-made) dew ponds, and none in the surrounding hills, coombes and minor valleys.' There are also precisely no ditches at Hog Cliff as they are not needed. But where does the water go?

It sinks first into the chalk fissures and joints, then slowly into the chalk itself: chalk is highly porous, with 35 to 47 per cent of its volume taken up with pores. The water sinks downwards until it reaches either completely saturated chalk or an impervious layer of some other material. The water will run into a river and sometimes from springs. Indeed, during heavy rain an impressive if troublesome spring forms in or near the allotments situated to the east of the village and a kilometre west of Hog Cliff. One year it was knee-high in the lower allotments and caused much muttering in the village pub. The spring seems to have mended its ways somewhat, content to appear just inside the village itself and making a walk to the doctor's surgery an occasional journey of adventure.

SOIL AND CLIMATE

We have already looked at the important role that soil plays in the ecology of grasslands. Soil, topoclimate (the climate of a small area) and hydrology as well as the present and historical management of Hog Cliff determine what grows where.

The great countryman William Cobbett, describing the soil of The Chalk in another county, wrote: 'The ground is loam, mixed with flints, and has the chalk at no great distance beneath it.'[10]

Soil qualities are fairly evident in the plants that grow there. The soil on the valley's sides where there is no overlaying clay is very thin. It also lacks multiple layers, consisting of what is known as a 'rendzina', a mixture of clay, sand, chalk particles and humus. It is very poor in nutrients and this, combined with it being so shallow, makes it perfect for the diminutive plants that grow there. The other soils on the site – those of the clay cap and the head – are relatively rich in nutrients and more acidic, producing a different mix of flora. Some areas are a 'halfway house' consisting of chalky clays – marls.

C. J. Smith, in his *Ecology of the English Chalk*, notes that this eponymous ecology is down to the happy coincidence of low rainfall and chalk hills. Indeed, more northerly and easterly instances of chalk hills have noticeably different ecologies.

The climate on the Dorset Chalk is as temperate as it comes, with no great extremes of temperature or rainfall. Overall rainfall is between 1,000 and 1,250 mm per year, which is not far from the average rainfall in Britain, typically 800 to 1,400 mm. Nevertheless, it is wet for the Southern Province Chalk Formation. This has an effect on what grows, or does not grow, on the Dorset Chalk. Most of the Southern Chalk, then, is relatively dry compared with more northern and western areas.

The amount of sunlight that makes its way is, of course, not entirely dependent on how much is available. The sunny aspect of an area will vary considerably between flat hilltops, valley bottoms and north, south, east and west slopes. South-facing slopes will receive most sunlight and have the highest number of plant species.

THE PLANTS OF HOG CLIFF

If any grassland can engender joy, it is that of chalk downland. The turf is famously short and springy, and, when sensibly grazed, there are few plants more than 10 cm tall. Indeed, the plants are often tiny – W. H. Hudson's 'bright little flowers of the chalk', with none consistently claiming dominance." While travelling in Dorset, Daniel Defoe wrote of the 'fine carpet ground, soft as velvet, and the herbage, sweet as garden herbs'. Poignantly, he repeats the leading phrase in reference to Salisbury Plain, recalling what has been lost: 'the many thousands of acres of the carpet ground being, of late years, turned into arable land, and sowed with wheat'.[12]

With so many species to boast and so many occurring in any small space, chalk downland is considered to be one of the most ecologically interesting of all the many grassland types, far out-stripping most others, even the much-fêted meadows. Some writers have compared chalk downland to tropical rainforests. More plants means more invertebrates and other dependent organisms.

Finally, note that species recorded at this and the other sites visited in Part Four are in **bold** type when first mentioned as an organism that has been recorded there. For Hog Cliff itself, most of the records of all the types of organisms – plant, insect, fungus and so on – are courtesy of the Dorset Environmental Centre, many are my own, and more come from supportive friends. I have not used records from other lists, so, excepting the plants, there will be many more species that are neither mentioned individually nor included in the totals I provide for each grouping of organisms.

THE PLANTS OF THE CHALK

One hundred and thirty-five grasses and wild flowers, plus an impressive twenty mosses, eight of them rare, have been recorded

Lesser Hawkbit

for the grasslands of Hog Cliff, and more are to be found with the ever interesting scrub. On a few of the nevertheless still beautiful locations I visited elsewhere in Britain while researching for this book, forty or fewer plants were to be found.

The plant records for Hog Cliff are almost as complete as one could ask for, and the odd one or two are added to the list most years. I was there with an ecologist friend just a month before writing this section, and he found something new: the uncommon **Fragrant Agrimony**, *Agrimonia procera*.

GRASSLAND COMMUNITIES AT HOG CLIFF

Crucially, these are not spread evenly but naturally arrange themselves into plant communities. Even a glance at the grasslands here (or almost anywhere) will make this clear when they are in flower.

At Hog Cliff these grassland plants are spread over nine grassland NVC communities and sub-communities (see p. 74). The original survey map showing these communities looks like an impossible jigsaw puzzle, so I have simplified it into just three broad grassland communities plus the scrub. See Plate 11.

The most interesting by far are the slopes where the soil is extremely thin. This is Defoe's glorious carpet ground. It ranges over three subcommunities within CG2: CG2a, CG2b and CG2c.* 'CG' refers simply to 'Calcareous Grassland', known for its low fertility. The first of these is the most valued and occurs primarily on the south-facing slope of Farm Hill Bottom.

Some of the slopes have a high component of clay but also incorporate chalk and thus are moderately calcareous. They contain many valued herbaceous plants, though not so densely as those found on the pure chalk. These are MG5b and are sometimes referred to as 'calcareous clay'. This community is not necessarily confined to slopes and is often seen in calcareous meadows.

The valley bottoms are the least interesting, consisting of clay, sand, weathered flint and at least some chalk – the 'head' as it is called. These are MG1 and MG6.**

I have given the above three broad community groups the following names: the Chalk, Calcareous Clay and the Head.

THE GRASSES AND SEDGES OF THE CHALK

Overall, there are a very respectable thirty species of grass, sedge and rush found at Hog Cliff – some restricted to the chalk, others

* There is also CG2d, which we will see later.
** MG is Mesotrophic Grassland, meaning of moderate fertility.

elsewhere. Although sometimes present in disturbed ground and on boundaries, there are few 'coarse' grasses: that is, weed grasses that can overwhelm an otherwise species-rich grassland. Coarse grasses require a much more fertile soil.

The headline grasses for species-rich Chalk Grassland (CG2) come in their overarching name, 'CG2 Sheep's Fescue, Meadow Oat-grass grasslands' (I am using the common names rather than the latinised terms here for clarity). Here **Sheep's Fescue**, *Festuca ovina*, takes the place of the near-ubiquitous **Red Fescue**, *Festuca rubra*, though the latter can sometimes be found in the Chalk too. It takes a little time with a loupe to see the fine differences between Sheep's Fescue and Red Fescue. **Meadow Oat-grass**, *Helictochloa pratensis*, and the more common **Downy Oat-grass**, *H. pubescens*, have a strong association with limestones.

One of the non-eponymous constants of the site is the exquisite, familiar and easily identified **Quaking Grass**, *Briza media*. *Briza* means 'nodding', a reference to the way in which the flower and seed heads bob up and down in a gentle breeze. Less well known is **Crested Hair-grass**, *Koeleria macrantha*, a fine, tufted grass. Again, it is restricted to calcareous soils, excepting that it is also found around almost the entire coast of Britain irrespective of whether or not the soil is calcareous.

THE WILD FLOWERS OF THE CHALK

Hemicryptophytes

Beautiful as these grasses may be, it is the flowers that gain our attention. Many times I have watched them come and go through spring, summer and autumn, the colours slowly changing. Close up they are prettier still, their intricate details always a marvel.

You will recall that most plants in Britain survive by having buds that grow at ground level, *below* the reach of grazing teeth.

These are the hemicryptophytes that form the major constituent plants at Hog Cliff.

Members of the Daisy Family, which includes members of the 'dandelion' and thistle persuasion, and those of the Pea Family, enjoy the highest head count by species. Overall, yellows, white and purples dominate, with a few pinks and pale blues, the various colours coming and going as each plant comes in and out of flower.

Dwarf Thistle, *Cirsium acaule*, also known as the 'Stemless Thistle' and, most tellingly, the 'Picnic Thistle', is very much a calcareous grassland species and confined mostly, though by no means entirely, to the southern chalk. As with nearly all the plants here, it is 'survival of the shortest'. There are three other thistles, mostly found in the less calcareous areas. These are all tall and rely entirely on their fearsome spines to protect them. None is common on the site.

Among the most trying of groups for the amateur botanist are those that bear flowers in the form of a dandelion. About forty species fall into this informal group within the Dandelion Family: the milk-thistles, hawk's-beard, cat's-ears, hawkweeds, hawkbits, lettuces, oxtongues, dandelions (of course) and Nipplewort, the last being a species which is seemingly endemic (epidemic even) to your author's garden. Attention to the more conspicuous details (e.g. hairy or not, more than one flower on a stem and whether or not the stems branch) will reap rewards, so they are not *too* difficult. Here are some of those found onsite.

The common **Mouse-ear Hawkweed**, *Pilosella officinarum*, is one of the prettiest of these. Its leaves look very much like the ears of a mouse and are appropriately hairy, as is the rest of the plant. It has attractively pale yellow petals that terminate with a distinct saw-toothed edge (common to many of these plants and known as 'pinking'), with the outer petals bearing attractive scarlet stripes

Small scabious

on their underside.

Although it is also a common plant of other grassland types, **Rough Hawkbit**, *Leontodon hispidus*, is a stalwart of the species-rich chalk. Superficially, it is similar to the dandelion but produces tough hairy stems, of which there can be several. It is these that provide its name, as 'hispid' refers to the hairs. Small details often help with identification, so it worth knowing that the hairs on the leaves are *forked*. **Common Cat's-ear**, *Hypochaeris radicata*, is similar but has small leaf-like structures on the flower stems known as 'stipules'.

The **Dandelion** itself is found at Hog Cliff and was recorded as *Taraxacum officinale* agg. The ugly appendage is an abbreviation for 'aggregate', indicating that the recorder is content that it is, indeed, a dandelion, but is not prepared to hazard a guess at which one. Like brambles, dandelions are apomictic: that is, they reproduce asexually, with all of their seeds producing only clones (apomicts) of the parent plant. There are over two hundred of these apomicts, and it takes a more than usually serious botanical specialist to distinguish them. The one at Hog Cliff is very small indeed, with a small number of 6-cm-long leaves on each plant. It is likely to be a named apomict, but my own researches have not discovered which one.

The largest 'clock' among the dandelion-like flowers is that of the splendid **Meadow Salsify**, *Tragopogon pratensis*. I have only found isolated instances of this, even though its conspicuous clock can be 5 cm in diameter.

The Pea Family is represented by five species, all common: **White Clover**, *Trifolium repens*, **Red Clover**, *T. pratense*, **Bird's-foot Trefoil**, *Lotus corniculatus*, **Black Medick**, *Medicago lupulina*, and **Horseshoe Vetch**, *Hippocrepis comosa*. Common though they may be, these will all provide a source of biologically accessible nitrogen to themselves and, subsequently, to other plants.

Clovers, incidentally, produce cyanide when damaged – that is, when chewed. This is a defence against attack by invertebrates. Grazing animals consume the nutritious White Clover with some relish but may do so carefully. Sheep, who can suffer female sterility and 'frothy bloat' from eating too much, have been reported to preferentially eat this plant in the morning, then move on to grasses in the afternoon. This is presumed to be a response to the high levels of cyanogen produced by the plants in, or more likely *from*, the middle of the day.[13] The result for the plant is that large grazing animals at least restrict their intake.

Cyanide acts by preventing the production of adenosine triphosphate (ATP) in the mitochondria of all living cells. Mitochondria produce energy, so consuming cyanide effectively turns off the power supply. I cannot resist relating that we produce our own body weight of ATP every day.

Two common bedstraws exist in these calcareous areas, **Hedge Bedstraw**, *Galium mollugo*, and **Lady's Bedstraw**, *G. verum*, the last of these providing an attractive cover with its frothy yellow flowers. Plants that grow on the chalk are noted for their long roots, needed to draw water and nutrients from deep down. Lady's Bedstraw is the master of this trick – a 7-cm-tall plant, with roots that can reach down 60 cm.[14]

Hoary Plantain, *Plantago media*, has a strong preference for the dry grasslands of the chalk and, like the Dwarf Thistle, keeps its head down, its basal rosette of broad, ribbed leaves remaining flat to the ground. The often inconspicuous Plantains occur throughout all of the grasslands at Hog Cliff and densely so, with barely a square metre devoid of them. Hoary Plantain, I have discovered, appears in *every* close-up photograph I have taken here of the calcareous sward.

Two violets occur in these species-rich areas: **Common Dog Violet**, *Viola riviniana*, and the **Hairy Violet**, *V. hirta*. One or other of these is a common and near-constant sight when in flower here. There are a handful of buttercup species at Hog Cliff, with the most frequent being the **Bulbous Buttercup**, *Ranunculus bulbosus*, which takes its name from its storage bulb in the form of a swollen stem that resides in the soil. It is easily distinguished in the field by having sepals that cling to the stem, rather than the underside of the petals.

The delicate pink **Field Scabious**, *Knautia arvensis*, is primarily confined to calcareous soils to the point where a map of limestone and chalk grasslands in Britain is much the same as the distribution map of the plant. As such, it is classed as 'near-threatened' by the International Union for Conservation of Nature.

Devil's-bit Scabious, *Succisa pratensis*, exists still at Hog Cliff, and is one of the species that helped in the site's ascendance to SSSI status. It is the obligate larval food plant of the Marsh Fritillary Butterfly. 'Obligate' means it is the only food plant it can use, though 'near-obligate' would be better here as they occasionally feed on the Field and Small Scabious. The plant is found in the nearby sites across the road but has had mixed fortunes at Hog Cliff, where it is less common.

Squinancywort, *Asperula cynanchica*, defines the southern chalk even more precisely than does the much more common Field Scabious. It forms a sprawling basal rosette of dark-green, oval-pointed and delicate, pale-pink, four-petalled flowers that bear markings in a darker pink. **Chalk Milkwort**, *Polygala calcarea*, is also a chalk specialist. Hog Cliff is its most westerly outpost, Dover its most easterly. Eastern Gloucestershire also has a population, no doubt on the Birdlip Limestone Formation.

The **Clustered Bellflower**, *Campanula glomerata*, is also at its westernmost outpost. It follows the chalk and scattered places further north where there is limestone. The Clustered Bellflower is one of Britain's prettiest plants, though I have not seen it at Hog Cliff for some years. At the infamous and invariably amusing Giant's Hill near Cerne Abbas, 6 km to the north-east, it is extremely common and a truly beautiful sight. Its close relative the **Common Harebell**, *Campanula rotundifolia*, is certainly still onsite. Seemingly unfussy about soil pH, it is indeed common throughout Britain, excepting the far south-west, with Hog Cliff yet again being its most westerly population.

Facing west from the top of Farm Hill Bottom

Facing southwest from the top of Camel Hill

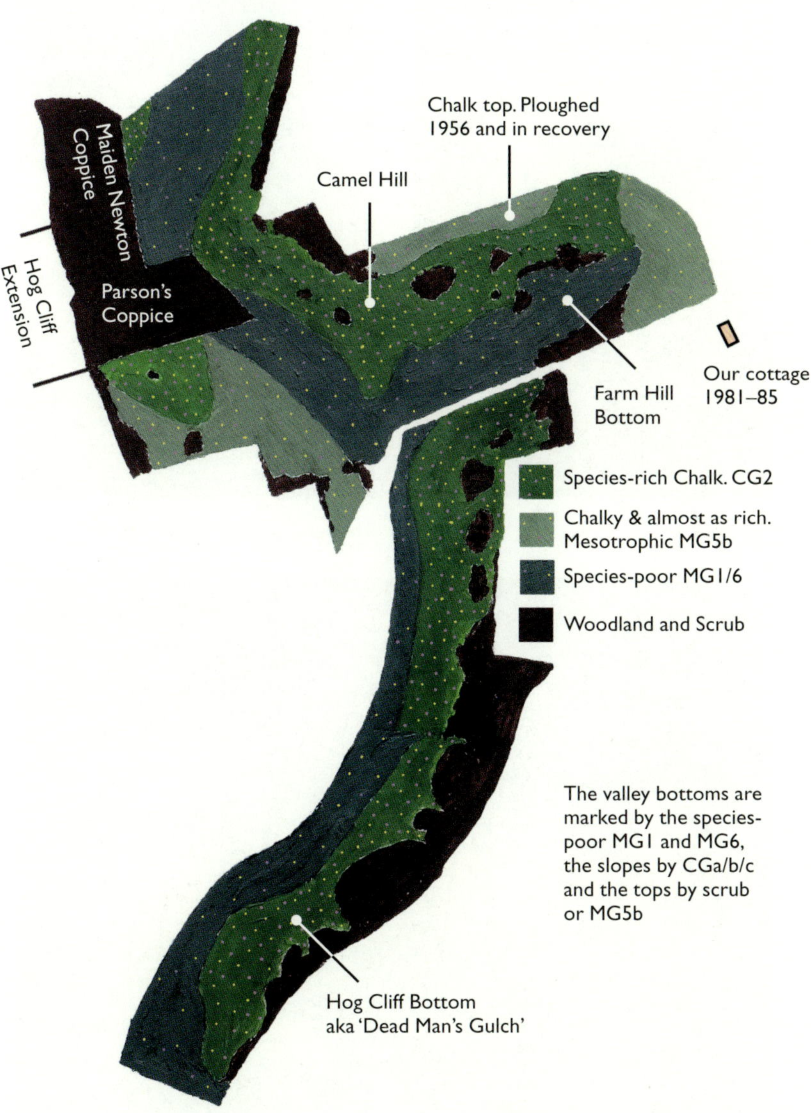

This is a highly simplified graphic of the plant communities at Hog Cliff. They are represented here according to their perceived value as communities. The brighter the green and the more flowers (coloured dots) the better. Note: the handy 'cut-out' that harbours the sample patches and descriptions is actually part of a neighbouring arable field, as are (nearly) all of the surrounding fields.

Cowslips

The very local Chalk Milkwort

Common Bird's-foot Trefoil, Common Rock-rose and Lesser Stitchwort

Field Wood-rush

Common Dog Violet

Eyebright

St John's Wort close up

A sedge

Mating Common Blue butterflies

Cistus Forester Moth

Marsh Fritillary

Wood Tiger Moth

Female Wilke's Mining Bee

Red-tailed Mason Bee

Waisted Bee-grabber Fly

Lurid Bolete, here associated with the Common Rock-rose

Tricholoma hemisulphureum, Common Rock-rose associate

Large ring of the Spotted Blewit

Younger Spotted Blewits

My grandmother, a Wiltshire lass who was raised at the edge of Salisbury Plain, often mentioned **Cowslips** (*Primula veris*), so the name has long been in my mind. Unfortunately, she never showed me one, or even a picture of its bright yellow flowers, and it was a couple of decades before I came to know this plant. It is less common than it once was but has seemingly received a boost in its fortunes as a commonly planted wild flower of roadsides and roundabouts. At Hog Cliff it graces its more natural habitat with an innocent beauty.

Therophytes (Annuals)

Since they generally grow anew from seeds each year, these plants require bare soil with comparatively high frequency, even if it is a very small patch. Such opportunities arise on the site of an anthill that has been devasted by badgers looking for a meal or a collapsed rabbit warren, and hundreds of tiny seedlings can be seen in such locations. Heavy hoof-fall can also create patches of bare ground. With the exception of the small proportion of plants whose seeds are only viable for the following year, therophytes are prepared to bide their time as a seedbank. As with the hemicryptophytes, this is a reproductive/survival strategy.

Therophytes are rare on the densely populated chalk and the grasslands in general, with only four therophytic wild flowers recorded. Three of these occur in the chalky slopes of Hog Cliff. They are the delicate **Fairy Flax**, *Linum catharticum*, and the pretty **Yellow Rattle**, *Rhinanthus minor*. The latter is well known as a hemiparasitic inhabitant of meadows and will be described on p. 230.* The fourth, its close relative, **Common Eyebright**, *Euphrasia nemorosa*, also a hemiparasite, is common in many grasslands.

* A hemiparasite is a parasite that does not depend entirely on its host
  for sustenance.

The 'Eyebrights' (for there are more than one) are so-called 'critical' plants, needing close examination with a loupe and consideration of precisely where it was found to determine which *Euphrasia* is before you. The 'where' is often the most useful determinant, as many are only found in a few localities (or even just one), with the north of Scotland hosting many of these 'badly behaved' species owing to the geographic isolation that encourages those differences. There are twenty-one 'microspecies' of *Euphrasia* in Britain, forty-eight being the total for Europe as a whole. Some are species, some are sub-species, and hybridisation muddies the waters even more. *E. nemorosa* is by far the commonest and presumably the ancestor of all the others, so it is the go-to species name for those who care not for the finer niceties of botanical taxonomy.[15] I am, nevertheless, confident that the one at Hog Cliff bears the name given above as it was determined by someone who knows his *Euphrasia* species. Another species of *Euphrasia*, found on lowland dry acid grassland, is mentioned on p. 265.

All *Euphrasia* and *Rhinanthus* species are hemiparasitic on various grasses and other plants, with the Pea Family a particular target. They still have chlorophyll in their leaves, hence their status as *hemi*parasites. They are in the Family Orobanchaceae, many of whose members are completely parasitic, having no chlorophyll of their own – the Broomrapes being the most familiar.

Geophytes

While the woodland to the west of Hog Cliff boasts a splendid display of the geophyte we know as the 'Bluebell', all three of those that occur in the chalk grasslands of Hog Cliff are orchids: the **Fragrant Orchid**, *Gymnadenia conopsea*, the **Common Spotted Orchid**, *Dactylorhiza fuchsii*, and **Autumn Lady's-tresses**, *Spiranthes spiralis*. The last of these is found chiefly around the

Heath Bedstraw

south coast of Wales, up and down the Bristol Channel and all the way around to Broadstairs in north-east Kent, having followed the chalk hills. It is a delicate beauty, with its white flowers neatly formed in helices on twisted stems.

The Shrubby Plants (Chamaephytes)
These plants dominate large areas of the prime grassland here and I consider them to be the most interesting plants at Hog Cliff. They are the only two that are routinely associated with chalk downland, and both occur here and in large numbers: **Wild Thyme**,

Thymus polytrichus, and **Common Rock-rose**, *Helianthemum nummularium*. The tiny flowers of Wild Thyme are pink/purple and very striking. The larger flowers of Common Rock-rose are a bright pale yellow, with the petals noticeably delicate. They are reminiscent of the buttercups, but more striking.

Both plants are wiry and diminutive shrubs (sub-shrubs) that form extensive, prostrate mats, often close together and jostling for space with each other and with other plants. Countrywide both follow the chalk and limestone geographically, though they can be found elsewhere.

Both support a massive ant population (as I will relate later), and the Common Rock-rose has a critical role in the mycota (fungi) of the site. See pp. 171–2 for its story. Their strong and spreading roots also provide the delicate soil with stability.

It is interesting to note that the Common Rock-rose is one of only seven species used as indicators of the age of a site. In a study of the Porton Ranges in Wiltshire the authors suggest that the existence of any of the seven indicates that the site has been undisturbed for at least 130 years.[16] I have already argued that this is an ancient site, so this adds little beyond mild confirmation, but it does indicate how long it may take to recolonise a damaged chalkland, should conservation work be required. More positively, six of those seven species are found at Hog Cliff, all mentioned here, with only Dropwort spoiling the party.

THE PLANTS OF THE CALCAREOUS CLAY (MG5B)

This community is also known as 'calcareous loam pasture', and more comfortably as 'old meadow pasture'. This is species-rich as, although not directly on the chalk, chalk is a strong component of the soil. Inevitably, there are plants here that also occur in CG2. It is found onsite on the south- and west-facing slopes of Farm Hill Bottom and on the irregular slope south of the woodlands. Since the calcareous clay occurs on some of the steep slopes, they are ancient grasslands, just like their chalky neighbours.

The Grasses

With its chalky component MG5b is the richest of the mesotrophic grasslands (those of moderate fertility) at Hog Cliff. There are several grasses: both Sheep's Fescue and Red Fescue, Common Bent, the almost ubiquitous **Cock's-foot**, *Dactylis glomerata*, **Perennial Ryegrass**, *Lolium perenne*, **Sweet Vernal Grass**, *Anthoxanthum odoratum*, and several more. The slightly wetter soils have encouraged **Spring Sedge**, *Carex caryophyllea*, **Glaucous Sedge**, *Carex flacca*, and also **Field Wood-rush**, *Luzula campestris*.

The Wild Flowers

As mentioned earlier, this community is very rich in wild flowers, though less so than the Chalk. They are not so densely packed together and with fewer species in any one area. Nevertheless, some of the plants here form spectacularly large patches. Here we see swathes of the dominant species.

A couple of the plants are 'definitive' for their community in that they are titular: **Common Knapweed**, *Centaurea nigra*, finds its name in the title of MG5 as a whole (the other being **Crested Dog's Tail**, *Cynosurus cristatus*), and Lady's Bedstraw, in the name of the particular sub-community under consideration – MG5b.

It is not necessary to visit a nature reserve to see the charming Common Knapweed, as it is found throughout Britain in many types of meadow and pasture and cheerfully inhabits waste ground and roadsides. As is obvious from a single glance at the flower, it is related to thistles in the Tribe the Cardueae (a Tribe being a rank between Family and Genus).

The brilliant yellow Lady's Bedstraw is widely distributed throughout most of Britain. Its frothy sprays of bright yellow flowers are a delight, frequently covering areas in swathes. They are often found adorning anthills.

When I lived there, I did not see **Pignuts**, *Conopodium majus*, on the site at all. It is a delicate beauty in the Carrot Family that flowers until midsummer, produces its seeds then dies back, its eponymous 'nut' now a little larger than it was. This species is effectively an indicator of mildly acidic or neutral soils, and about twenty years ago it started to appear at the north-facing slope at the eastern end of Farm Hill Bottom. Since then, its numbers have gone from twenty or so into the hundreds, forming the largest of those swathes. Being a perennial geophyte, with that nut-like storage root, it insists on undisturbed ground, but I cannot say why it was not there before as, at a one-in-five gradient, the ground is too steep to be disturbed with a plough. Perhaps the area was cleared of scrub many years ago, but however it came about, it shows how long it takes (maybe forty years in this case) for plants to re-establish.

Betony, *Stachys officinalis*, is common across most of these areas, showing the same soil preference as Pignut. A great beauty both individually and as a carpet of purple-pink, it can flower from June to September. **Common Mouse-ear**, *Cerastium fontanum*, is related to Lady's Bedstraw (and Chickweed), with upright flower stems, while the rest of the plant straggles amongst the other vegetation. Both White and Red Clovers occur here, plus **Lesser Trefoil**, *Trifolium dubium*, a plant that could be mistaken for a medick because of the round, compact flower heads, made up of half a dozen tiny yellow florets. Here it forms dense blankets. The exceedingly common **Meadow Buttercup**, *Ranunculus acris*, replaces the Bulbous Buttercup of the chalk. A lookalike for buttercups is found here in the unrelated form of the common **Creeping Cinquefoil**, *Potentilla reptans*, which is (much) botanically closer to a strawberry than to a buttercup.

Its close relative, also common in these areas, is **Tormentil**, *Potentilla erecta*, another indicator of neutral or mildly acidic soils. It too has yellow petals, but they are smaller and there are only four on each flower. The least commonly found species in this group (Tribe Potentilleae) is **Parsley-piert**, *Aphanes arvensis*. It has no particular business here; it simply arrived and took up residence on an anthill.

The flora listed above do not paint the entire picture of this area of calcareous clay, as one other community exists within it. There has evidently been a flushing out of soil down the north-eastern corner of slope at Farm Hill Bottom. This has lowered the pH along a narrow strip that runs down the hill. Encouraged by the relatively low soil pH, mildly acid-loving plants such as the Foxglove and a handful of species with 'heath' in their name have made a home here.

The key species here are **Heath Bedstraw**, *Galium saxatile*, and **Heath Violet**, *Viola canina*. As their names suggest, they prefer a low pH, being found chiefly in woodland, rocky places, moors and heath. Towards the bottom of the still grassy slope a couple of **Foxgloves**, *Digitalis purpurea*, sit proudly and conspicuously at odds with the expected ecology.

A botanist friend who went with me to this spot suggested that it might qualify as another CG community or even a 'U' – that is, an acid grassland, possibly U4: *Festuca ovina-Agrostis capillaris-Galium saxatile* grassland. Soil type really does determine what grows where.

THE PLANTS OF THE HEAD (MG1 AND MG6)

'Head' is the name given to the superficial deposit found on many valley bottoms. The soil is nutrient-rich and species-poor, though the areas classed as MG6 are considerably better. It is certain that most of them were ploughed seventy years ago.

MG1 is the poorest on the site and dominated by the coarser grasses such as **False Oat-grass**, *Arrhenatherum elatius*, **Yorkshire Fog**, *Holcus lanatus*, and **Cock's Foot**, *Dactylis glomerata*.

Perennial Ryegrass is a constant of MG6, along with **Crested Dog's-tail**, *Cynosurus cristatus*, with both almost ubiquitous. Both are also among the easiest grasses to identify, the first from having a simple spike of flowers, the second a distinct *spine* on the flower spike. Other grasses are Red Fescue, and **Creeping Bent**, *Agrostis stolonifera*.

MG6 is *the* permanent pasture in much of lowland Britain and primarily used for fattening stock or for dairy, and generally forms a tight and moderately short sward.

The wild flowers are mostly very common and many of them are generally classed as weeds. They include the **Daisy, Creeping Thistle, Lesser Stitchwort, docks, Sorrel, Silverweed** and the (only) therophyte **Shepherd's Purse**, a tiny plant in the Cabbage Family.

SCRUB AND GRASSLAND

As is typical of landscapes such as Hog Cliff, long-established scrubby areas occur at the tops of the hills, sometimes stretching like stubby fingers down the slopes. There is also scrub that appears as islands in what was once open grassland. The initial stages of the establishment of scrubby areas are clearly to be seen in these islands. Here intractable shrubs, perhaps Bramble or a gorse species, were left ungrazed, perhaps because they were protected in a collapsed rabbit burrow and became established to form an ever-spreading disc of scrubland.

Soon larger shrubs such as Hawthorn, Elder and some Blackthorn appeared in the centre. The overall structure is of Hawthorn and Elder in the middle, a ring of relatively short vegetation, an outer, broader and taller ring of Brambles and a leading edge of tall herbs and grasses. The last of these, the so-called *saum* zone, forms the major interface between the shrubs and the grass. Left unchecked, standard trees will establish to form a small climax forest, something that has happened in the very old scrub high up some of the slopes.

Commander Eyre kept the scrub as cover for his precious foxes, only occasionally cutting it back when it threatened to encroach too far into the grassland. When Natural England acquired the site over forty years ago, they had an opportunity to clear the scrub completely and begin the long process of turning the cleared areas into species-rich grassland. They did clear some, notably extensive patches of bramble that were very productive of blackberries (50 kg one year), but certainly not all.

This was not an opportunity missed but a policy to maintain the greatest number of habitats and species. Such a policy came with the understanding that the plagioclimax nature of chalk downland requires scrub to be kept from spreading and overwhelming the grassland. Scrub clearance is discussed on p. 306.

The above-mentioned *saum* is what is classed as a type of 'ecotone'. The word 'ecotone' derives from *oîkos* and *tónos*, 'habitation' and 'tension' respectively, nicely describing the somewhat pugilistic nature of these halfway houses between two communities, here between scrub and grassland. Interesting things happen within and across borders: birds may nest in the scrub and feed in the field; a bee can collect nesting material in the scrub and construct the nest in the grass; a butterfly may feed on pollen from scrubby plants and lay its eggs on a particular grassland plant. An ectomycorrhizal fungus may live on the roots of a tree and produce it fruiting bodies in the grass. In high season, sitting quietly in the grass alongside a mass of gorse, Hawthorn and Bramble will keep a naturalist amused for hours.

At the top of Camel Hill all stages of development can be seen. I saw this a few years ago during a visit with my knowledgeable friend. Here **Purging Buckthorn**, *Rhamnus cathartica*, **Pedunculate Oak**, *Quercus robur*, and **Field Maple**, *Acer campestre*, have robustly survived, effectively descendants of a patch of scrub. A little to the west of the oaks is a relatively wide area of tall grasses and plants below a tangle of prickly scrub alongside which were two plants recently added to Hog Cliff's species list, one beautiful, one simply interesting.

The beauty is the **Slender St John's-wort**, *Hypericum pulchrum*, its brilliant yellow flowers adorning a tall flower spike. Its Latin name means 'beautiful thing that grows above heath', *pulchrum* meaning 'beautiful', *hyper*, 'above' and *-ericum*, a reference to heathland. This is another plant that is not found on the thin soils above chalk, but upon the more acidic clay-with-flints.

The 'interesting' plant goes by the frankly ugly name of **Gromwell**, *Lithospermum officinale*. My friend who pointed out this unassuming plant in 2023 noted that it was quite rare in Britain. I was impressed by this, but more so when I noticed that it was the same species as one that was growing uninvited in my flowerbed at home. It reaches about 1 m in height and has two dozen or so leafed stems rising from a substantial woody root that looks rather like a baked potato. The stems bear small, dull, white flowers, but more exciting is the seed, which has the appearance of a 3-mm-long, teardrop-shaped pearl. The name, *Lithospermum*, means 'stone-seed', and indeed it is rock-hard, almost like glass. These seeds (in fact they are 'fruits') have been used all over the world for necklaces and to ornament wooden boxes.

The plant has one gall, caused by the midge *Dasineura lithospermi*, its specific epithet indicating its association with the plant, and it appeared on the plant in my garden. The midge eggs and larvae thicken some of the leaves, which twist and produce hairs for protection. Galls are structures built by a plant, but *under instructions* supplied by the parasite. They form what is effectively a defended dining room for the developing larvae. There are thousands of galls in the UK alone, and they are among the greatest wonders nature has to offer.

Also there were two new records for grasses, **Smooth Brome**, *Bromus racemosus*, and **Yellow Oat-grass**, *Trisetum flavescens*, both vigorous plants of edge habitats, notably roadsides.

Finally, in the scrub at Hog Cliff Bottom, and in addition to the usual oaks, Hazel, Blackthorn and Hawthorn, are two trees of calcareous soils: a small **Yew**, *Taxus baccata*, and a **Wild Privet**, *Ligustrum vulgare*. There is only one of each species, both recorded when I lived there and both still going strong.

THE MOSSES

It will come as no surprise to owners of a lawn that mosses occur in grasslands. They are usually considered to be a nuisance, but old mossy lawns often support colourful populations of waxcap fungi (see p. 113). Waxcaps are always associated with mosses, and indeed never appear without them.

The grassland (species-rich chalk, neutral and acid) at Hog Cliff is well provided with mosses – no fewer than twenty species. Seven are recorded from the chalk turf, five from pockets of bare soil, one from the north-facing turf where the chalk was overlaid by a neutral or acidic soil, three from various positions on anthills plus one that was found on both anthills and soil pockets, one that was attached to exposed chalk in the turf and two from the halfway house where grass and scrub meet. Most, by far, are mosses of the chalk or limestone. Some of them are rare; all are delicately superb.

The bryophytes (mosses, liverworts and hornworts) suffer more than any other macroscopic plant from being visible in general but not in particular – a clear expression of the 'sizeism' described in the introduction. The grasses are a close second, but most people can name three or four species, or at least have heard of them. To the untutored eye mosses and their allies are all the same – a mass of small and oddly shaped leaves, with the occasional tiny 'lollipop' of a fruiting capsule to be seen. Yet Britain hosts more than its fair share of the European species – 1,098, which is 58 per cent of those found in Europe as a whole. This compares strikingly with the percentage of the European flowering plants, of which Britain hosts just 20 per cent. No doubt it is down to Britain's wet and mild climate and its complex geology.

As to their beauty – this is hidden from us by both their overall diminutive size and that of the details of leaf and capsule sat on its supporting seta (a hair-like stem). To see such minutiae with any clarity a loupe is required.

The leaves of mosses (on liverworts the comparable structures are called 'thalli') are almost indescribable in their form. They are also highly variable between species, sometimes like tiny, emaciated Christmas trees, sometimes palmate like a sycamore leaf, sometimes compressed like a cypress leaf and occasionally no more than a single thread. Many of the individual branching parts are only a single cell thick.

All bryophytes are non-vascular: that is, they lack vessels in which material may be moved from one part of a plant to another, something that is inherent in flowering plants and ferns. In a way, each cell looks after itself. The setae are the stems on which the capsules are formed, the capsules producing reproductive spores. The most striking part of bryophyte biology is that their spores contain two sets of chromosomes (diploid), but not the plants themselves, which have only one set (haploid). This is the 'wrong way round', though not particularly surprising as reproductive processes have proved endlessly inventive.

The leafy stage comes in two parts: a filamentous 'protonema' that emerges from the germinating spores, followed by the familiar leafy stage. Bryophytes are also capable of vegetative reproduction, sometimes growing from fragments dislodged from the parent plant, and sometimes 'intentionally' forming propagules on the central rib (nerve) of the otherwise single-cell-thick leaf.

I will not describe all twenty-one species of moss, just half a dozen or so (there were no liverworts or hornworts). With customary regret I have included the common names, most of which are of new coinage and little respected by the serious bryologist – or your author. Some of these common names are longer than the scientific names, and no more memorable.

So I will begin with the **Oblique-mouthed Beardless Moss**, *Weissia brachycarpa* var. *obliqua*. (See what I mean?) This is the species found on anthills and in soil pockets. A glimpse at the distribution maps for this species suggests that it is rare and that it occurs mostly on calcareous soils. One of the more imaginative names belongs to the **Spiral Extinguisher Moss**, *Encalypta streptocarpa*. 'Spiral' derives from the striking twisted shape of the protonema, and 'Extinguisher' from the shape of its capsule.

Slightly discouraging for my claim that Hog Cliff is a splendid example of chalk downland are *Oxyrrhynchium hians* and *Brachythecium rutabulum*, respectively **Swartz's Feathermoss** and **Rough-stalked Feathermoss**. These are very common species, which the British Bryological Society has described as 'unexpectedly common [...] especially in neglected or reversion swards'.[17] Perhaps there was a little too much clay where they were found. Perhaps worse still is **Springy Turf Moss**, *Rhytidiadelphus squarrosus*, the species most likely to infuriate gardeners. However, it has a strong association with waxcaps and is thus welcome.

The species found on lumps of chalk is the **English**

Rock-bristle, *Seligeria calycina*. It is uncommon in Britain and very rare everywhere else. Even for a moss it is tiny, with leaves barely 1 mm long, though with setae and capsules towering a few millimetres above them. Fortunately for the moss enthusiast, it often congregates in large numbers on a single piece of chalk, generally appearing as a slight green fur when alive and a grubby brown fur when dead.

The genus *Microbryum* (literally, 'small moss') contains species of similar size. Two occur at Hog Cliff, **Smallest Pottia**, *Microbryum davallianum* var. *davallianum*, and **Upright Pottia**, *M. rectum* (it means 'upright'). Again, they are rare and largely confined to Britain and calcareous soil pockets. The capsule of this species is only 0.5 mm in diameter and coloured like a toffee apple. Even the sedate British Bryological Society describes it on its website as being 'very, very cute'.

THE FUNGI OF HOG CLIFF

Nearly two hundred species within the Basidiomycota – that is, mushrooms, toadstools, puffballs and club fungi – have been recorded at Hog Cliff. Many are in the coppices and scrub, but around seventy-five are found in the grasslands. All but one of the two dozen Ascomycetes recorded here grow in wood or scrub, the exception being the tiny, orange and very common **Cowpat Gem**, *Cheilymenia granulata*, which is very often found just where you might expect it.

It was most fortunate that I found myself at Hog Cliff back in the 1980s, and that when we left the farmhouse, we moved into the village within the same parish. Fungi had fascinated me since my teenage years, and here was a place where they grew in peace and in plenty. My first notable encounter was with the **Field Mushroom**. It grew in the long-established pasture in the top field to the north, which was outside what was to become the nature reserve. The field was covered with a hundred distinct rings, one of which, I recall, made out an almost perfect outline of Australia.

Of the recorded grassland fungi, sixty-three live by digesting dead organic matter in the soil via external enzymes (saprotrophs), nine have a mycorrhizal relationship with a living plant or plants and three are plant parasites. Saprotrophism is the simplest mode of nutrition in the larger fungi, with several of them forming spectacular and long-lived rings.

Waxcaps grow at Hog Cliff, but only on the less calcareous areas. A lack of grazing when the reserve first came under the control of Natural England greatly reduced the waxcap population, and it has taken most of the forty intervening years for them to recover.

I have divided the fungi into five groups: the saprotrophs, the associates of the Common Rock-rose, the waxcaps, the ring fungi and the microfungi.

Saprotrophic Fungi

The Field Mushroom still occurs in the more fertile grass at Hog Cliff, next to the field where it once grew in abundance and on the relatively nutrient-rich soils. Three more *Agaricus* species occur within the current circumscription of the reserve, *Agaricus comtulus*, *A. dulcidulus* and the **Yellow Stainer**, *A. xanthodermus*. The first two are diminutive members of the genus, measuring barely 3 cm and 6 cm in diameter respectively: both smell of almonds or anise. They are in the 'section' of *Agaricus* species known as 'the Minores', members of the genus having been divided into groups based on response to a chemical reagent and various physical characteristics such as the colour of the flesh when cut. One such group is the Xanthodermatei, characterised by the various parts of the fruiting body staining chromium yellow on bruising. The Yellow Stainer is a very common mushroom and the cause of *much* intestinal grief (though not death) for those many who pick it on the misunderstanding that it is a Field Mushroom.

The statuesque **Parasol Mushroom**, *Macrolepiota procera*, makes an occasional appearance, while the much less common **Slender Parasol**, *M. mastoidea,* is found every year all over the steep slopes. Both, incidentally, are edible and good. *Agaricus* and *Macrolepiota* species are near-constants of grassland, but there are many others.

Conocybe species, the **Conecaps**, are also common but relatively dull, with the words 'small' and 'orange' coming to mind. Still, five species have been found on the site, two of them rare or at least either under-recorded or confused with the commoner species such as *Conocybe tenera*. They often live on dung.

Although they may look dull to the uninitiated, the similarly small but generally grey Bonnets, *Mycena* spp., are quite exciting. *Mycena* is a large genus with easily one hundred species occurring in Britain. Many are the very devil to identify, with the minutest of details requiring examination for an answer to be found. Some, however, have 'tricks' that make identification easy: the stem may 'bleed' white (or red); it may smell of nitric acid or radishes; it may buck the trend and be pink or yellow; it may have a slimy stem, or glow in the dark; or it may grow densely and in enormous numbers on a log. Most of them are found in woodlands, growing on dead wood, but a few are found in grasslands. Only three species have been recorded at Hog Cliff, one of which has a 'trick' – it has a brown edge to the gills, hence its names: **Brownedge Bonnet**, *Mycena olivaceomarginata*.

The grassland at Hog Cliff boasts three species of *Lycoperdon*, a genus of puffballs: the **Meadow Puffball**, *L. pratense*, the **Grassland Puffball**, *L. lividum*, and the **Mosaic Puffball**, *L. utriforme*. The second of these I have seen only once, over thirty

Waxcaps

years ago, when it covered every anthill on the site. The Meadow Puffball does not entertain such flamboyant displays but seldom misses a year, growing in ones and twos here and there. It is a pretty thing: soft, slightly oval when seen from above and white with a flush of peach.

The uncommon Mosaic Puffball always requires old pasture. Here it is well established, and I have seen it there every year since 1982. It is large, at typically 12 cm in diameter and 20 cm high, and covered with distinct greyish scales: hence its common name. As with all *Lycoperdon* species, it is pyriform (pear-shaped), but upside down. All *Lycoperdon* species have a spongy sterile base growing in and just above the soil, with the fertile mass vaguely spherical above. This fertile mass is white while it is growing, with the appearance of marshmallow. Once fully grown, it exudes vast quantities of water, turning a green/brown colour, with billions of dry, brown spores forming in the top section.

With the Mosaic Puffball the skin at the top breaks down to reveal a cup of spores which are exposed to the distributing winds and splashing raindrops. Owing to some surface bumps, the spores never become waterlogged, and a pile of them can often be seen floating on a pool of rainwater within the cup. The Grassland Puffball follows a more considered strategy, forming a small hole (ostiole) at the very top of the intact and papery skin. When a raindrop falls on it, a small puff of spores is ejected.

Not all puffballs are pyriform; some are more or less round. Once, in what I presume to be a shallow, hillside chalk pit at Hog Cliff, I found a **Giant Puffball**, *Langermannia gigantea*. A splendid sight, sadly not to be repeated at Hog Cliff to my knowledge. As you will guess, this is the largest of the puffballs, averaging 35 cm in diameter. The entire structure, excepting the thin skin, turns into spores held in a branching matrix of cottonwool-like fibres (the capillitium). When mature, the skin tears and falls away, and the spores disperse in the wind. Often, mature specimens detach from the ground and roll around while still dispersing their spores – trillions of them.

'Trillions' is beyond the ready reach of our imagination, so I once considered how to make it understandable, for this puffball at least. Fungal spores are very small – up to 5 µm in the case of the Giant Puffball, which means that 200 fit side by side in 1 mm. If they were the size of a haricot bean, the 7 trillion spores that have been estimated for a large specimen would fill the Millennium Stadium in Cardiff to the roof four times over.

A similar technique of dispersal is adopted by the final two puffballs found at Hog Cliff: the **Grey Puffball**, *Bovista plumbea*, and the **Brown Puffball**, *B. nigrescens*. These are around 3 cm in diameter, spherical, with a thick outer skin that peels away at maturity to reveal a thin, papery inner skin. The inner skin forms a large and often irregular pore, and the entire fruiting body detaches from the soil. It then rolls around the countryside, blown by the wind and spreading its spores. Almost indestructible, they can persist in this state for a year or more.

Fungal Associates of the Common Rock-Rose

When I first moved to Hog Cliff, I discovered a species called the **Panther Cap**, *Amanita pantherina*. It was one I had seen before in a most definitely wooded part of the New Forest in Hampshire. It is a mycorrhizal species, so I wondered why it might be growing in open grassland with the nearest suitable tree a hundred metres away.

Subsequently, I found several other woodland species growing on the slopes of Hog Cliff, including two species of *Cortinarius* (Webcap). It was barely known at the time, but it transpired that the plant with which these species had a mycorrhizal relationship was under my feet all the time – the Common Rock-rose.

The Common Rock-rose is, first of all, not a rose in the Order Rosales but belongs to the Malvales, an Order that includes the mallows. It is a shrubby plant, and I have a couple of cultivars of it in my garden, both of which reach about 40 cm in height. Wild populations, however, barely reach 10 cm. This is an adaptation common to nearly all of the plants found on well-grazed downlands. Small as it is, from the perspective of mycorrhizal fungi it is just another tree.

The list of its associated fungi at Hog Cliff is now nine: **Tawny Grisette**, *Amanita fulva*; Panther Cap, *A. pantherina*; the **Grisette**, *A. vaginata*; the **Lurid Bolete**, *Neoboletus luridus*; an unidentified **Fibre Cap**, *Inocybe* sp.; ***Tricholoma hemisulphureum***, a knight; *Lactarius evosmus*, a milkcap; and two webcaps, ***Cortinarius cisticola***, and **C. epsomiensis**.

Those of you who know about the webcaps (there are hundreds of them in the UK) may well doubt the determinations above, but they were provided by Peter Orton, who visited the site with me many years ago. In fact, it was a fungus foray by what was then the 'Southern Recording Group'. I was in awe of my companions, of whom I now appear to be the sole survivor. All of them were vastly more experienced than was I at the time, and it could not have been a better day as an extraordinary number of species were found. Peter was then the leading authority on *Cortinarius* species, and I mentioned to him that there were a couple onsite. He knew them both, but I remember that when he picked one of the webcaps, he said, 'Ah! *Cortinarius epsomiensis*! I haven't seen this since I found it on Epsom Downs in 1956 and gave it its name.' The full name for this species is: *Cortinarius epsomiensis* P. D. Orton.

It still astonishes me that these species are found in grassland, as it is difficult to believe that they can produce such large fruiting bodies when the source of their food comes from so small a plant. All that I have seen are in the same size range, whether they are growing in woods or in fields. No doubt they manage because a single mycelium may connect to many plants, and the roots of Rock-rose form a dense and wiry mat. Unlike forty years ago, *Helianthemum*—fungus associations are now well recognised, to the point where '*Helianthemum* grasslands' have garnered much interest from botanists and mycologists.

WAXCAPS

I consider the Common Rock-rose associations described above as the headline ecological feature of Hog Cliff, but there is one other contender: the waxcaps, with fifteen species found at Hog Cliff, all in the slightly acid/neutral soils. All belong to the Family Hygrophoraceae, within which they form a monophyletic group.

The waxcaps, discussed at greater length on p. 113–14, are among the most beautiful of all the fungi, as most display brilliant colours that can match any flower – crimson, scarlet, purple, orange, green, pink, yellow, black, white and grey. As one would imagine, their appearance is vaguely 'waxy', though their surface textures range from extremely slimy to dry.

I once compared the waxcaps at Hog Cliff to a box of children's toys scattered down the hillside.[18] On that hillside there were the **Scarlet and Crimson Waxcaps**, *Hygrocybe coccinea* and *H. punicea*, the bright yellow **Golden Waxcap**, *Hygrocybe chlorophana*, the pale orange **Meadow Waxcap**, *Cuphophyllus pratensis*, and the common **Snowy Waxcap**, *Cuphophyllus virgineus*. These were largely restricted to the neutral/acid slope near the head of Farm Hill Bottom. The waxcaps suffered a long period of under-grazing when Natural England first acquired the site, but forty years later they are showing signs of recovery.

There are another seven species of waxcap found at Hog Cliff, a little short of providing the site with the status of national importance. Among them is the uncommon **Bitter Waxcap**, *Hygrocybe mucronella*, and the well-named and larger **Splendid Waxcap, *H. splendidissima***.

A member of the Family Hygrophoraceae that is *not* a waxcap has been found at Hog Cliff: ***Arrhenia obscurata***. It is a small, grey fungus, with gills that run down the stem slightly, giving the whole thing a funnel-shaped appearance. Hog Cliff is one of only fifty sites in Britain where it has been recorded. Small, pale brown species in grasslands are none too conspicuous, so observational bias will have had some hand in this poor showing, though there is little doubt that it is rare – I have seen it only once. It too grows with mosses, and the questions about nutritional strategy have been asked. Some in the genus are known to parasitise mosses, so it is likely that *A. obscurata* does just this.[19] Some *Arrhenia* species take their parasitism to the extreme of dispensing with a stem and forming a cap, complete with fertile gills, directly from a living thread of a moss frond.

This is creepy enough, but I cannot resist the story of the 'Powdercap Strangler'. This mushroom parasitises another powdercap by germinating its spores on its victim, plumbing itself into the victim's stem and growing its own cap upon it, instead of that of its host. You can see the join – really! This freeloader fungus is exceedingly rare, though its host is common.

The pinkgills, *Entoloma* spp., are mostly small species with, well, pink gills. They are relatively easy to identify to species owing to some distinct characteristics such as cap and stem colour (metallic blue, cream, brown or white), whether or not there is a black edge to the gills, or smell, with one species (apparently) smelling of mouse pee. One of those found onsite is much larger than the others, the **Big Blue Pinkgill**, *E. bloxamii*, and quite splendid with its metallic blue cap. This 'species' is often rendered as '*Entoloma bloxamii* agg.', as there is a complex of difficult-to-separate species surrounding this name. A remarkable nine species of pinkgill occur at Hog Cliff, not all of them associated with the grasslands.

RING SPECIES

An aspect of at least some grassland species, and some woodland species too, is that a few grow in rings. This is an extraordinary display, as you will no doubt have seen somewhere on your travels, and perhaps on your lawn in the highly troublesome form of the Fairy Ring-champignon. Of the one hundred species of fungi that can form rings, sixteen or so are found at Hog Cliff, though I have only seen six do so. All six have been 'Type 1' rings.

The **St George's Mushroom**, *Calocybe gambosa*, boasts about five rings, though they are all short lengths of arch. Three of the others are also large mushrooms, and their rings are simply spectacular. They are the **Clouded Funnel**, *Clitocybe nebularis*, the **Grooved Cavalier**, *Melanoleuca grammopodia*, and the **Spotted**

Blewit, *Lepista panaeolus*. The last of these is considered to be uncommon; indeed, I know it from only four locations, three of them in West Dorset. It always occurs in grasslands that are conspicuously permanent, always grows densely and is most often seen in very large rings. These natural structures are so striking that I devote a page or three to them in the introduction to grassland fungi on pp. 117–21, but for now I will just repeat that one is now 31 m in diameter and at my last count in 2023 had produced 400 substantial mushrooms.

MICROFUNGI

Not all fungi produce large fruiting bodies. Although few have been recorded onsite, there are also the 'microfungi' that parasitise or otherwise depend on plant species, with few British plants escaping their attentions. We are fortunate to have a book that provides information about these organisms, with the vast majority being described within its covers. It is the previously mentioned *The Microfungi on Land Plants*, by Ellis and Ellis, 'micro' in this sense meaning small, not necessarily microscopic, although some optical aid will be needed to see the details of nearly all of them. They range over most of the fungal Divisions: Basidiomycetes, Ascomycetes and other more obscure corners of the Kingdom Fungi.

With 130 or so species of plant in the grassland plus scores in the scrub, and with anything from one to twenty species able to colonise each species, Hog Cliff has a *potential* for these fungi that runs into four figures. Unlike the macrofungi, they must be searched out, and it is beyond doubt that there will be many more than those few recorded. A common group, the Rust Fungi (mostly Pucciniales – formerly the Uredinales), are conspicuous as (usually orange) discolorations and pustules on leaves and stems. Betony is sometimes infected with the rust fungus, **Puccinia betonica**, the

Latin name reflecting the only plant it grows on. It discolours the top of the leaves and forms multiple, small, dark orange-brown pustules on the underside. Slightly more cosmopolitan is *Puccinia arenariae*, which is found on **Thyme-leaved Sandwort**, *Arenaria serpyllifolia*, but can also infect chickweeds (*Stellaria* spp.). Thyme-leaved Sandwort is one of the top colonisers of anthills.

SLIME MOULDS

It is the fate of slime moulds, organisms that are most definitely not fungi, to be lumped in with the fungi when it suits the convenience of the writer – as is the case here. They were once thought to be fungi; indeed, the name assigned to them was, and mostly still is, the 'Myxomycota' – the 'myco' part indicating 'fungus'. Those we see most often are known as the 'true slime moulds'. Quite where they fit in the classification of organisms seems to change from week to week, but many place it in the Kingdom Chromista or in the Protista, both ragbags of the weird and wonderful, including some terrestrial algae, amoebae of various stripes and many types of seaweed.

Mucilago crustacea is one of the plasmodial slime moulds. It is certainly one of the largest and invariably comes as a shock when encountered for the first time. Famously, it has received the very informal name of the **Dog's-sick Fungus**, for reasons that become obvious when you see one. This name has been misapplied to its bright orange relative *Fuligo septica*, though this is just my opinion, and it is up to people to decide what they call things.

In general, it forms a slowly moving mass of plasmodium that looks (dog's-sick aside) like scrambled egg when fresh. I have seen it at Hog Cliff, where it occurred as multiple masses spanning a metre or so. Having slithered around on the grass for a while, consuming (mostly) bacteria, it settles down to form a pale crust, within which is a mass of billions of spores that together look like cocoa powder. It is a species I see two or three times late in summer or autumn but always, it seems, on permanent grasslands.

THE INVERTEBRATES

As is well known, and as I have belaboured at length in this book, invertebrates will invariably and greatly outnumber the combined total of all the plants, larger fungi and other animal species that occur on any terrestrial habitat. It is they that put most of the 'diversity' into the much-lauded biodiversity.

Including the nineteen butterflies, 180 invertebrate species have been recorded at Hog Cliff. This is a reasonably good number, but unlikely to be more than a small fraction of what is there.

Some inspirational work was done by Dr Rob Wolton in Devon, who published the remarkable results of his efforts in *British Wildlife* in 2015.[20] Over a two-year period he recorded *every living thing* he found in a 70-m length of what is admittedly a very good, very old hedge. The number was 2,200 species and counting, most of them by far invertebrates. Hog Cliff is orders of magnitude larger than that single hedge; indeed it includes hedges and scrub just as likely to contain large numbers of invertebrates. Therefore I would say with considerable confidence that Hog Cliff contains many, many more species than those that have been recorded.

Every terrestrial animal will depend on plants directly or indirectly, with many of them depending on a particular plant. This, and Wolton's brilliant survey, have provided a very rough rule of thumb: count the plant species on a site and multiply by eighteen, though this is my interpretation, not his.

Unfortunately, unless one is an expert on all terrestrial invertebrates (a degree of expertise that has been acquired by no one) and has a great deal of time with nothing else to occupy one, it is impossible for an individual to discover the number of species in almost any area of land. Help from specialists will always be required. There are records for most important sites, but they will seldom be comprehensive. Which brings us back to observational bias and sizeism. To repeat: large species and common species are over-represented; species that are small, difficult to identify or both are under-represented.

The resultant number of invertebrates occurring at Hog Cliff could be well into the thousands. We know only a few, but here are the stories of some of these, starting with the most conspicuous by far.

Ants, Anthills and Aphids

I often encounter anthills on the walks I take and always tell people to resist the seemingly irresistible temptation to step on the anthills, pointing out that each tiny clump of earth, particle of sand or chalk had to be excavated by an ant, carried to the surface between mandibles only 0.65 mm across and placed in position *one at a time*.[21] An anthill, I point out, is likely to be older than their grandmother.

Like the Starkadders and Cold Comfort Farm, there have always been ants at Hog Cliff Farm, nearly all of them the extremely common **Yellow Meadow Ant**, *Lasius flavus*, a species that produces herb-rich mounds. All ants that live in the grassland will make their nests in soil, with perhaps a few other species that could be found on foraging expeditions from the wood or scrub.

Now that Natural England owns the site, there are many more Yellow Meadow Ant mounds than when I lived there, as cattle grazing has been limited and largely replaced by sheep. Sheep will live happily with the hills that the ants form, while cows will sometimes trample them out of existence. Anthills have always existed on the slopes, but the gentler grazing has given the bottom of the valley, especially the part to the east of Parson's Coppice, the opportunity to accommodate hundreds of new hills. The view of them in a good light is magnificent: hundreds of tiny green castles capped with flowers, their unseen residents busy with their work. This is the richest population of Yellow Meadow Ant I know, and, although common enough, one of Hog Cliff's great treasures.

Yellow Meadow Ants often form these familiar hills, though elsewhere in Britain, and indeed worldwide, their colonies may simply live under a small rock. The ecology of anthills is extraordinary, most notably the micro-habitats they form, with plant communities that are different from those that surround them. First, however, to the ants and their engaging lifestyle.

Unless you visit them in the spring, when most of the annual refurbishment is done, you are unlikely to see a single Yellow Meadow Ant wandering about and searching for food. The reason for this is that their food is in the nest. It has long been known that ants live (mostly) on the honeydew created by aphids that live on the roots of living plants. Honeydew is the sticky, sugary substance that drops onto any car parked under an aphid-infested tree. Here it quickly accumulates dust.

The aphid taps into the nutrient sap in the phloem, the complex vessels that transport sugar-rich material from the leaves. The sap has a high sugar content but a low concentration of other required nutrients, so most of the sugar is excreted. An aphid may simply form a droplet, though some species spread the honeydew onto hairs around the anal area. Some squirt the honeydew from their rear end, but 'ant-attended' aphids, as in Yellow Meadow Ant nests, are unable to perform this trick to rid themselves of their honeydew. Having ants to clear up what would become a troublesome waste product underground, this association with ants is essential for both their lives. But of course, aphids would not easily feed underground without the tunnels they feed in.

There is an arguably appealing story told in ant circles (there are such) that the rear end of an aphid is remarkably similar in appearance to that of a worker ant's head. Fed by worker ants when they are juveniles, they come to associate that shape with food. The word 'appearance' does not refer to sight as it is completely dark in an anthill; the ants sense shape through touch, using their antennae.

The food collected by a worker is regurgitated into the mouth of another ant, which passes it on to another ant and so on, each absorbing some of the food. The entire process is known as 'trophobiosis': the provision of food from one species to another in a mutualistic relationship.

While ants can recycle nutrients within their bodies using the services of gut bacteria, the nutrient content of phloem sap is low, with the aphid taking most for itself. The ants need to find more. The aphids are bred in the nests, their young tended by the ants. The aphid population is maintained at a constant level (typically 3,000 excluding the first instars, or life stages). They are rapid breeders, and the first instars are frequently consumed by the ants, also estimated at about 3,000 a day in a single anthill.[22] Many of these will be fed to the brood ants, who need a high-protein diet. It is possible that the ants consume other prey, but it will need to be a creature that has found itself inside the nest.

Apart from a little attention to the aphids' hygiene, what are the advantages they enjoy that makes their status any better than that of farm animals? There are several: the chambers and galleries in which they and parts of the sap-full roots are found provide the aphids with room to move. Ants defend them from predators and will carry them from one place to another. The microclimate within the hill is relatively steady and benign, and the aphid eggs are kept free of fungal spores as the ants 'lick' them off.

The anthills at Hog Cliff are substantial examples, typically around 70 cm wide and 50 cm tall. There are larger specimens on the hillsides, many of which are taller, if not wider, giving them to appearance of a tower rather than a bell. The eastern face is usually steeper than the other faces because this is the side on which most building takes place. This may explain why anthills can move across the landscape, with indications that this is so provided by a famous pair of studies of anthills in Wytham Woods in Oxfordshire.[23] The studies were made sixty years apart, in 1960 and 2020. The majority of the anthills were still there, and a few of these appeared to have moved a short distance.

The amount of soil that is piled up to make the mounds is extraordinary if one considers the size of the workers – each about 4 mm long and weighing in at 2 mg. A hectare of grassland with a high population of Yellow Meadow Ant anthills will have had between 150 and 240 tonnes of soil moved above the level of the pasture. Anyone who has examined a disturbed anthill (or disturbed one themselves) will have seen the consistently fine soil from which it is made, a result of the small particulate sizes.

Most ants and ant activity occur below ground level, with the hills themselves vegetated spoil-heaps containing only a small proportion of the aphids and their attendant ants. The below-ground galleries extend well beyond the footprint of the hill.[24]

In addition to being consistently fine, the soil of an anthill is lower in organic matter and nutrients than the surrounding soil. One study found the surveyed soil to be lower in nitrogen, sulphur, manganese and zinc, and higher in phosphorus, iron, calcium and potassium.[25]

Anthill soils display greater porosity, allowing easier growth for plants, more air and better drainage. In their digging and hill-making, ants also provide similar soil services to those of earthworms, cycling lower soil – notably the friable chalk – to the top. This chalk will raise the pH in anthills and to some extent in the immediate vicinity. I tested this at Hog Cliff and found anthills to have a pH averaging 6.8, falling to 6.0 some 60 cm away and to 5.5 at 1.5 m away. The raising of chalk particles to the surface is an important feat of eco-engineering by the ants in that it improves overall diversity.

The Vegetation of Anthills

Wandering around anthills is like wandering around village gardens on 'Open Garden Day'. All the gardens we see as we amble from house to house differ one from another, allowing us fulsome opportunities for both admiration and (much more fun) disdain. Apart from abandoned hills that tend to revert to grass or monoculture moss, little disdain is possible with anthills. No two anthills bear the same mix of vegetation, with some a mass of the shrubby Common Rock-rose, some a mass of shrubby Wild Thyme and others a blinding yellow with Lady's Bedstraw or green with mosses. Most, however, show more flair, with displays of multiple species.

The biology and behaviour of Yellow Meadow Ants are endlessly interesting in themselves, but the effect that their anthills have on the landscape is profound to the point of them being described as 'antscapes' made by 'ecosystem engineers'.[26]

Ten of the top eleven plants with an affinity for chalkland anthills listed in C. J. Smith's *Ecology of the English Chalk* can be found on anthills at Hog Cliff. They are Common Rock-rose, Wild Thyme, Thyme-leaved Sandwort, Common Mouse-ear, Black Medick, Fairy Flax, Eyebright, **Wall Speedwell**, *Veronica arvensis*, **Fern-grass**, *Catapodium rigidum*, and 'mosses'.

In the spring, and at later times of year in the case of damage, new soil is brought to the top of the mound at a rate of up to one litre per year. This is a conspicuous process, and it is possible to see the fine young blades of grass shoots stood in a rising tide of otherwise bare soil. While some plants cannot withstand this annual inundation and disappear from the anthills, some can. For many plants it will form a welcoming new seedbed – something that is rare in grasslands and sometimes embraced by annuals.

At Hog Cliff the chief beneficiaries of the anthills have been Common Rock-rose and Wild Thyme, which together dominate them. Perennial, with tough, wiry and spreading roots, they form large surface areas on which aphids can feed. In addition, and of some importance, are the mosses. Although they die back in the warmer months, some mosses live on the anthills. Of the twenty mosses found at Hog Cliff four have been found on the anthills, two of which are rare – *Encalypta streptocarpa* and *Fissidens taxifolius* **var.** *taxifolius*.

THE ASSOCIATED ANIMALS OF ANTHILLS

With no one, including your author, prepared to dismantle an ant hill at Hog Cliff, the species below are taken from the Wytham Woods studies.

Over thirty animal species were recorded as associates of the anthills in the grasslands studied at Wytham Woods. This excluded microscopic species such as tardigrades and nematodes, as they were unlikely to be exclusive to anthills. Hog Cliff is likely to have as many species, and many of these will be the same as those of Wytham Woods because the associations are well established.

Although a few larger invertebrates have an association with the Yellow Meadow Ant, most of the animals found habitually within the nests were small, and generally known as 'myrmecophiles', literally, 'ant lovers'. Those that spend time within an ant colony will attempt to avoid detection by smelling of nothing at all, matching their odour ('cuticular hydrocarbon profile', no less) to that of the nest or by acquiring the odour by simply being there for a short period, presumably while keeping their heads down.[27]

Thirteen species of aphid were found at Wytham Woods,

though there are twice as many UK aphid species able to take on the task. At Hog Cliff, one of them is very likely to be *Aphis helianthemi*, as it is (rather obviously) known to feed on the roots of the Common Rock-rose.

Mites

Mites are arachnids that are found in nearly all terrestrial habitats, most of them barely a millimetre in diameter. The Red Spider Mite and the common tick are the most familiar to us, but tens of thousands of species are known.

Five mites were recorded, all of them known to be frequent occupants of Yellow Meadow Ant anthills. Although 'myrmeco-phile' means 'ant lover', the relationships are often unclear and not necessarily affectionate. It may be that only one or the other in a relationship benefits (commensal), that both benefit (mutualistic), that one of them is a parasite on the other or, as is most likely, nobody knows.

Antennophorus pubescens is uncompromisingly classed as a parasite, the other four simply noted as myrmecophilous. A tedious review of the literature found that most students of mites were interested in the naming of new species, with few interested in their behaviour, even with those they were naming. One source noted that it was difficult to know what they (mites) are up to, but that consuming otherwise troublesome detritus (detrivory), using ants for transport (phoresis, a common behaviour in mites) and being predatory are the general range of behaviours.[28] *Myrmecological News* (really) was more direct, saying that although the behaviour of mites was diverse, they were 'mostly antagonistic (parasites, parasitoids, predators, kleptoparasites)'.[29] Since all five species are in the group of mites known as the Parasitiformes, my money is on *Myrmecological News*.

Hoverflies

Some hoverflies have a relationship with anthills: a predatory one. The larvae of three genera of hoverfly feed on the aphids that are so carefully tended by the ants. Using chemical signals, they mask their presence and are ignored by the ants. Since the ants tend aphids for food, this is effectively stealing and is called 'kleptoparasitism'. It is likely that one or two such species occur at Hog Cliff, but none has been recorded there.

Looking more like a bee than most bees is the hoverfly the Downland Ant Fly, *Microdon devius*, although the recorders were unsure about their determination. It is a rare species and unlikely to be at Hog Cliff. Nevertheless, it is interesting in that it is an obligate parasite of *L. flavus*. Its larvae consume both the eggs and the larvae of the ants.

OTHER INVERTEBRATES

A much more friendly and common myrmecophile is the beetle, *Claviger testaceus*. One hundred individuals have been found in a single anthill. Only a little over 2 mm long, they are a dull orange in colour and brandish antennae that look like remarkably like kebabs. They consume dead insects and the excreta and secretions of larval ants, all of which behaviours are beneficial to the colony, as well as sucking out the contents of ant eggs, which is not so welcome. Nevertheless, like a resident elderly aunt who helps with the laundry and has promised you her estate in her will, they are highly tolerated by the ants. The beetles will even carry ant larvae to safety when needed, and in preference to their own larvae.[30]

One silverfish species was recorded and the isopod (woodlouse) *Platyarthrus hoffmannseggii*, the latter worth mentioning for its specific epithet alone, as it boasts four pairs of letters in a single word (possibly a record). Unlike the silverfish, all species of which are strangely unappealing, the woodlouse is a 4-mm beauty, neat and, needing no protection from ultraviolet light, a translucent white. It is a detrivore, effectively keeping the place clean. Fittingly known as the 'Ant Woodlouse', it is specific to the Yellow Meadow Ant.

Among the less intimate invertebrate relationships found at Wytham Woods were those of two butterflies (of which more shortly), two grasshoppers and a burnet moth whose given identity is dubious as it is otherwise reported as unknown in England. The **Meadow Grasshopper**, *Chorthippus parallelus*, and the **Common Grasshopper**, *C. brunneus*, both lay egg pods in the form of an encompassing membrane and a protective layer of fixed soil particles. They contain up to fifteen eggs. Using an ovipositor, the pod is laid in the soil. Where anthills are available, their homogeneous and soft soil will be preferred, and in spring they will be covered in fresh plant growth on which the juveniles may feed.

Butterflies

The Lepidoptera consists of two groups, the butterflies and the moths. Out of 2,400 UK Lepidopteran species, only about sixty are butterflies. Their relative value is higher than this stark ratio suggests, as they are 'poster children' for conservation and valuable as indicator species of the quality of the land on which they live and for the general ecological trends their populations reveal. Having said this, I consider that their hyper-sensitivity to unsuitable weather makes them over-dramatic in their responses and unreliable for such a task, though at least they are conspicuous and easy to identify close up – and on the wing for some species and some observers.

First, and to follow the ant section as neatly as possible, there are those that have a relationship with ants. Of the Family

Lycaenidae the **Common Blue**, *Polyommatus icarus*, Chalkhill Blue, *P. coridon*, **Adonis Blue**, *Polyommatus bellargus*, **Brown Argus**, *Aricia agestis*, and **Green Hairstreak**, *Callophrys rubi*, have all been recorded at Hog Cliff, though the Chalkhill Blue is not found there now. These can all be ant-attended to one degree or another. This 'degree' is expressed as either 'obligate' (the butterfly cannot survive without the ants) or 'facultative' (they can take them or leave them).

The overall deal is that the larvae of the butterfly supply sugars and amino acids to the ants from specialist structures on one of their segments known as the 'dorsal nectar organ'. The ants return the favour by protecting the butterfly larvae from predation. This happens outside the anthill and on the larval food plant.[31] With a facultative relationship the nectar reward is relatively poor, as there is little trust between the two partners.

An obligate relationship will have a single species of ant associated with a single species of butterfly, the loyalty rewarded with more and better nectar. Ants in obligate relationships will also attend the larvae in much greater numbers. Ants will continue their care even when the nectar-free pupal stage is reached.[32]

The most famous of these obligate behaviours is that of the Large Blue, *Phengaris arion*. It became extinct in Britain in 1979, suffering the fate of all fussy eaters in difficult times. None of the Lycaenidae at Hog Cliff is an obligate myrmecophile, and it is difficult to know how much or how often the facultative myrmecophiles avail themselves of the services of ants. Not much, according to my lepidopterist friends.

The overall butterfly count at Hog Cliff is moderate, at around eighteen. Those that I have seen other than the Lycaenidae species above are the **Green-veined White**, *Pieris napi*, **Small Tortoiseshell**, *Aglais urticae*, **Red Admiral**, *Vanessa atalanta*, **Meadow Brown**, *Maniola jurtina*, and the **Silver-washed**

Fritillary, *Argynnis paphia*. I was particularly pleased with the last one.

With butterflies, and very many other invertebrates, their existence in a particular area will depend on their larval food plant being present. Pollen and nectar are secondary considerations.

Butterflies fall into two vague categories – the specialists and the generalists – based on whether they have a restricted or a broad range of larval foodplants. This is somewhat misleading because it is really a continuum as opposed to a binary distinction. Nevertheless, this allows a rough but useful division between specialists and generalists.

More helpful, perhaps, is the concept of species found in high-value environments (such as chalk downland), many of which will require a plant or plants not normally found in 'ordinary' farmland – or anywhere else. The Chalkhill Blue, for example, is firmly in the specialist category as it can only survive with Horseshoe Vetch, *Hippocrepis comosa*. Similarly, with the Small Blue it is the Kidney Vetch. The Small White larvae seem capable of consuming almost any member of the cabbage family, plus, bizarrely, the Wild Pansy.

One might imagine that being a generalist is the more sensible choice, but it is thought to have some disadvantages. These include the extra biochemical costs of obtaining and supporting the adaptation to more than one food plant. Specialists, it has been argued, will cope better with environmental change, and they are generally better suited to sites of high botanical value.[33]

Butterflies in general have had a difficult time in the UK. A major drop in population occurred courtesy of the catastrophic drought of 1976 ('Bath with a friend' being the most memorable – and most followed – piece of government advice at the time). The butterfly population dropped off a cliff, with the numbers falling to half of what they had been before the drought. It has never truly recovered. It is unlikely that the drought alone could have such a long-term effect, but there was a great deal of habitat loss over subsequent years owing to strong governmental encouragement to grow corn. Habitat specialists did slightly worse than the generalists, something to be expected from the loss of species-rich seminatural grasslands.

Of the twenty-one butterfly species that have been recorded at Hog Cliff since it was established as a nature reserve, one is seen only occasionally year to year and one is missing, presumed locally extinct. This is particularly sad as they are 'headline' species, respectively the **Marsh Fritillary**, *Euphydryas aurinia*, and the Chalkhill Blue, even though their foodplants are still there.* What has happened? There are multiple possibilities.

It is almost a truism that when an authority or new private owner takes over a nature reserve, something immediately goes wrong. This is a familiar situation in companies and other organisations, as some of you will know, perhaps to your cost. This may be simple abandonment for a year or three while the management is planned and put in place. It may be that, although the nature reserve is good, perhaps it could be made better. This always sounds suspect to me – if it was good enough to save, it is good enough to leave alone. A typical thing to change in grasslands is the grazing regime. Get it wrong, and you can lose species very quickly.

Hog Cliff suffered two or three years of virtual abandonment while stock for grazing was arranged. Some cattle have almost always been kept onsite since the time of Snowy, but sheep were brought in too – a major change to the grazing. The sheep were something of a blessing, however, as they managed to remove nearly all of the **Common Ragwort**, *Jacobaea vulgaris*, that was making a bid for dominance in the all-important grassland and

* Marsh Fritillary may still be there but not observed. It is still found immediately to the east in one of the extensions to Hog Cliff.

nearly everywhere else. Sheep, incidentally, are able to perform this function because they can eat the basal rosette of the plant whereas cattle cannot.

Was this enough to remove these butterflies? I do not know, though the new grazing regime as planned, or just badly or irregularly applied, may have had this effect. One of those lepidopterist friends often says, 'What the hell have they done at [enter site name here]? It's been grazed to within an inch of its life.' The essential point I wish to address here is why, once something disappears from a site, it does not come back when conditions are more to its liking. The answer is fragmentation and isolation. See p. 40. As a matter of interest, the nearest Chalkhill Blue is now fifteen miles away southwards.

Moths

Considering the large moth-to-butterfly ratio, and assuming someone had put in the work to find them, one would expect over seven hundred moths to have been found onsite, not twenty-two. This is partly plain observational bias in action, but only four out of the twenty-two were night-flying, even though they outnumber day-flying moths by an extraordinary twenty to one. Since night-time moth traps are heavy, and require a great deal of power and expense, what one might call 'circadian observational bias' will certainly be at play here.

With a good book, a little work and an attention to details, anyone can identify a butterfly with ease. Moths, however, are a different matter. There are many, many more of them, and those fine details are much more critical, and some may even require dissection under a microscope. Also, a large proportion are very small. They have been divided up into macro-moths and micro-moths, the former being (mostly) the substantial creatures we see. This differentiation is not as obvious as it sounds as it is based on how the genera are related, their phylogeny, not necessarily how big they are. Micro-moths appeared on the planet first, macro-moths much later. This also means that size really is not that important, with some macro-moths being smaller than many micro-moths.[34] Another categorisation is between night-flying and day-flying moths; this too has a phylogenetic connection.

Common species include the stunning **Six-spot Burnet**, *Zygaena filipendulae*, which warns potential predators with its red spots against black of the cyanide that will come their way if they get too close, and the **Cinnabar Moth**, *Tyria jacobaeae*, with its tiger-striped larvae, which is always found on Common Ragwort. Then there is the **Burnet Companion**, *Euclidia glyphica*, a moth of calcareous lands, so named because it often flies alongside other moths, including the various burnet species. Its larvae feed on Wood Sage, though the moth itself is common enough in scrub and rougher areas of grasslands.

The enchantingly named **Mother Shipton**, *Euclidia mi*, earns its common name from the presumed similarity of its wings to the face of the eponymous sixteenth-century Yorkshire prophet. This was no compliment as she is reported to have been exceedingly ugly. It is, in fact, an attractive moth of browns, yellows and white. It has numerous larval food-plants that are found in grasslands.

Less common in Britain are the **Common Purple & Gold**, *Pyrausta purpuralis*, and its companion, the **Silver-barred Sable**, *P. cingulata*. These are the two micromoths, though not so very 'micro', with a wingspan of about 25 mm. The larvae of both live on Wild Thyme, which is common onsite.

One moth that I found in the scrub a few years ago is the **Small Eggar**, *Eriogaster lanestris*. In fact I did not see the adult moth but fifty caterpillars seething within a nursery web that encompassed a branch of its host tree, a Blackthorn.

The Beetles of Hog Cliff

Famously, the British geneticist and evolutionary biologist J. B. S. Haldane noted that if God was responsible for all of life on Earth, he had an 'inordinate fondness for beetles'. Indeed, one in four animal species is a beetle, and beetles were long thought to account for more species than any other group. It is now the wasps that take this prize.[35] A fair number of beetle species have been recorded from the grassland, scrub and woodland at Hog Cliff. Some will live only on the grassland, while others have a connection with both grassland and the Hawthorn, Blackthorn or gorses of the hillside scrub, or with the trees of the bordering woodland. Some, of course, will require only scrub or woodland – a slightly educated guess for these being 30 per cent.

Among the commonest, and certainly the most memorable, is the **Hogweed Bonking Beetle**, *Rhagonycha fulva*. Its alternative name, the Common Red Soldier Beetle, has fallen out of fashion, presumably because it is much less fun and not in truth accurate as it is distinctly orange.* It nevertheless lives up to this military name because it preys on insects on flowering plants, though content to eat pollen and nectar as well. In my opinion, it richly deserves the more colourful name as mating pairs, sometimes in unseemly numbers, can be all too easily seen on Hogweed and Cow Parsley flower heads.

The most familiar of the brightly coloured and distinctive beetles, in the south at least, is the common **Swollen-thighed Beetle**, *Oedemera nobilis*, the male (though not the female) fitting the description perfectly. It has a comparatively dull fellow species in **O. lurida**.

There are 40,000 leaf beetles, 280 of which are found in Britain. For those with time on their hands, all or most of the British

---

* The words 'orange' and 'pink' are of recent coinage, with 'red' applying to both. Cf. 'Red Campion', which is pink!

species are to be found in a book devoted entirely to this group.[36] At Hog Cliff only *Cryptocephalus fulvus* has been recorded in the grassland, with one other, *C. pusillus*, in the woods. The generic name means 'hidden head', and it is true that when seen from above there is no head visible. Leaf beetles tend to be host-specific; in this case it is with **Sheep's Sorrel**, *Rumex acetosella*.

Weevils are beetles, though it is usually the larval stage infesting ship's biscuits in historic maritime adventure movies that catches the public imagination. Some weevils still infest foods, and heroic (if not swashbuckling) human efforts are made to stop them. (Rest assured – while the larvae of some of their number are agricultural parasites, very few will ever trouble a Rich Tea.)

Weevils are characterised physically by their long 'snouts' (rostrums), and some are only 2 mm long. Of the nearly 100,000 named species, twenty-three are recorded from Hog Cliff. We will content ourselves with just two – the **White Clover Seed Weevil**, *Protapion fulvipes*, and *Mecinus pyraster*.

Better known is a beetle in the Scarabaeidae: not the commonest and largest of them – the startlingly named Common Cockchafer – but the **Summer Cockchafer**, *Amphimallon solstitiale*. In flight both sound like small helicopters and they are substantial creatures, the Summer Cockchafer being about 20 mm long and 8 mm in diameter. It has an association with wood edges.

Only three ladybirds have been found at Hog Cliff. In the peculiar nomenclature of the ladybirds, they are the Seven-, Fourteen- and Twenty-four-spot Ladybird. Ideally, Latin names should provide at least a nod in the direction of what the named organism looks like, but in the case of ladybirds this ambition has run away with itself rather. Both respectively and in ascending order of unpronounceability, they are *Coccinella septempunctata*, *Propylea quattuordecimpunctata* and *Subcoccinella vigintiquattuorpunctata*.

Much loved by children and just about everyone else, ladybirds, beetles within the large Family known as the Coccinellidae, are not as 'nice' as is often thought. They are fearsome predators of aphids and scale insects, and they *bite*.

During the drought of 1976 I spent some time on Southsea beach in Hampshire. Failing to find sustenance or water, ladybirds had flown in search of both. Evidently realising that they would find no respite out to sea, they accumulated in their many millions on the beach, forming dense ladybird swarms. Hungry (and angry) as they were, one bit me on the hand. It stung a bit. Years later one bit me on the tongue after taking a swim in a pint of beer I had been enjoying. This one really hurt.

Most by far are predatory and will even lay their eggs near colonies of their chosen prey. They are famous for their fondness for aphids, and it is often said that if you wish to rid your garden of aphids the best thing to do is encourage ladybirds. Since *having aphids* is the greatest encouragement possible, it seems like empty advice.

The Diptera of Hog Cliff

The name of the zoological Order for flies, the Diptera, means 'two wings': in this case, 'an insect with two wings'. The common name for this group is the 'flies' or the 'true flies'. All other insects that have wings have four. Those that have no wings are assumed to have lost them at some point in their evolutionary history.

In the Diptera there are, however, the remnants of another pair of wings, just behind the forewings. They are small, club-shaped and known as 'halteres'. Incidentally, another, much smaller (and weirder) Order of flies has only two wings – the hindwings – with halteres where the forewings would have been. Halteres have an essential purpose in flight, taking the part of a gyroscope in detecting in-flight rotation in three axes.

In the popular imagination flies are creatures that buzz around the house and require either capture-and-release or swatting, and indeed many flies are of this form. However, there are also Crane Flies, Horse Flies, Midges, Hoverflies, Soldier Flies and many more. Unfortunately, many species have *undeservedly* acquired 'fly' in their name, with Caddisfly, Dragonfly and Sawfly coming immediately to mind.

Worldwide, there well over 100,000 named species of fly, one-thousandth of which have been found onsite at Hog Cliff. I was surprised to see such a relatively long list, and some of the determinations between two or more closely related species require the observational skills of specialists. When I asked my very knowledgeable friend in the village why that might be, he told me that the Dipterist Forum had visited the site fifteen years ago.[37]

Those one hundred species are encompassed within twenty-two Families. Much as I avoid common names for organisms, it is often helpful for the non-specialist to have a common name for a group and most helpful when it applies to Families. Continuing the list above, we also have the Blowflies, Dance Flies, Thick-headed Flies, Robber Flies, Fungus Gnats and on and on. There are many more.

You will no doubt be delighted to hear that I will not be relating the stories of all one hundred species but will instead pick out a few of the more interesting dipteran denizens of Hog Cliff. They are more interesting than beetles.

'She swallowed the spider to catch the fly', is the line from the familiar and robust nursery rhyme. But does a fly ever catch a spider? Yes, the 'Spider Fly' does. There are two resident flies that have a predatory connection to spiders, both in the Acroceridae Family: *Acrocera orbiculus* and **Ogcodes pallipes**, both of them 'nationally scarce'. The eggs are laid in the same habitat as that of the target spider species, most often the helpfully ground-nesting Wolf Spiders (Lycosidae).

The eggs are laid in large numbers (4,000 have been recorded from a related species), no doubt because of the more than usual amount of luck required for the tiny (0.3 mm long) emergent larvae to encounter their prey. If and when they do, the larvae will adhere to the spider and find their way into the spider's book-lung lamellae situated towards the front of the abdomen and conveniently near the ground. Once inside the spider carapace they will proceed to consume the contents. The adult flies have no mouth parts, so they only live long enough to mate and produce eggs.[38] These adults are small, and odd in appearance owing to the pronotum (thorax) being nearly hemispherical. This has informed the basis of a common name for British species as in (respectively) **Top-horned Hunchback**, *Acrocera orbiculus*, and **Black-rimmed Hunchback**, *Ogcodes pallipes*. As an ironic aside, it is not unknown for these flies to be caught in a spider's web.

Robber Flies (Asilidae) are also known as Assassin Flies, the latter name being more appropriate for their fearless predatory be-haviour. They have powerful 'jaws' (mandibles) with which to kill their prey and will often take on bees and wasps, provided they are not much bigger than themselves. One species is the **Kite-tailed Robber Fly**, *Machimus atricapillus*, which predates flies and other insects at the adult stage.

The small Order of flies the Chamaemyiidae consists of species that are truly tiny. Ignoring the wings, from head to the tip of the abdomen can be as little as 2 mm. Despite this, they are predatory, living on appropriately small prey: aphids. They are sometimes known as Aphid Flies and have been put to work as a biological control agent. Three have been recorded at Hog Cliff, including ***Chamaemyia aridella***.

Many more dipteran Families found onsite are parasites or

predators – the Polleniidae whose larvae feed on earthworms, the Snail-killing Flies the Sciomyzidae, whose larvae feed on those snails that cannot lock up the house with a trap door (operculum), and the Dagger Flies, the Empididae, from whom few small terrestrial arthropods (insects, spiders, woodlice, etc.) are safe.

One Family of flies, the Tachinidae, are parasitoids of other insects. An impressive fifteen species were found in twelve genera. Parasitoids are parasites that always kill their host, usually slowly, often consuming non-vital parts first to keep their prey alive for as long as is convenient.

A final note on parasites in general is that for those who record species in the field the existence of a parasites is highly suggestive of the presence of its prey. Sometimes this will be member of a Genus, Family etc., but sometimes it is down to a single species.

Not all flies are so predatory. The **Golden Dung Fly**, *Scathophaga stercoraria*, for example, makes beneficial use of a waste product, as do some of the Flesh Flies, the Sarcophagidae, who feed on dead flesh, though sometimes the open wounds of live animals.

Hoverflies

Two hundred and eighty-three hoverflies (Syrphidae) have been recorded in Britain, with Hog Cliff boasting sixteen recorded species in eleven genera, though there will doubtless be many more. These are familiar in gardens, where they dart from one pollen- and nectar-bearing flower to another and amaze us every time with the precision with which they hover. Most of these garden species will bear black and yellow bands on their abdomens, providing them with a striking similarity to wasps, and sometimes bees. The patterning is, of course, a matter of mimicry and a survival trait. Look like something dangerous and few predators will trouble you, and there is none of the investment in resource-heavy weaponry required of wasps and bees. They are, however, easily distinguished as they have only two wings and do not possess a 'waist'. Many hoverflies, however, are plain, dull and unlikely to be recognised for what they are, though in flight the hovering will usually give away their nature.

The larvae can live much longer than the adult, and it is usually *their* food source that places a hoverfly in a particular habitat. However, adults may just flit about among the flowers, with many preferring grass pollen.

A splendid book by Graham Rotheray entitled *Colour Guide to Hoverfly Larvae* lists the larval food sources and particular feeding preferences: 'mycophages in fungal fruiting bodies; predators attacking aphids, coccids, psyllids and larvae of beetles, moths, ants and wasps … saprophages occurring in media as diverse as dung, tree sap, nests of social insects, wet decaying wood and wet decaying vegetation'.[39] Coccids are the scale insects that can easily cover the trunk and branches of a tree, where they suck out the sap, and psyllids are charmingly known as 'jumping plant lice' and suck sap from leaves and stems. The book is out of print, but helpfully available online.

The most common, with a countrywide distribution, and one of the confirmed aphid-eaters, is the **Marmalade Hoverfly**, *Episyrphus balteatus*. It is quite the beauty, with yellow/orange coloration between stylishly placed moustache-shaped black bands. Its larvae consume the aphids; the adults consume nectar and pollen. It is reputed to possess the unusual ability to crush pollen grains, allowing easier access to their protein-rich contents.[40]

Rhingia campestris larvae live on fresh dung, filtering out bacteria and larger organisms. Its adult form is very distinctive owing to a projecting snout, which encompasses a long proboscis. This specialised kit enables it to reach the nectar of plants where it is deep within the flower, such as with Red Campion.

The oddest pair of hoverflies recorded at Hog Cliff are **Eristalis horticola** and **E. tenax**. Considering the dry situation of a chalk hill where even ditches are superfluous, it is surprising to find these species here as the larvae are aquatic. Perhaps those specimens captured for identification were on a search for a new home, one with water, and not 'born' there. Nevertheless, where there is stock there is poaching near water troughs and gateways and the murky puddles thus created. Also, the woodland often acquires substantial and long-lived puddles where they may breed. The larvae of these two are true ugly ducklings. Their side profile looks like the thing that appeared out of John Hurt's stomach in *Alien*, down to a long, whip-like appendage at the rear end. There is a common name for these monstrosities: rat-tailed maggots. The appendage is a breathing tube that enables them to breathe through the rear end while filter-feeding through the front end. The 'swan' that emerges as the adult looks superficially like a Honeybee.

Bees, Wasps and Sawflies

The Hymenoptera is an enormous Order, containing 150,000 described species and counting. It includes bees, wasps, sawflies and ants, plus some less familiar and mostly older groups in the Order. At Hog Cliff eighteen have been recorded, though it is certain that many, many more are there: my knowledgeable friend has identified twenty-five or so solitary bees in his tiny back garden!

Those we know about consist of one sawfly, the **Honeybee**, *Apis mellifera* ('bee that bears honey'), six bumblebees, five solitary bees and five parasitoid wasps. The sawfly is **Cladius pectinicornis**, a common species whose larvae infest the leaves of roses. Sawflies are obviously not flies, though they can look a little like them. The impressive antennae and four wings place sawflies firmly in

Hymenoptera, though they lack a 'wasp waist'. The larvae of some of the Sawflies consume the leaves of trees within a hammock that encompasses a small branch.

For many people there are only two types of bee: Honeybees and Bumblebees, both members of the same Family, the Apidae. But there are many other bee species in many other Families. The Honeybee needs no explication here, except to say that they were unlikely to be wild stock. A few people in the village keep bees, and they can easily travel the mile to Hog Cliff. Honey Bees were kept in a small clearing in Parsons' Coppice forty years ago.

I did slightly worry at the time that they would compromise the food supply of the local invertebrate species, but their tenure was short-lived as the officer who gave permission for them evidently forgot that he had done so and was horrified when he discovered they were there.

Bumblebees

The bumblebees are all in the genus *Bombus*, the name appropriately deriving from the Latin word for humming or buzzing. There are twenty-four in Britain, with seven widespread. Only two are recorded at Hog Cliff. One is the **Red-tailed Bumblebee**, *Bombus lapidarius*.

While the females can sting when they feel threatened, Bumblebees are thought of kindly by most people. Not all, however, behave well in human terms. The larvae feed on pollen brought to them in the nest, and the workers and queen feed on pollen and nectar. Life, one might think, is sweet for this bee. But nothing is left in peace, and in this case it is the **Red-tailed Cuckoo Bumblebee**, *Bombus rupestris*, that disturbs it.

There are six cuckoo bumblebees in the UK, all of which parasitise one or more species of bumblebee that are *not* cuckoo bumblebees, that is, the 'social bumblebees'. Like the bird, they are

Lady's Mead

Aerial view of Lady's Mead

Lady's Mead at the end of June

Choke – asexual phase

The sward close up in late June

Common Knapweed

Machimus atricapillus, a robber fly

Derbyshire Meadow

Bistort and Buttercups

An aerial view of Derbyshire Meadow

Tufted Vetch

The ubiquitous Self-heal

A Lady's Mantle

The meadow

Another view

Grassington

Melancholy Thistle

The sward close up

Near Grassington

The spoil heaps and sparse vegetation of a calaminarian grassland

Near Grassington

Alpine Pennycress

Spring Sandwort

Malham Cove

Malham Cove and its limestone pavement

Malham Cove

Flowers among the boulders

Common Harebell

Malham Tarn

Marsh Lousewort

Bird's-eye Primrose

ultimate freeloaders; indeed they are considered to be parasites *par excellence*, helping themselves to *everything*. The females collect no pollen to feed their brood, lacking even the pollen baskets to carry it, produce no workers, just fertile males and females of their kind, and neither tend nor feed their young.

A fertilised female Red-tailed Cuckoo Bumblebee enters the nest of the Red-tailed Bumblebee after the latter bee's first workers have been brought to development by their queen. The confusingly similar names indicate a degree of required mimicry. She may hide in the nest for a while to acquire the necessary scent, then kill the queen, although sometimes she will simply dominate her. The parasitic female has the advantage in a fight of a longer sting and tougher coat, and thus will usually triumph, though if there are enough workers to defend the nest, she may be overwhelmed. She will then proceed to lay her eggs in the wax cells made by the resident workers, who will also feed her larvae once the eggs have hatched.

This brutal strategy works well, with 11 per cent of bumblebees adopting it. However, they account for less than 6 per cent of individual bumblebees out of a million records for the genus, and this species is relatively rare. This is nothing other than might be expected for a single species that depends entirely on one (or two or three) other species.

There is an appealing hypothesis on how this behaviour evolved. It is suggested that these social parasites originated as a southern species at the northern limit of their range. Southern species, used to warmer climes, would emerge later in the spring than northern species adapted to a colder climate. Faced with little time to build a nest, they parasitised other nests and gradually lost the behaviour and equipment required to build successful nests themselves. The idea is given some credence by the fact that UK bumblebees that are not career parasites will take over nests if they fail to build one or have their own destroyed. This behaviour is known as 'facultative parasitism', and that of *B. rupestris* and its five companion species as 'obligate parasitism'. The behaviour adopted by the latter is more precisely known as 'brood parasitism' and is a rare phenomenon in nature.[41] 'Kleptoparasitism' is another term that applies. Incidentally, humans are kleptoparasites when they collect honey or milk from their respective owners.

Solitary Bees

Solitary bees are by far the commonest of all bees, though only a mere five on a large nature reserve like Hog Cliff seems poor indeed. It is. My knowledgeable friend provided his own list based on a single trip we took together and accounting for those I mention here. Many solitary bees are informally named according to their behaviour, with 'Mining' and 'Mason' the most common.

The most common species he found was **Gwynne's Mining Bee**, *Andrena bicolor*. No amount of research has discovered the who, what and why of 'Gwynne', but 'Mining' is self-explanatory as they burrow tunnels in the turf as nests. *Andrena* comes from the Greek for 'wasp'; unhelpfully so, considering that members of this genus are conspicuously bees.

It is a common species on chalk downland, but not exclusively so. Most solitary bees will have one brood a year ('univoltine'), but this bee is 'bivoltine'. Having two broods requires a major investment, but it is based on the principle shared with royalty of 'an heir and a spare'. If, owing to poor weather conditions or parasitism, the first brood fails, there is still hope. The adults of the second brood frequent Common Harebells and Clustered Bellflowers, both of which occur onsite. Parasitism, as we have seen, is an almost universal problem for individual species, and *Andrena* species suffer a much as their cousins, the bumblebees. *Andrena bicolor* faces the attentions of the nomad bee **Nomada** *fabriciana*. Interestingly, it matches its victim species by following the bivoltine lifestyle.

One mining bee we saw, the uncommon **Trimmer's Mining Bee**, *Andrena trimmerana*, found several females busily excavating their burrows in short turf between two **Salad Burnet**, *Poterium sanguisorba*, plants. More exciting was the **Red-tailed Mason Bee**, *Osmia bicolor*. The female of this species lays her eggs in empty snail shells, usually those of the genus *Cepaea*, the stripy shell of which is reminiscent of one of the sweets in the vile confection known as 'winter mixture'.

There is considerably more to this than 'lay the eggs and run'. Shells are assessed for suitability, and one is chosen. Four or five brood cells are created using chewed vegetation, and pollen and nectar are introduced into each cell as food for the larvae. Each cell is sealed with chewed leaf material. Not content with this level of security, the bee fills the rest of the shell with soil and whatever particulate matter comes to hand. The part of the operation that I was delighted to witness was that of camouflaging the nest. She made repeated flights collecting pieces of grass and other debris and, like the helicopter I once saw on a Swiss mountain delivering liquid concrete to a mountain-top building project, hovers above the nest and lets go. Then it is on to the next snail shell to do it all over again, with about half a dozen shells being used by a single female.

Wasps

The common understanding is that the wasp that makes a nuisance of itself on picnics is the *only* wasp, apart from Hornets and the occasional and troublesome wasp species that has made its way to these islands. Even what we might call the 'Picnic Wasp' comes in at least two flavours: the native Common Wasp, *Vespula vulgaris*, and the German Wasp, *V. germanica*, a species that arrived in Britain about 130 years ago.

The two *Vespula* species are known as 'social wasps', reflecting the community effort of a large nest. There are, however, many more types. They include gall wasps, wasps that hunt spiders, wasps that consume fruit, cuckoo wasps, parasitoid wasps and more.

Only two of the thousands of wasp species found in Britain are recorded from Hog Cliff. They are both in the Ichneumonidae, a very large Family of parasitoids: **Promethes sulcator** and **Scambus brevicornis**. The latter parasitises the larvae of hoverflies by positioning an egg inside the larva, resulting in a larva inside a larva. Obviously the wasp must perform this grim violation multiple times.[42] Such unpleasant behaviour is typical of the parasitoid wasps and is reflected in their Family name – 'tracker', as in 'hunter'. There are numerous and sometimes baroque variations of method.

The Ichneumonidae, otherwise known as the 'ichneumonid wasps', consists of 25,000 species worldwide, with easily the same number estimated to await discovery. Two thousand five hundred have been recorded in Britain, making up almost 10 per cent of British insects, and comparable to the entire British flora in species numbers.

The number of ichneumonids is daunting, but their small size and the fine and invariably microscopic differentiations that need to be studied to identify them to species make them all but impossible for the amateur. Even deciding which sub-Family a specimen might belong to requires much experience and the navigation of long and impenetrable diagnostic keys. The ichneumonids are for the true specialist. Incidentally, all but a few of these wasps have a common name: who would invent them, who would need them?

Ichneumonids are mostly slim and elegant in appearance and often decorated with colours that warn off potential predators.

They range in size from the Sabre Wasp (sometimes called the Giant Ichneumon), *Rhyssa persuasoria*, at from 10 to 40 mm long, down to 3 mm, both values excluding the long ovipositor that protrudes from the end of the abdomen (an ovipositor is a tube via which organisms can place her eggs). ***Promethes sulcator*** is an attractive species, its black body decorated with a broad orange band wrapped around the abdomen, orange spots and patches elsewhere, and orange legs.

The ichneumonids are the commonest of the parasitoids and, although I will always maintain that not every living thing has a purpose (many organisms just *are*), the 'point' of these wasps, and hypothetically all parasitoids, is to stabilise the populations of their hosts. Without them, the world would be overrun, in this case with hoverflies.

True Bugs

While they can certainly be victims, the True Bugs (Hemiptera) are *mostly* benign creatures that abstain from the dog-eat-dog world we have seen over the last few pages. They obtain their nutrients from plant sap via a strong, modified proboscis that is able to pierce the outer parts of plants. The one group that *does* consume other animals is the Family the Reduviidae. These are the assassin bugs, a few of which occur in Britain but not, it seems, at Hog Cliff. The rest consist of aphids, shieldbugs, leafhoppers, planthoppers, cicadas and bedbugs. Around forty have been recorded at Hog Cliff.

Some Hemiptera are very appealing. The cicada, ***Evacanthus interruptus***, for example, is bright yellow all over, but decorated with bold black markings. From the side it looks a little like a boat. The commonest True Bug is the **Common Froghopper**, *Philaenus spumarius*. It is one of the instars of this that causes the froth that appears on many plants. It needs no nature reserve to survive as it is extremely common and often found in gardens as the small patches of froth on vegetation. It is one of the most remarkable creatures on the planet.

The froth is created by several complex processes, including parts of its outer anatomy being used as bellows to blow the bubbles. But the unique and scarcely believable triumph of this harmless creature is that the adult form possesses partial gearwheels at the top of each rear leg. Their purpose is to precisely synchronise the thrust of these legs when it jumps. It certainly works, with an acceleration equivalent to 550 G occurring over a single millisecond, beginning its arc at 45 degrees. Such a jump requires 'feet' that are firmly attached to the ground in that they do not move horizontally backwards. This is achieved with tiny spines that pierce the vegetation. Its take-off velocity is up to 5 metres per second, and it has the longest jump for its size of any animal.[43]

Spiders

No spiders have been officially recorded from the site, so I will merely report just the two that I have found and succeeded in naming. There are 670 British species, and it takes skill and familiarity to identify all but a few.

One is the **Labyrinth Spider**, *Agelena labyrinthica*. It will be familiar to everyone from its funnel-shape webs among grasses and other vegetation, and it is often possible to see it just inside, waiting to pounce on passing prey. These are by far the most frequent spiders that one will encounter in grasslands.

The most splendid of the spiders I found was a large orb-web species, the **Wasp Spider**, *Argiope bruennichi*. (Not to be confused with the Spider Wasp!) Even a novice such as your author could identify this species at a glance as its body is decorated with the black and yellow stripes of a common wasp. The orb web is constructed vertically, as usual, but is close to the ground in open grassland, attached to tall herbaceous plants. At this height it is able to catch grasshoppers and crickets. These will have no reason to avoid a wasp, but larger animals, which can easily and inadvertently destroy the web, may be deterred from venturing too close. The web possesses a mat-like stabilimentum at the centre. In some related species this is a thing of beauty: vertical or radiating zigzags or spirals. The Wasp Spider is less concerned with artistry, producing a stabilimentum that is a dense and largely random mat of silk. Quite what these are for is open to question too, with the aforementioned increased visibility to avoid accidental damage being one hypothesis, the reflection of UV light that is attractive to some insects being another and that the stabilimentum attracts males being yet another.

The Wasp Spider was first recorded in Britain in 1922, and confined to the central south coast of England, with Dorset and south-east Hampshire being its stronghold, a status it has retained.

Although they are not spiders, mites and ticks are in the same biological Class as the spiders, the Arachnida. Mites have been mentioned in relation to ants and their hills, but many more will probably be in the grass of Hog Cliff. The ticks, however, are definitely there in abundance – as I know to my slight cost. I do not find *them*; they find *me*. Over my forty-five years in Dorset, I have found many hundreds of these creatures attached to my skin, half a dozen at a time on bad days. Very little in the countryside is inherently dangerous, but ticks certainly are, due to Lyme disease. The tick itself is harmless, apart from discomfort, but it is the helical (spirochete) bacteria in the genus *Borrelia*, which they carry and introduce into warm-blooded animals, that cause the disease. Between 2.5 and 5.1 per cent of ticks carry the bacterium, varying from year to year, so I have been very lucky indeed to not catch the disease, or at least not symptomatically. A young nephew from the city visited for a week some years ago, suffered one tick bite and hit the jackpot first time. Luckily, he was successfully treated with antibiotics. The disease is thus easily dispensed with, but if not treated soon after infection, it can reappear bearing much more serious problems than a fever and an initial ring rash around the bite. Diseases aside, the **Deer Tick**, *Ixodes ricinus*, is most definitely there.

THE MAMMALS OF HOG CLIFF

I have seen all of the eleven species of mammal at Hog Cliff. One of them, the **Wood Mouse**, rather found me, as it infested the house we lived in, at one point nesting in a tunnel it had dug in the soil of my ancestral Aspidistra. I saw a **Stoat** just the once in the nearby hedge where there was a rabbit burrow and **Brown Rats** darting in and out of the barn. The two deer were the **Roe** and the **Fallow**. I will not describe all eleven species, just the three that affect the grassland.

Rabbits

To wildly varying degrees, Hog Cliff is alive with rabbits. Mr Elsworth told me that it was once a warren: that is, a place where rabbits were encouraged, and provided a secondary income for the farmer. It was once closely fenced with wire, the fence having many little doorways (think cat-flap) that only opened *inwards*, ensuring an extra supply of rabbits from neighbouring fields where they were not so welcome and also preventing inbreeding.

These were 'informal' warrens, not those built and closely maintained when the then highly prized animal was introduced into Britain in the late eleventh century. The word 'warren' is related to 'warden', showing that they were cared for and guarded. These were banks (pillow-mounds) that were constructed to house the rabbits, sometimes with entrances placed in them for encouragement, and sometimes an entire burrow system would come ready-made. Such extreme effort was required because, having been brought from southern Europe, the rabbits found the British climate too harsh.

Eventually, natural selection was to favour the hardier lineages of escapees, and they became established as the wild rabbit we know today. It was, however, a long process, one that was not complete until the late nineteenth century, encouraged by an increase in hedges for their burrows and changing agricultural practices which provided them with food that was all too easy to obtain. By the 1950s the population had exploded to between 60 and 100 million. Then myxomatosis was introduced. This was a mild disease endemic to a related species, the North American Cottontail, but to the European Rabbit it was deadly. Within a very few years the population crashed to a mere 1 per cent of what it had previously been.

The fortunes of the rabbit rise and fall even today, with myxomatosis returning every few years. On occasions, a walk over Camel Hill in early evening will see hundreds of white tails bobbing away, while many rabbits will stamp with their hind legs, or simply watch me to gauge how dangerous I might be. I visited Hog Cliff very recently, and there was little sign of them, but I do not worry: they will be back.

Myxomatosis is a truly vile disease, and while living there, I would carry a hefty stick to quickly dispatch any that were suffering. Being unable to see, they would sit in the open, not moving, so they were easy targets. A friend who was unfamiliar with the countryside came to stay at Hog Cliff for a weekend and proudly showed me numerous, very grim, close-up photographs of what she called 'surprisingly tame' rabbits. She was horrified when I explained why they were so 'tame'. There are now two types of viral haemorrhagic diseases to add to their problems.

When the population was healthy, a couple of old boys would come with nets and ferrets to collect two or three dozen for the pot. I managed to shoot a few for my own pot with an air-rifle.

There are easily a dozen burrows at Hog Cliff, a testament to the rotten and fissured nature of the top metre or two of the chalk bedrock. It is odd that Rabbits have much, or any, particular association with anthills, but the connection takes the form of a simple behaviour for which there is no immediately obvious explanation, though dogs and lamp posts come to mind. Where there are anthills, rabbits preferentially deposit their droppings on them. Since anthills have a distinctive flora, it is likely to be that they are effectively planting the seeds they excrete on the fresh soil of anthills to ensure a supply of the food they require. Of the fourteen plant species that have this three-way association, six have been recorded at the site, Parsley-piert, Thyme-leaved Sandwort, Hairy Bitter-cress, Lesser Trefoil, Wall Speedwell and **Squirreltail Fescue**, *Vulpia bromoides*.

Rabbits are considered to be highly beneficial in species-rich grassland and especially chalk downland, owing to their close-cropping. There should, however, not be too many of them – too many and the turf is over-grazed. They should also graze alongside other animals, as with rabbits alone the turf becomes thin and not firmed into place by the feet of large grazers. It will then start to lift and leave bare soil, as sometimes happens at Hog Cliff. The existence of a large population of rabbits at Hog Cliff has helped with the widespread establishment of certain plants that would otherwise struggle through the grass, such as the bright yellow Lady's Bedstraw and, critically, the Common Rock-rose.

Badgers

There are several badger setts at Hog Cliff, some of them of great age. A few are in the scrub-line above the eastern valley side;

three are in coppices. One of the latter is half in and half out of the neighbouring grassland. It is a monster at a (visible) 15 × 12 m. A long way from the road, all Hog Cliff badgers are safe from traffic, and they have always thrived. I used to worry about their setts being 'stopped' with sacks prior to the hunt, preventing foxes from hiding in them, but they were always unstopped soon afterwards. I have seen families with seven cubs in the spring, and badgers may simply walk up to you if you are quiet, their forward vision being so poor. The first thing they do when they appear from the sett at sundown is to scratch themselves, with a distinct ripping sound. All animals have fleas, often ticks and no doubt intestinal worms, adding to the biota of the site, if not the comfort of their hosts.

Their main food is earthworms, as can be deduced from the extremely sticky black mess often seen in their latrines. Their taste for insects can also be revealed in their latrines, this time in the shiny external parts of beetles. Sometimes the tiny bones of small mammals can be found by anyone brave enough to deconstruct a badger dropping. They can eat almost anything, and at Hog Cliff they seem to stay mostly within the woods and coppice, where the earthworms are abundant in the relatively thick soil.

Badgers do, however, venture into the grassland, and their effect can be conspicuous, chiefly on the anthills. The occasional digging in grasslands for roots or earthworms will obviously affect the turf. The roots are usually Pignut, which grows on the lower pH soils at Hog Cliff. This does little damage (though see below), but the anthills that receive the attentions of a badger are seriously compromised or even destroyed, the badgers eating the ants and, much more nutritious, the eggs and larvae. Fortunately, this seems to be a last-resort behaviour as there is no shortage of anthills. An anthill that has suffered the attentions of a badger is always excavated from one side. Some are rebuilt, others abandoned, soon to become an area of bare soil adorned with a tangle of tough, wiry and dead roots.

Very rarely, badgers will make a complete mess of grasslands. This happened at Hog Cliff twenty years ago. The 'attack' was chiefly to the most important part of the site, the south-facing slope and the slope to the east of the coppices. It looked as though someone had taken a harrow up and down the hills, with barely a patch undisturbed. The damage was so extensive that I thought it might be escaped Wild Boar. These were causing problems elsewhere at the time, having been released from a farm by activists. However, boar always 'delaminate' the turf in their efforts to find Pignuts, turning large patches of turf completely upside down. This was not to be seen at Hog Cliff, so the finger pointed to the badgers.

Distraught as I was, I contacted DEFRA, and one of their ecologists kindly came to take a look. The DEFRA fellow agreed, noting that for this to happen, the badger population density at the time must be as much as thirty times the normal. Starving, they were looking for anything edible they could find. Quite how this could happen for just one year I have no idea, so it is still a mystery.

We often have a decidedly anthropomorphic view of nature, mourning the loss of a single badger on the roadside or objecting to deer culls. But, as my mother *always* said when the third wildebeest fell to a lioness in a television documentary, 'Isn't nature cruel?' It is not actively so, of course, it just *is*. Applying Malthus: for a stable population a mating pair of badgers (or anything else) will leave only two offspring that will live to breed. Taking lower estimates and ignoring bachelors, badgers will breed for three or four years, producing an average of around 2.5 cubs each year. If ten are born, eight must die before they successfully breed.

The Fox

I have mixed feelings about fox hunting. I like the ancient absurdity of the endeavour, the bright pinks of the jackets and the occasional glass of wine that was handed out on good days. I have always taken a robust view of the natural world – survival of the fittest, and all that – and know that most of the offspring of any wild population of animals will fail to reach maturity, and that death from old age is rare indeed. Most animals will be predated, die of disease, freeze to death or die of starvation. Indeed, even a death in old age will mean only that the debilitated animal will starve or be predated.

What I did not like was 'cubbing', the unpleasant practice of unearthing a family of foxes and killing them, and the arrogance of some members of the hunt about whose land they could trample: everyone else's, it seemed to me at the time. There are always two sides to any story, and my distaste for cubbing is moderated somewhat by the fact that inter-litter cannibalism is sometimes practised by the vixen on behalf of her cubs, the vixens seemingly not above raiding another's litter if times are hard.[44]

We do have the hunt to thank for one thing, and that is the survival of Hog Cliff. The landowner from the early 1950s to 1984, Snowy Eyre, was secretary of the local hunt and kept Hog Cliff fox-friendly. He never expressed much of an interest in wildlife beyond foxes, so his saving of this lovely piece of chalk downland was a mere side-effect. Hurrah for welcome side-effects. And for Mr Fox.

There are two or three fox earths at Hog Cliff, the one I see most often being on the south-facing chalk slope of Farm Hill Bottom. The foxes are less visible than in, say, the urban setting of Surbiton, where my daughter once lived and where they are unavoidable. The earths of country foxes are invariably old rabbit burrows or sometimes old badger setts, sometimes taking over just a part of a sett, with their badger neighbours still in residence next door.

Foxes nearly match humans in their omnivory, consuming anything that is remotely edible: voles are a major part of their diet, as is carrion from dead stock when available, and insects. They are also very fond of fruit. Earthworms are commonly eaten and often fed to the young.

BIRDS

Twenty-five species have been recorded at Hog Cliff. Of these, the **Fieldfare**, *Turdus pilaris*, is perhaps the most welcome to ornithologists as it is Red-Listed in the Birds of Conservation Concern of 2021. More important to the grass are the **Buzzard**, *Buteo buteo*, and the **Green Woodpecker**, *Picus viridis*. Their close relationship with the land comes in the form of their prey: respectively, the resident rabbits and the ants.

Buzzards fly high over the downs, sometimes four at a time. Stacked one above another, they are reminiscent of planes waiting to land at Heathrow Airport. Their main prey here is rabbits, usually the lightweight young. I once observed this directly, albeit slightly after the event. On my arrival home some years ago, I was asked by my wife if I could explain the existence in our garden of a dying juvenile rabbit that had bounced there noisily from next-door's roof. There is no other explanation than it had been dropped by a Buzzard that was either clumsy or, more likely, had been mobbed by crows.

I have always been fond of the Green Woodpecker. Its undulating swoops and rapid, creaking-gate call are always a joy and, compared to the many dull brown birds that inhabit Britain, they are iridescent beauties. They have long lived at Hog Cliff and depend almost entirely on ants and anthills for their sustenance. They peck away, eating adult ants, larvae and eggs, using their long, sticky tongues. Their feeding is a relatively gentle affair, so it is difficult to believe that they cause the excavations found on about a twentieth of the anthills. That would be badgers.

FINALLY

This long section relating the types, names, numbers, loves and lives of the inhabitants on an area of species-rich grassland is here to show how gloriously rich they can be. There are a little over one thousand records of species at Hog Cliff, of which I have only been able to mention a few. Nevertheless, and as I have been at perhaps tedious pains to point out, that one thousand might easily be multiplied by four or more. These many, many species are not just *on* Hog Cliff: they *are* Hog Cliff. It is a magnificent and detailed painting, an arable field or ley a mere blank canvas.

Hog Cliff, its partner nature reserves across the road and the extension to Hog Cliff towards the west are mere tiny islands in a sea of heavy agricultural land. So, critically, the large numbers of species found in and on species-rich sites are more than a representation of what there *is*; they are also an indication of what can be so easily *lost*.

Part Four

PASTURES NEW

One of the great pleasures of writing this book has been the opportunity it afforded to examine other grasslands within Britain. I have been to Wales to examine some Rhos pasture, Derbyshire to see an exceptional meadow and a piece of 'limestone downland', Yorkshire to view an upland hay meadow, the New Forest for lowland dry acid grassland, and revisited with a new eye the grasslands near my Dorset home that are not chalk downland.

Often my wife joined me on these expeditions, invariably taking notes of what was found and where, but with the proviso that she did not have to carry my camera tripod. Again. On others I was alone or accompanied by one or other of the many kind naturalists for whom grasslands are a speciality.

Hog Cliff is exemplary of chalk downland, and my deep dive into its resident species is an indication that this is what species-rich grasslands *are* – rich in species. Other grasslands can easily be as species-rich, but they will be different in many other ways, and it would be a dereliction for me to ignore them. Since my main aim is to interest the reader in grasslands, just writing about chalk downland is not enough as they are confined largely to the south. Revisiting Kipling, we must find our own beloved places.

This part examines other types of grasslands, such as meadows, upland acid, lowland acid, floodplain and calaminarian grasslands. There are eleven in total. These will each be described in much less detail than I provided in Part Three for Hog Cliff, but enough to show that they are species-rich or at least worthy of protection. To varying degrees, the numbers of species and the interactions between them will be much the same as those we encountered at Hog Cliff.

The sites that I have selected as examples here are not necessarily the best or worst of their type: either extreme would give a false impression of the broader character of these types of grassland.

This section is also an opportunity to see that other grasslands have their own and often very different complexities. They also allow reviews of the problems faced by different grassland types and allow us to see other communities and their constituent plants, fungi and animals.

Meadows

Meadows are the most fêted of all the many semi-natural species-rich grasslands in Britain. The figure of 97 per cent of them being lost in the last fifty years is not one that I would argue with, and efforts should and have been made to save those that remain and to establish new ones. Unfortunately, they are often considered the *only* type of grassland worth saving. They have distracted us. I love meadows with a passion, but they are not always as species-rich as several other semi-natural grasslands (lowland calcareous and some wetlands, for example). Nevertheless, as with all the grasslands discussed in these pages, they are rich in species. What makes them so different is how they are managed to make them what they are: meadows are cut for hay every year.

There is more to it, of course, with what precisely we mean by a meadow being open to much debate. Some places look like meadows, yet do not fit this definition because they are not or seldom cut for hay. There is one such at Kingcombe Meadows in Dorset: Coarse Mead. Here it is irregularly managed, with the cattle sometimes grazing from early in the year, sometimes not until early July. In the latter circumstance it looks like a glorious meadow in full flower, even though it is not subsequently cut for hay. For 'meadow' and 'meadow-like' grasslands, it is the lack of 'improvement' and soil type that truly defines a meadow, to which we must add a diversity of plant species.

Not all fields that are used for hay, and thus technically classified as meadows, are species-rich. Not by a long way. Many will have been ploughed relatively recently and even periodically, and most will have had fertilisers applied. Hay is still a major fodder crop in Britain but is mostly cut from land that has been 'improved', with relatively little from meadows of ecological value.

When lowland neutral grassland is spoken of, it almost invariably means 'meadow'. Indeed, meadows are usually on soil with a pH between 5.5 and 6.5. The amount of water in the soil is also of considerable importance. Meadow soils fall more or less between extremes: not too acid, not too alkaline, not too wet, not too dry, but with a slight tendency towards the alkaline and the wet.¹ Meadows are seldom homogeneous, so wet and dry patches can occur, but never heath or bog, though marsh is sometimes found in otherwise well-behaved meadows.

Such variation, to which we could add geographical location, produces a wide variety of meadow types. One firm distinction, however, is between lowland meadows and upland hay meadows, each containing their own collection of species. Nevertheless, there are few constant plants of meadows, with nearly every instance possessing a different flora.

THE CUT

Every owner of a meadow where conservation is a consideration will worry about when to cut their hay. Too early and many plants will not have seeded; cut late and the hay will decline in quality as the days go by until it is useless. Often the weather will make the decision for you.

The harvesting of hay often seems like sacrilege to those unfamiliar with the principles involved. I read an online post a couple of years ago where someone posted a photograph of a truly splendid hay meadow full of flowers, and a photograph of it the next day when it had all been cut to the ground. He was horrified, and perhaps no less so when others chipped in with 'Well, that's what happens in meadows: without the cut they wouldn't be meadows!'

It is surprising how little the generally accepted dates of hay-cutting have changed over the years. In *The English Husbandman*, of 1635, Gervase Markham advises: 'it is held of all the best English Husbandmen generally to be a weeke or a fortnight after Midsummer day, as namely about the translation of Thomas, which is ever the seventeenth day of July.'[2] This seems moderately late, but Markham was using the Gregorian Calendar, and his 'ever the seventeenth' is what we know as 'ever the seventh'! This is very much in accordance with modern practice, with UK government advice to cut no earlier than late June, or by mid-July for cooler upland areas.[3] By then the grasses and most of the wild flowers will have set seed.

Plantlife, one of the UK conservation organisations devoted to wild plants and their management, recommends the path most likely to result in the greatest species diversity: cutting between mid-July and September. The later dates, as noted, will result in poor hay quality, but the point here is biodiversity, not good-quality hay.

'Once again the fields we mow, / And gather in the aftermath', writes Longfellow in his appropriately entitled poem 'Aftermath'. The 'aftermath' in the poem is what grows after the hay has been cut. It is a resource in itself, and not to be wasted. Livestock is let out a few weeks after the cut and allowed to graze until November or whenever the grass stops growing. It may be for a shorter period if the ground becomes too wet, and grazing may recommence in February or thereabouts in meadows that are reasonably dry. All stock is removed ('closed up') by May to allow the meadow plants to grow.[4]

Such grazing is an essential part of meadow management, as without it the herbaceous plants would form a thatch of dead plant material for the new growth to struggle through while leaving them insufficient light to do so. Abandoning a meadow after the cut will also encourage coarse grasses and other troublesome ruderal plants. There are, of course, benefits that will accrue to the fertility of the meadow soil from grazing and, for those whose interest lies in diversity, it adds dung fungi and dung invertebrates to the species list.

The word 'aftermath', you will be pleased to hear, derives from 'after-moweth'. It is interesting that so agricultural a term as 'aftermath' has taken on the figurative usage for anything that is a result of some dramatic occurrence. Cutting hay is certainly dramatic, at least for the plants that are cut.

Another word for the aftermath, one that is sometimes used in preference, is 'fog'. The first reference in the *OED* is from *c.* 1380: 'He fares forth on alle faure, fogge watz his mete', which I assume translates as: 'He goes forth on all fours, fog was his food.' 'Foggage' is also used in place of 'aftermath', though an alternative meaning is 'the right to use the aftermath' (or 'fog', of course) under common law.

I have already mentioned Yorkshire Fog, a grass that is considered to be a weed species that can dominate grasslands. It can form dense and conspicuous patches and displays a tendency to fall over. Anything that falls over is difficult to cut, and livestock take little interest in eating it fresh, except when it is young. It may therefore be a derisive name aimed, for reasons unknown, at Yorkshire meadows, and nothing to do with a 'thick mist'.

Meadows vary very considerably in which plants they contain. The first meadow I write about contains upwards of one hundred plants, the next a mere twenty. George Peterken, in his brilliant and comprehensive *Meadows* of 2013, estimates that three hundred plants can be found in British meadows, with each meadow 'choosing' which ones. Whichever plants appear will grow at differing rates and flower and seed at different times. It is essential that they do set seed; otherwise, and rather obviously, the plants will soon disappear. This limits which species can be found in meadows since many flowers seed after the time of the cut. Still, exceptions occur. Meadowsweet, *Filipendula ulmaria*, for example, is perpetually found in the wetter areas of Lady's Mead (described shortly), even though it produces no seeds until August.

Finally, meadows are usually classed as MG5 and divided up in the NVC system into three sub-communities. Taken together, and with one other rather rare community type, MG4, they constitute almost all British lowland meadows.

LADY'S MEAD AT KINGCOMBE MEADOWS, DORSET

My first visit to Kingcombe Meadows, over forty years ago, was to a spectacular and ancient ash wood that was being felled by a local lad who had been contracted to do the work. The task he was undertaking was to clear the wood and replace it with arable. 'The idea is to make it look like that field over there,' he told me, pointing to a distant hillside on another farm which was glowing bright green from the application of nitrogenous fertiliser.

A cabinetmaker at the time, I was there with a view to buying timber. Expecting to find some much younger thinnings, and not a complete old-growth woodland, I could not bring myself to do so. I believe that the felling stopped soon after and most of the woodland was left in peace. I must mention that while I was there another young farmworker greeted me with: 'Oi be Sam, yoom don't know I.' Although many of my friends have Dorset accents, this young man's mode of speech was as near as one could hope for, in the 1980s, to that championed by William Barnes.

This story aside, the modern world, more particularly modern farming methods, had seemingly passed Kingcombe Meadows by, and it was already known to be a rare gem of rural history, meadows, thick hedges, small fields and pasture that had long been permanent. It was declared a Site of Special Scientific Interest in the mid-1980s and is now a National Nature Reserve (NNR).

When the farmer died at the age of ninety, the Dorset Wildlife Trust and other bodies considered purchasing it. Unfortunately, the money was not forthcoming. Soon after its purchase in 1987 the new owner put the entire farm back on the market but parcelled it up into fifteen lots. Desperately concerned that another opportunity for salvation would slip away, some brave individuals launched a campaign to save Kingcombe. There is nothing like publicity, so when the BBC and the *Telegraph* took a strong interest, the money rolled in. I chipped in with £25, which was a considerable amount at the time, and, having done the sums, I consider that I own a plot 15 × 15 m, approximating to the footprint of my cottage two miles away.

Dorset Wildlife Trust managed to purchase most of the lots of high diversity, and like-minded people, determined to maintain the semi-natural state of the site, purchased more.[5] The 180 ha of Kingcombe Meadows was saved, and champagne corks popped in the valleys – well, fizzy cider. One of the organisers of the campaign was Richard Jennings, a first-class mycologist and a kind and respected friend. Very sadly, he died long before his time and shortly after Kingcombe was secured. There is a stone memorial to him there, close to a magnificent oak tree, but his true memorial is Kingcombe Meadows itself.

I have visited Kingcombe hundreds of times, most often when taking people on walks, or being taken on walks by a specialist in a subject other than fungi. I took over the fungus walks from the great John Keylock when he became unwell and have run them there for nearly thirty years. As indicated, many other specialities are taught at Kingcombe, from bats to birds to bryophytes and much more.

Quaking Grass

LADY'S MEAD

Lady's Mead is the lowest of three meadows that troop up the hill towards the north-east, with another to the south-west. The last of these is appropriately called Lord's Mead, though it is not truly a meadow, being mostly too wet and seldom cut.

Lady's Mead, which is much more mainstream, sits on Fuller's Earth from a mudstone bedrock in the form of the Frome Clay Formation. It forms a long rectangle 3.5 ha in size and surrounded by hedges consisting mostly of oaks and Ash, though the Ashes are mostly lost. Whether or not these mature trees count as a hedge is a matter of opinion. The meadow is moderately uniform in character, but with the predominance of some plants in certain areas indicating different soil conditions, most particularly the wet ones. Most of these form areas of rushes, and I have excluded the plants found only in these. The dominant community is MG5a, the classic lowland meadow of Britain.

THE PLANTS OF LADY'S MEAD

I took a walk across Lady's Mead with my friend Bryan at the end of May 2023. We found forty-three plant species. Bryan, able to identify almost any plant at a glance, even when it is not in flower, seldom misses anything, so the number found is likely to be reasonably close to the number there at the time.

However, since Kingcombe Meadows has run so many nature identification days and been visited by so very many loupe- and clipboard-wielding naturalists, the species list for any part of it will be staggeringly comprehensive. The list for Lady's Mead as a whole contains over six hundred species of plant, animal, fungus etc. Two hundred of these are higher plants – that is, plants that are not mosses, ferns etc. – though these are in the overall list too.

Many of the plant species would have been found in the surrounding hedgerows or were ruderal species that occurred around the edges, paths and gateways. Subtracting these left 110 species that would have occurred at one time or another in the meadow itself. Many of these would have been 'blow-ins', appearing in odd corners for a year or two, and thirteen plant species have been designated as 'negative indicators', meaning that they really should not be there and could possibly be removed with careful management. ‘ They are weeds. Creeping Thistle is, inevitably, one such, though I have always rather admired it because of the splendid and dramatically swollen fly-galls that form halfway up the stem. Weeds have interesting associated organisms too.

This abundance of species is in part down to its being a 'good' meadow, but it is also because of the different soil conditions that prevail, most of these being the wet bits that do not quite count as rush pasture – or meadow, come to that. These account for some of the sedges and all of the rushes found there and for four wild flowers with 'marsh' in their common name. I will come back to a handful of those on the list that Bryan and I did *not* record that day and first discuss some of those that we did.

The two titular species in the NVC MG5 designation were there, **Crested Dog's-tail** and the purple/pink thistle-like **Common Knapweed**. **Meadow Vetchling**, *Lathyrus pratensis*, is also a common here. The latter's survival strategy in a tall environment like meadows is to clamber over neighbouring plants. It is a member of the Pea Family, the Fabaceae, a Family well served here with a striking twelve pea species making an appearance. Two more of these are worth a mention, **Zigzag Clover**, *Trifolium medium*, so named because of its periodically bent stem, and **Tufted Vetch**, *Vicia cracca*, a striking purple/blue 'pea' that also uses other plants as a climbing frame.

As is the case with most meadows, few species found there count as being rare. Yes, there are five orchids in Lady's Mead, but they are all fairly common: the **Common Spotted**, **Heath Spotted**, **Southern Marsh**, **Early Purple** and **Bee**. There are many thousands of sightings of each of these species recorded in Britain. This is unlike their rare compatriots, some of which barely reach treble figures, with around only 120 for the Lady's Slipper Orchid and a mere forty-five for the fittingly elusive Ghost Orchid.

While very nearly every naturalist will crack out the champagne on finding something truly rare, few are disappointed if none are found during a survey or merely a walk across the fields. It is the rightly vaunted 'diversity' that counts. Better one hundred common species in a field than a single Lady's Slipper Orchid, though I might be tempted to trade all one hundred for a Ghost Orchid. Searching out these rarities is sometimes little more than trainspotting. As I have stressed, *everything* is interesting, even the pernicious weed Common Ragwort, on which over two hundred invertebrate species have been recorded.

The Lady's Mead records mention forty-five species as 'Dorset Notables', indicating either that they are Dorset specialities (though all occur elsewhere), or the opposite: that naturalists were just very pleased to see them because they are relatively rare in Dorset. The most striking (notable even) of these are the un-common **Saw-wort**, *Serratula tinctoria*, and **Pepper Saxifrage**, *Silaum silaus*, which is generally uncommon, though not found on the day of our walk, and **Corky-fruited Water-dropwort**, *Oenanthe pimpinelloides*. This last is largely restricted to south-west England, excluding Cornwall, but also found in Hampshire and, strangely enough, to the south-east of London but *inside* the M25. It is exceedingly common over much of Kingcombe Meadows, to the point of being taken for granted. Even the rarest of organisms are likely to be common *somewhere*.

Yellow Rattle inevitably occurs here too. I say 'inevitably' because it is an almost essential ingredient in every meadow, a constant, though agriculturally speaking it is nothing but a pretty pest. It is a member of the Broomrape Family, the Orobanchaceae. Most of the plants in this Family are hemiparasitic on other plants, and having one's grass crop parasitised will not lead to commercial success. It is, however, conducive to diversity as its restricting of the vigorous grasses, and some other plants, allows for the growth of plants that will not tolerate a heavy grass cover.

I saw this in action recently when an ecologist friend showed me what had happened on a newish roadside that he was attempting to make more interesting. He had bought a kilo of seeds (about 300,000 of them!) the previous year and sprinkled them over the wide and upwards-sloping verge. Wherever the Yellow Rattle failed to appear, the grasses grew tall; wherever it grew, the growth of grasses was weak and sparse. New wild flowers duly appeared, including Bee Orchids. Yellow Rattle suppresses the growth of host plants by up to 60 per cent, a quite extraordinary feat.

To enable them to parasitise plants, Yellow Rattle, and other parasitic members of the Family, produce structures called 'haustoria' that partially penetrate the roots of host plants, tapping into the host's vascular system and stealing nutrients. Unlike the occasionally seen Broomrapes and Toothwort that lack both leaves and chlorophyll, Yellow Rattle possesses both. They are thus 'hemiparasitic'. Surprisingly, Yellow Rattle is an annual. It produces its seeds in numerous, almost spherical and highly conspicuous pods. If you collect a sprig of pods and shake it, you will hear the eponymous rattle.

Bryan spotted a plant not recorded in Lady's Mead before: **Ragged Robin**, *Lychnis flos-cuculi*. This striking pink plant is not as common as it once was, earning the status of 'near-threatened'. This is due to loss through drainage and sometimes ploughing of the wet meadows and pastures it requires. It earns its 'ragged' common name from the untidy arrangement of the petals, though no doubt 'Robin' is merely a pleasing alliteration. *Lychnis* is from *lychnos*, the Greek for 'lamp', from the use of its stem as a wick for oil lamps. *Flos-cuculi* simply means 'cuckoo-flower', providing the plant with more than its fair share of avian names. Being a very close relative of the campions, it is unrelated to other tall plants with similarly shaped flowers, such as knapweeds, most of which are in the Daisy Family.

Among those on the Lady's Mead list that were not recorded on my survey with Bryan there are a few bedstraws, six more 'Carrots', six more daisy-like plants, nine dandelion-like plants (mostly hawkbits, hawkbeards and hawkweeds, all members of the 'hawkish complex'), six members of the Dock Family (which includes sorrels) and three buttercups, including the welcome **Bulbous Buttercup** and the considerably less welcome **Creeping Buttercup**, *Ranunculus repens*.

It is interesting to note what different reproductive strategies these two buttercups adopt. The latter species produces about one ramet (a vegetative propagule, or clone) each year and, on average, only a single seed, its creeping habit allowing it to take the long view on reproduction. The Bulbous Buttercup, by contrast, produces only seeds, and then not very many – about fifteen each year.[7]

The dominant species in Lady's Mead are grasses, something that cannot be said for all grasslands – chalk downland, for example. No fewer than twenty-two species occur in Lady's Mead – about 10 per cent of the UK list. Many, such as **Sweet Vernal Grass, Heath Grass**, *Danthonia decumbens*, **Yellow Oat-grass, Quaking Grass, Red Fescue** and **Squirreltail Fescue**, are welcome there for varying reasons: good manners in not taking over the meadow, the nutritious hay they produce and simply their beauty. Others are unwelcome for their boorish behaviour, even though they may be inevitable: **Perennial Ryegrass, Cock's Foot, Yorkshire Fog** and **False Oat-grass**. Sedges occur in nearly all grasslands, and Lady's Mead hosts nine.

Meadow plants will not all flower or seed at the same time; there is a distinct succession in all communities that follow the seasonal progression of whatever local climate they find themselves in. There are two broad strategies that might be followed: grow short and early, or tall and later. Early in the growing season the fresh growth herbaceous plants will be lush but, obviously, short. This provides the opportunity for flowers to form, attract pollinating insects and produce seed, before taller plants make such ambitions too difficult or simply hopeless.

Lesser Celandine, *Ficaria verna*, also known as 'Pilewort', is usually a hedgerow/wood-edge plant but is often found flowering in meadows early in the year, when most other vegetation is still largely dormant. A typical and extremely familiar early adopter is the humble **Dandelion**. It, and several other dandelion-like species, live their lives as a basal rosette of leaves, throwing up their leafless peduncle when preparing to flower. When the Dandelion flowers (typically in late April), it produces its single inflorescence on this single stem (peduncle), one that is sufficiently tall to allow insect pollination and subsequent dispersal of the seeds. **Bluebells**, *Hyacinthoides non-scripta*, flowering in early May, adopt the same strategy and are frequently found in meadows. There is a conspicuous line of them in Lady's Mead, possibly marking the position of a long-forgotten hedge.

At least one relatively tall plant makes an appearance around the end of April, the **Cuckoo Flower**, *Cardamine pratensis*, its flowers towering conspicuously above everything else. It is an understated beauty that can appear in any damp meadow or moist, open grassland. Some plants, such as the Common Dog Violet, flower early and for three months after, but must be content with a briefer period in meadows, where competition soon sets in. One more early flowering plant is the **Field Wood-rush**. This is a lovely plant, but you will need to get close and maybe use a loupe to appreciate its appeal.

I will not catalogue the entire flowering calendar of this or any other meadow; the point is that they certainly have one, forming an ever-changing palette of colours. In May the splendid purple **Bugle**, *Ajuga reptans*, will come into flower, plus the yellow **Tormentil**, some early **Pignuts** (white) and the above-mentioned Yellow Rattle. Sweet Vernal Grass, with its young bronze flower heads, is a clear early adopter. This grass, as its name indicates, is very much a spring plant, and invariably the first grass to flower. By June the meadow is yellow with buttercups. By July it will be purple with **Betony** and yellow with dandelion-like flowers. Sadly, or not, there is little or no further development because the meadow will, of course, soon be cut.

THE FUNGI OF LADY'S MEAD

Fungi are relatively uncommon in meadows despite never suffering from the plough or, more usually, from inorganic fertilisers. This is largely due to the dense sward that appears from spring until the cut in July.

One might point out that the sward is short, or at least much shorter, in late summer and throughout the autumn, when the fungal fruiting bodies almost invariably appear, but the fungi do not know this and, photo-sensitive as they are, must 'assume' that fruiting will be pointless. I have seen this in fungi-rich grasslands that have been abandoned for a few years, then cut in the autumn. The fungi rarely reappear, save a few of the very tall fungi such as parasols.

Nevertheless, a few grassland fungi have made an appearance in Lady's Mead over the years, though nowhere near as many as in the exclusively grazed areas of Kingcombe. Two were waxcaps: the truly magnificent **Ballerina**, *Porpolomopsis calyptriformis*, and the **Goblet Waxcap**, *Hygrocybe cantharellus*. In addition, there are the **Field Mushroom** and two puffballs: the **Meadow Puffball** and the conspicuously large **Mosaic Puffball**.

One fungus that is common but nevertheless *seen* extremely rarely is Choke, described on p. 105. In all the grasslands I visited in preparation for this book, the single specimen I saw at Lady's Mead was the only one I encountered on my travels.

THE INVERTEBRATES OF LADY'S MEAD

Bryan and I found a few insects on our short walk around the meadow, though we were not particularly looking for them. There were two common butterflies, the ubiquitous **Meadow Brown** and the **Common Blue**, and an impressive six bees: four bumblebees, **Wilke's Mining Bee**, *Andrena wilkella*, and the **Honeybee**. Also, there was a relative of bees and wasps (though it looks more like wasp) in the form of the sawfly *Tenthredo brevicornis*, as well as three hoverflies – *Eristalis arbustorum*, *E. tenax* and *Sphaerophoria scripta* – and two beetles – the **Soldier Beetle**, *Cantharis rustica*, and the **Swollen-thighed Beetle**. In addition, and to acknowledge that even a peaceful meadow has its conflicts, we saw *Tachina fera*, a tachinid fly that *masquerades* as a bee to avoid predation. It is, nevertheless, a predator itself, laying its eggs on leaves grazed by the caterpillars of (mostly) moths. The caterpillar consumes these eggs (presumably unchewed), and the first one to hatch successfully proceeds to eat the caterpillar from the inside out. Bryan's record of this species was the first for the site.

THE INVERTEBRATE INTERACTIONS BETWEEN HEDGES AND MEADOW

Which of the insects recorded at Lady's Mead are dependent on the meadows, which on the hedgerows, which on *both*? With the butterflies, of which a remarkable thirty-one species have been recorded (around half of all those known from Britain!), it is reasonable to say that most benefit from having both habitats. The Brimstone Butterfly, for example, whose sole larval foodplant is the Buckthorn found in hedges, will nevertheless feed as an adult on nectar and pollen from plants growing in the meadow such as knapweed and thistles. But how often do invertebrate species in general require both hedge and grassland? I decided to find out.

Taking one hundred species from just three groups of insects (the Hymenoptera, Diptera and Lepidoptera), I divided them into groups according to where their larval stage was situated and where their adult food was situated. The calculations were somewhat 'back of the envelope', owing to a few essential if arguable assumptions.

The overall results were that fifty-nine out of the one hundred were restricted to one or the other habitat. Forty-five of these spent their entire life in the field and fourteen in the hedge – or the ditch for some larval stages, notably some of the hoverflies.

Forty-one used or (more often) *required* both. I also noted the order in which the habitats were used. Taking the larvae as coming first, field-then-hedge accounted for just seven species, hedge-then-field for thirty-four.

The point of this exercise was to demonstrate how much richer a habitat can be if it is near a different one. It is reasonable to suggest that around 40 per cent of the insect species recorded at Lady's Mead would either struggle to survive or not survive there at all if the hedges were not present. Similarly, the hedgerow is much richer by being next to a species-rich meadow. Yes, all of these insects can fly elsewhere, but the close proximity of the hedges here makes life much easier for those organisms that require more than one habitat. Hedges are often isolated in a sea of arable land, and their biodiversity invariably diminished; much the same can be said for at least some meadows.

I return briefly to the larval/adult food choices made by some of the insects found at Lady's Mead by providing some examples – the subject is irresistible. The first observation is the large number of butterflies whose *larvae* feed on grasses. Eight of the thirty butterflies recorded do just this, including the Meadow Brown, the **Speckled Wood** (*Pararge aegeria*) and the **Small Heath** (*Coenonympha pamphilus*). The plants employed by *adult* butterflies range through Bramble and several herbaceous plants of meadow or hedge (the path followed by five of the eight) to various strictly meadow plants, to honeydew (the Speckled Wood).

The larvae of the hoverfly **Rhingia campestris** feed on cowpats, while the adults attend many flower species. Another hoverfly, the elegant **Sphaerophoria scripta**, feeds on aphids found at soil level as larvae and various flowers in the Asteraceae and Apiaceae as an adult. A third hoverfly, the **Tiger Hoverfly**, *Helophilus pendulus*, spends its youth consuming the dead vegetation found in ditches and ponds, before following the more respectable path of the adult form by feeding on pollen and nectar. *Helophilus*, incidentally, means 'marsh-lover'.

Several of the insects formed galls on trees or herbaceous plants, but with a large proportion being on surrounding trees, most particularly oaks.

COARSE MEAD

Every field at Kingcombe has a name, and usually an *interesting* name. My favourite is the charming 'Yonder Cowleaze', so called from being the next field after 'Cowleaze'. The word 'cowleaze' once meant 'land let for cattle', and it is a sadness that the pleasing 'yonder' has gone out of fashion. Another is 'New Graffs'. This may (just) mean 'new ditches' (*graff* = 'ditch', from the Dutch for 'grave') but is much more likely to be a corruption of 'New Grass' where the long *ʃ*, a character that went out of fashion (mercifully, this time) by the nineteenth century, was mistaken for an 'f'. A little to the south of Lady's Mead, but still in the Kingcombe reserve, is a field known much more plainly as 'Coarse Mead'. This one indicates that it is (or was) a meadow, just not a particularly good one.

This negative judgement is doubtless due to the fact that the field is often very wet. A highly productive spring some 200 m uphill from Coarse Mead means that much of the lower part of the field has been claimed by rushes and other plants that prefer their soil to be wet.

Since I see it mostly while taking fungus identification walks, I am most familiar with Coarse Mead when it is bearing its autumnal aspect. In October it is generally very drab, and even wetter than usual. But by late June, its summer flowers in full and dense bloom, it looks as good as any meadow one could name.

Cattle appear to be introduced around the date that hay would have been cut, but not consistently so. Sometimes they are put out much earlier. Nevertheless, while Coarse Mead is mostly neutral lowland grassland of high species-diversity, the lack of 'the cut' effectively disqualifies it as a meadow; it is 'mere' permanent pasture. But it is none the worse for that. Here are some of the plants I found there.

The most notable plant is **Lousewort**, *Pedicularis sylvatica*. This unassuming little plant is in the Broomrape Family. It has small, pink, labiate flowers and grows as a biennial. Here, in the more wet and acid soils, it does the job fulfilled by Yellow Rattle in dry, neutral soils – it parasitises grasses, leaving more space for wild flowers. Like its cousin, it is a hemiparasite, making at least some of its own sugars by photosynthesis. It has a very restricted and predominantly western distribution in England as its requirements for acidic and wet soils are missing from most central and eastern areas. Unsurprisingly, it is common in the New Forest, north Hampshire and the Weald of Sussex, all of them acidic and wet to some degree. It is common in Wales and Scotland. The acid theme continues with **Pignuts**, a common plant at Coarse Mead, that is always found on neutral/acid soils, if not necessarily in wet ones.

One of the reasons I chose this field was the fungi. There are not very many, relatively speaking at least, as the sward is too tall and much of it wet, but some that are found here represent a

Rough Meadow-grass

seldom appreciated aspect of permanent grassland. So, I have seen **Horse Mushrooms** a couple of times, several species of puffball, and the ubiquitous **Cowpat Gem**, plus any number of other coprophagous fungi. More interesting, however, are the fungi that are found in the field but really belong to the hedge.

Kingcombe boasts some extraordinary hedges. Many are dominated by mature trees, and the resulting hedges can easily be 12 m thick. Some have paths or even streams running down the middle. Some of them effectively form spinneys.

It is some of these trees, such as Oak and Hazel, that provide the main support for fungi in the form of a mycorrhizal relationship. Since most fungi demand light and air in order to grow fruiting bodies, anywhere inside a dense hedge is unsuitable, and so the fungal fruiting bodies (mushrooms) form in the nearest open space – the field. Along the south-eastern hedge, and for easily fifteen Octobers, I found a webcap fruiting in the grass. It was the fairly common **Variable Webcap**, *Cortinarius anomalus*.

Other hedges at Kingcombe have associated fruiting bodies from other mycorrhizal fungi. A few from my list are several brittle-gills (*Russula* species): *R. foetens*, *R. adusta* and *R. vesca*, respectively the Stinking, Winecork and Bare-toothed Brittlegills, and the Death Cap, *Amanita phalloides*.

Nestling in one of the corners of Coarse Mead, a couple of metres from the hedge, there was once a patch of **Wood Mushrooms**, *Agaricus sylvaticus*. It grew there for half a dozen seasons. This is not a mycorrhizal fungus but a saprotroph: that is, it lives on dead organic matter. Woodland clearings are well known to support fungi, and here the fungus had simply found an extremely large clearing.

Such situations are common, but it should be remembered that the fruiting bodies of any fungal mycelium would not have appeared if the field had been cultivated. Without both the woodland (hedge) and pasture there would be no such mushrooms at all.

THE DERBYSHIRE MEADOW

Sometimes one comes across a secret treasure, one known to little more than a few locals, one with no mention on any natural history database and ignored by, or unknown to, the national bodies that deal with nature conservation. I fancy that there are many of these scattered across Britain, their owners wishing for neither the attention nor the interference of others, and willing even to forgo the subsidies they might otherwise receive. The

Crested Dog's-tail

natural custodians of these gems merely want to be left in peace, farming with methods both old and new that work for them. If my fancy expresses a reality, there would be more high-value grasslands than are generally believed to exist.

Derbyshire Meadow is the name I have given to this particular unconsidered treasure. Since I promised the farmer anonymity, I have used pseudonyms throughout this section and dispensed with gender-specific pronouns.

My discovery of Derbyshire Meadow was serendipitous. Just after a talk I was giving in Derby a few years ago I met an extraordinary person from the audience whom I will call Mel, and they told me they had admired my book on hedgerows. I mentioned that while I was in the county I would be looking for interesting grasslands for a new book – the one you are reading. They said that, if I was around the next day, they could take me to a lovely meadow that was farmed by a friend up in the hills nearby. I was delighted with this invitation and the next day duly set off for the meeting place – a pub not far from the meadow. This had been chosen because the meadow and associated farmhouse were almost impossible to find without a guide. They were right about this, as I was to discover over the next couple of years while trying to find it again, and on one occasion driving around the narrow, intricate lanes for three-quarters of an hour in the hope of coming across it by accident.

We met Jay, who looked in every way a farmer. They were quietly spoken, but also helpful and inviting. Jay expressed a deep love for the meadow, and a passion for protecting it. They told me that one year a contractor was engaged to cut the hay because the one on the farm was awaiting maintenance. The contractor arrived with a massive tractor that noticeably sank into the lightly farmed land. Jay told them to go away and come back with something smaller. Perhaps one of the reasons that the meadow is so magnificent is that the soil remains light and aerated.

After a cup of tea and several pieces of cake, we set off to the meadow. Its extent is just 2.5 ha and it is perched on a one-in-eleven gradient slope running upwards from behind the farmhouse and flattening at the top. The slope faces north-east, the coldest and least hospitable of aspects. I was immediately struck by the understated beauty of what I saw. I say 'understated', because there were not many species to be seen, but some of those that were there were colourful and occurred in vast numbers, all accommodated by a dense, waist-high sward.

There was, as always, variation. The bottom of the slope was wet, with **Bistort**, *Bistorta officinalis*, in full pink flower and dominant among the wild flowers. The land dried progressively with height: a consistently rich sward for most of it, with the flattening dry top sparse and dominated by grasses. On my third visit, a few sheep had been allowed to graze the thin grass at the top, which was of little use for hay, while the sheep were waiting for the aftermath.

On the main slope I found a total of around twenty species of plant. The dominant grasses were **Crested Dog's-tail**, **Sweet Vernal Grass** and **Tall Fescue**, *Lolium arundinaceum*. **Pignut** was nearly everywhere, indicating a moderately acidic soil, which is what one might expect on the bedrock of mudstone, sandstone and siltstone.[8] More dominant still were **Ribwort Plantain**, *Plantago lanceolata*, of which there must have been more than 100,000 in the field (I did the maths), **Meadow Buttercup** and **Great Burnet**, *Sanguisorba officinalis*. The last of these is a splendid plant that I seldom see as it is rare in the south of England, patchy further north and not particularly common even in this part of Derbyshire. **Red Clover** was common, with a lesser cover of **White Clover**. Inevitably, there were very many **Yellow Rattle** plants to be seen.

Less common, but still in abundance, was **Devil's-bit Scabious**, a plant that is something of a poster child for grasslands owing to its being the larval food plant of the Marsh Fritillary butterfly. **Common Knapweed** was, well, common, if irregular in where it grew, as was **Bugle**. There were individual patches that hosted **Sheep's Sorrel**, some splendid **Tufted Vetch** and patches of the often ubiquitous **Oxeye Daisy**, *Leucanthemum vulgare*.

Last on the list, because I have never determined its name for certain, is an *Alchemilla* sp., otherwise known as a Lady's Mantle. Anyone with experience in field botany will know that these are 'critical species': that is, species whose precise name is almost impossible to determine because their close relatives are almost identical. Fortunately, of the twenty or so *Alchemilla*

243

species in Britain (five of which are introductions), some can be found throughout the country. Most, however, are restricted to small areas, usually in the north of England and Wales and, most particularly, Scotland. These are not so much *species* as 'ecotypes', which have drifted in their morphology owing to geographic isolation and adaptation to the local environment. Incidentally and irresistibly, there is one species that glories in the name *Alchemilla falsadentata* – the False-toothed Alchemilla, a reference to the uneven 'teeth' that ornament the edges of the leaves.

Anyway, I am suggesting *Alchemilla glabra* as a tentative diagnosis because it is a common species of the north, known from the area and more or less matches the description in my treasured *Alchemilla, Lady's Mantles of Britain and Ireland*, by Mark Lynes.

Where, one must wonder, does the Derbyshire Meadow fit in to the generality of meadows? It is not quite a northern upland meadow (commonly found in the Yorkshire Dales, Lancashire and parts of Cumbria and Co. Durham) as, in addition to being too far south, it lacks the essential ingredient of such meadows, the Wood Cranesbill, *Geranium sylvaticum*. However, it is otherwise close, forming a welcome halfway house between northern upland and southern lowland meadows. I so hope that it survives.

Upland Hay Meadows

These are rare beasts, indeed, with only a thousand hectares remaining.' Anything with the term 'thousand' in it one would imagine to be large in some way, but this area is only one-third of the area of my own, average-sized parish in West Dorset. Hog Cliff, described earlier, plus the new nature reserve that has been added to it and described later, is easily 130 ha in extent. Upland Hay Meadows are mostly in the north of England, with just a few in Scotland. Wherever they are, they tend to be isolated, with all the problems that come with the lack of connectivity with the same or similar habitats. The typical size is just 2 ha.

Upland Hay Meadows are characterised by the NVC designation of MG3 Sweet Vernal Grass-Wood Cranesbill. They are typically on moderately dry, brown soils or humus-rich soils on flat or slightly sloping land at the head of sub-montane valleys. They generally occur between 200 and 400 m above sea level.

GRASSINGTON HOSPITAL GROUNDS MEADOW

This was the most northerly of the meadows I visited on my travels, and I was introduced to it by Tony Serjeant, then a Senior Wildlife Conservation Officer for Yorkshire Dales National Park Authority. He kindly took me there in late June 2019.

It will come as no surprise that the meadow is in the grounds of a hospital, though one long closed and now demolished. The hospital was built on a site that consisted of a large area of old

Downy Oat-grass

meadowland in 1919, with some of the land retained as meadows. It was built as a sanatorium for sufferers of tuberculosis, a place where they could sit out on the purpose-built balconies to enjoy the fresh air – something that could be enjoyed in vast quantities on the breezy summer day of my visit.

Long of interest to naturalists, the meadow evidently survived the years, obtaining its notification as an SSSI in 1988. Its Special Area of Conservation designation is a 'North Pennine Dales Meadow'.[10] At 230 m, the meadow is above the 200 m height above sea level for an upland hay meadow.

It is a real beauty, described in its SSSI citation as 'one of the finest examples of an unimproved herb-rich neutral grassland in the Yorkshire Dales National Park'.[11] It is framed nicely by mature trees with understories, though the trees tend to shade the meadow slightly, with ruderal flowering plants and taller and ranker grasses at the meadow's edges. The meadow itself was a blaze of colour on that bright and none too warm day.

I found twenty-two plant species in total and was pleased with this count. Perhaps I could have done better had I strayed from the east–west footpath that runs across the meadow. A few others were walking this blessed path, and my trampling over the exquisite meadowland on either side would have felt sacrilegious, and publicly so. Anyway, the meadow itself had no right of access. Having said this, the entire meadow would have been mowed to stubble within two weeks of my visit!

The most obvious plant was **Oxeye Daisy**, its white and yellow dominating much of the meadow, with some areas nevertheless devoid of it. The others in full flower, and densely interspersed with Oxeye Daisy, were **Rough Hawkbit** and the closely related **Common Cat's-ear**, *Hypochaeris radicata*. Also conspicuous was an eyebright, presumably (to my not entirely untutored eye) *Euphrasia nemorosa*, the commonest eyebright by far.

Also present in quantity were **Great Burnet**, **Common Knapweed**, **Sheep's Sorrel**, **Bird's-foot Trefoil**, **Ribwort Plantain** and **White** and **Red Clover**. Sparse, but nevertheless very welcome, was **Melancholy Thistle**, *Cirsium heterophyllum*, with its generally single flower head on each stem. In wetter areas there was the **Marsh Thistle**, *Cirsium palustre*.

I did find an abundance of an *Alchemilla* species (Lady's Mantles) but did not collect any for (an attempt at) identification. However, *Alchemilla glabra* has been recorded there too, so no doubt that was what I found. This is precisely the *Alchemilla* required for Upland Hay Meadows.

Mostly no longer in flower, but with their large seed capsules in clear evidence, was a large number of **Yellow Rattle** plants.

This abundance goes most of the way towards explaining the low density of grass species. My grass identification skills having not reached their current moderate level, back in 2019 I could name only eight: **Crested Dog's-tail, Cock's-foot, Quaking-grass,** *Briza media,* **Red Fescue, Sweet Vernal Grass, Yorkshire Fog, Perennial Ryegrass** and **Tufted Hair-grass,** *Deschampsia cespitosa.*

What I did not see were some of the rarer species that are noted in the SSSI citation. Most of these were in the wetter areas that required trampling to reach – a sedge and a rush among them – the common **Carnation Sedge,** *Carex panicea,* and **Soft Rush,** *Juncus effusus.* **Marsh Valerian,** *Valeriana dioica,* **Marsh Ragwort,** *Senecio aquaticus,* **Devil's-bit Scabious,** and **Water Avens,** *Geum rivale,* have also been recorded there. In the drier area I missed **Sneezewort,** *Achillea ptarmica,* a moderately uncommon relative of Yarrow.

A more fulsome list for the *entire* site was kindly supplied to me by a stalwart of the Upper Wharfedale Field Society, Christine Bell. The list was the result of a field trip she led for that organisation that found no fewer than eighty-six species of plant. The twenty-two on my list compared badly, of course, but not *quite* so badly once everything that was not in the meadow was excluded. This left fifty-seven plants that were almost certainly found in the meadow itself.

These consisted of forty-three wild flowers, eleven grasses and three rushes. The three grasses I had missed were **Meadow Foxtail, False Oat Grass** and **Crested Hair-grass.** I missed all of the sedges – they were **Glaucous Sedge, Pale Sedge,** *Carex pallescens,* and **False Fox-sedge,** *C. otrubae.* Pale Sedge is fairly uncommon, and False Fox-sedge is common in many places but rare in this area. As to the flowers, the most interesting (though not rare) were three orchids – the **Common Spotted, Northern**

Marsh and **Bee Orchid**, plus **Fairy Flax** and **Ragged Robin**.

One of the two titular plants of Upland Hay Meadows is the Wood Cranesbill. Without it, one would need to reconsider the status of the meadow. For a long time I considered it to be somewhat like the Derbyshire Meadow – a near-miss – but much later discovered that Wood Cranesbill does grow there. It is an Upland Hay Meadow, and undoubtedly the best and most colourful meadow I have ever seen.

Calaminarian Grasslands

The name 'Calaminarian' derives from the Latin for 'zinc' and is familiar to the general public as calamine lotion, the chief ingredient of which is zinc oxide. This gives a clue to their nature – they are grasslands contaminated with heavy metals, zinc among them, with chromium, copper and lead being three more. These can occur naturally in so called 'river shingles', where the metals are washed down from metal-rich rocks. Many more are the result of mining, mostly in the form of slag heaps, and it was to one of these that Tony and I went.

NEAR GRASSINGTON

Having completed our visit to Grassington Hospital Grounds Meadow by three o'clock in the afternoon, there was time for Tony to show me an area of calaminarian grassland that was fairly close by to the east and a little higher up.

The bright weather had given way to a cold, overcast sky, the devastated wasteland all around us matching its leaden rocks to the leaden sky. Mordor came quickly to mind. The grim scene was one of low spoil-heaps in a sea of unhappy-looking grasses, mostly **Sheep's Fescue** and **Common Bent**, plus some wild flowers. Rocks were everywhere, and stronger areas of grass were interspersed with partially vegetated fields of stones. Very few grasses are able to survive on these grasslands, with the only one seen here in quantity being the Sheep's Fescue. What grass was there was short, and almost no wild flowers grew above 30 cm in

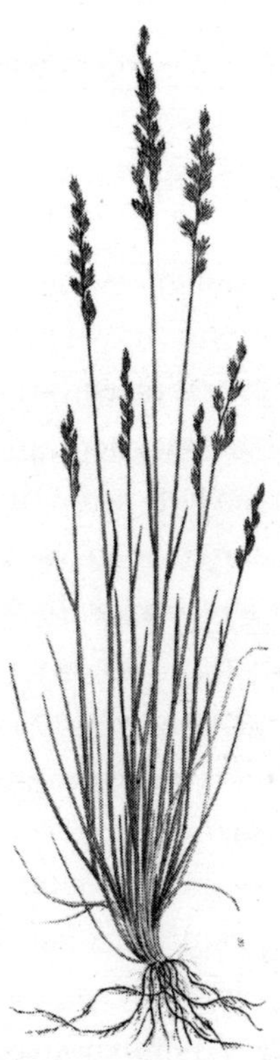

Sheep's Fescue

height. Plants adapted to this environment occupied the patchily distributed toxic areas, with less tolerant plants in the marginally safer areas between. Such observations have allowed prospectors to find the minerals they seek.

The tallest plant was a severely stunted group of **Stinging Nettles** (*Urtica dioica*), one of which was infected with the fungus **Nettle Rust**, *Puccinia urticata*, and the best and largest specimen I have ever seen. Perhaps the nettle's sickly condition made it easy prey. That the plants are so short is due to the low nutrient levels and some rabbit and sheep grazing, though one must suspect that the toxicity of the soil had a hand in this too. Plants that can tolerate these extreme conditions are often adapted strains of a species, as with Sheep's Fescue, or descendants of species that have both adapted and changed sufficiently in appearance to warrant their own name. Any plant that is so adapted is known as a 'metallophyte'.

Among the pebbles and sparse grass was a lichen, possibly *Cladonia portentosa*. The existence of a thriving lichen in this toxic habitat is no anomaly: several often rare lichens will thrive there. Mosses, too, and cyanobacteria, perhaps familiar to the person in the street as the black/green jelly blobs that infest pathways in very wet weather, are also known to grow on such sites. The bushy, trailing fern ***Asplenium septentrionale*** can also be found.

Other metallophytes that have been recorded here or nearby are **Pyrenean Scurvy-grass**, *Cochlearia pyrenaica s.l.*, **Mountain Pansy**, *Viola lutea*, **Thrift**, *Armeria maritima*, and **Moonwort**, *Botrychium lunaria*. The last of these is in the Polypody group of ferns and extremely bizarre in appearance. It is odd to see Thrift so far inland, it being a familiar plant of the coast, but it is an adapted form, perhaps primed for such a harsh habitat through its ability to tolerate high levels of maritime salts.

We saw only two species that were calaminarian grassland specialists that day, but they were the chief indicator species of this type of community: a substantial area of **Spring Sandwort**, *Sabulina verna*, and a single **Alpine Pennycress**, *Noccaea caerulescens*. Spring Sandwort is also known as 'Leadwort', owing to its being an indicator species for seams of lead-rich rocks. Both populations looked fresh, healthy and in full flower. Inevitably, both are restricted in their range and both rare; however, the pennycress has few records and was thus an exceptional delight. The Pennines bear the largest populations of both, followed by the Peak District, North Wales and, perhaps surprisingly, the Mendip Hills east of Weston-super-Mare, where an estimated 100,000 tonnes of lead have been mined over the centuries.

Are such grasslands threatened? Only 450 ha exist in the UK, amounting to one-third of those found in Europe. While the natural calaminarian grasslands may survive, those such as the one I visited are products of human endeavour and will eventually fail once the toxic metal compounds have leached from the soil. Much more rapid loss has occurred through lack of grazing, over-grazing, the reworking of mines and the advancement of scrub. Would it matter if they were lost? I believe so. The one I visited was an example of life on the edge, a stark contrast to the meadow we had just left, but it had a cold beauty of its own.

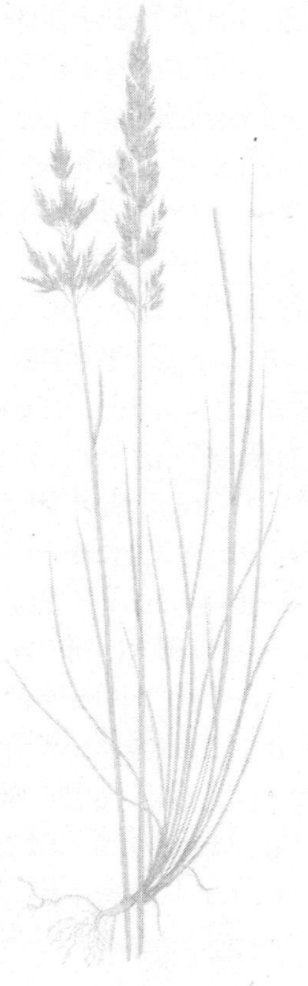

Upland Calcareous Grasslands

Upland calcareous grassland is invariably found on limestone, not chalk. There is also a height qualification of around 300 m above sea level. This will exclude lowland limestone areas such as those at Purbeck in Dorset. The difference between limestone and chalk (ignoring for a moment that chalk is also a limestone) is down to the former being more dense and much harder than the more friable chalk. Friability enables chalk particles to be accommodated in soils, something seen less in limestone. There are usually limestone boulders everywhere, providing places for wild flowers, bryophytes and lichens to grow.

The high rainfall in most of the upland calcareous grasslands slowly leaches out any limestone particles from the soil. This happens through the weak carbonic acid that forms from water and carbon dioxide dissolving the calcium carbonate particles in the soil. These gradually reduce, lowering the pH of the soil. The upshot of this is a soil more acidic than one would expect, something reflected in the plant species that grow there.

The floral component by species count is much less than that found in chalk grasslands such as at Hog Cliff, with many of the calcicoles (plants adapted to a high pH) missing. This is moderated somewhat by a number of plants that grow only in the north or at high altitudes, several of them beginning with the word 'Alpine', such as Alpine Lady's Mantle, Alpine Bistort, Alpine Speedwell and Alpine Cinquefoil, though only the last of these is to be found in the area I visited, the rest having a more northerly distribution. There is a greater proportion of grasses in upland calcareous grasslands, with wild flowers being relatively sparse.

Areas of upland calcareous grassland are chiefly central eastern Scotland and parts of upland northern England, with a small amount in central Wales. In total there are around 22,000 ha in Britain.

MALHAM COVE AND MALHAM TARN – NORTH YORKSHIRE

Both of these sites are within the unromantically named Craven Limestone Complex (CLC), an area designated as a Special Area of Conservation. Most of the CLC is around the 400 m mark, so it easily qualifies for Upland Calcareous, if rather patchily. It stretches to 5,328 ha, about twenty square miles, only a small fraction of which is occupied by Malham Cove and Tarn.

With both sites graced by extensive car parks, they are popular destinations for day-trippers. Malham Tarn is the quieter of the two as, despite the splendid lake from which it earns its name, it lacks the dramatic escarpment of Malham Cove. The Jaguar-threatening stone walls on both sides of the narrow, winding road up the hill to Malham Tarn may also be a discouragement. With two daughters at Leeds universities in the 2010s, I have visited both sites many times.

Malham Cove is best known among the general public for its 'limestone pavement'. It was here, at the top of the impressive cliff, that a dramatic scene was filmed for one of the Harry Potter movies, resulting in it being Selfie Central for young fans. Limestone pavements are exceptionally unsafe places to walk, especially with some of the boulders wobbling treacherously. There must an accident nearly every day. Fortunately for the plants, with very nearly all of them growing here in the deep cracks, they have survived the heavy footfall much better than they would had they been on the surface.

The limestone pavement forms only a small part of what one would see on a walk; most of it is open grassland. Calcareous grasslands form 85 per cent of the CLC and it is characterised as 'dry grassland' in the Joint Nature Conservation Committee designation. It forms the second-largest area of such grassland in England.

Ten per cent of the CLC is noted as 'inland rocks, screes, sands and permanent snow and ice'. Three per cent is made up of bogs, marshes and fens. In a way, these wet areas form the most interesting of the various communities, with Great Close and Ha Mire being rare examples of alkaline fens supporting several rare species of plants.

There is also a small amount of deciduous woodland and even some heathland and acid grassland. To the west of the lake at Malham Tarn there is an 'active raised bog' known as Malham Tarn Moss. Such bogs form over thousands of years and achieve a domed aspect caused by the accumulated peat that raises them above the groundwater. Thus raised, all of its water is derived from direct rainfall.[12]

MALHAM COVE

A walk that follows the main footpaths and roads around Malham Cove forms a closed loop. Going anticlockwise from the village takes one alongside some pleasant meadows to the south of the car park, through a wood that boasts a small waterfall, along a road, then up a long slope to the top of the escarpment 110 m above the car park. Then it is down the 400 steep steps to the bottom and a walk through lower grasslands and then the village of Malham itself. Since walking down 400 steep and irregular steps is harder than walking up them, I prefer clockwise.

Most of the site is grazed, with only the intractably steep grassy

Yorkshire Fog

slopes and screes left to fend for themselves. Rabbits are clearly evident. This has produced a tight, short sward for the most part, and it is, frankly, and as indicated above, a little disappointing. I found about forty species in total, many of them common on undisturbed grasslands almost anywhere.

A quick run-through: an **Eyebright**, **Zigzag Clover**, some splendid **Common Harebells**, an occasional **Betony**, the welcome **Bulbous Buttercup**, brilliant displays of **Lady's Bedstraw**, then **Sheep's Sorrel**, **Self-heal**, *Prunella vulgaris*, and **Wall Lettuce**, *Mycelis muralis*, with only the last of these being at all uncommon. The most conspicuous and frequent wild flower was **Creeping Thyme**, *Thymus praecox*, which was most often to be found carpeting exposed rocks, of which there were very many. On account of it being unpalatable, the most conspicuous grass was **Yorkshire Fog**, though at least it must have felt at home here.

The fissures within the limestone pavements, most of which contain some plants, can hardly be described as grasslands; they just exist *within* grasslands, and not quite even that. They were slightly more productive, with three ferns: **Wall Rue**, **Maidenhair Spleenwort** and **Hart's-tongue Fern**, respectively *Asplenium ruta-muraria, A. trichomanes* and *Phyllitis scolopendrium*. Also found in the cracks in the pavement were the **Welsh Poppy**, *Papaver cambricum*, and **Common Valerian**, *Valeriana officinalis*.

MALHAM TARN

Malham Tarn is just to the north of Malham Cove and can be reached from there by foot. From its own car park, the approach northwards towards the Tarn is a footpath across a grassy plain. One arrives at the vaguely square lake at its south-eastern corner. My favoured destination is the hill that rises immediately to the east of the lake. To access it without climbing its escarpment one follows the path northwards along the lakeside and turn eastwards to ascend the 60 m to the top of the hill, a little over 450 m above sea level.

My walks there have found a handful of species, though nothing new except an *Alchemilla*. It was very small indeed, with leaves barely 15 mm in diameter. Although this was something of a prize, I did not feel I could pick either of the two I found, so its precise name will remain unknown.

Returning, invigorated by what is always a gruelling climb but disappointed by the relatively dull flora that added little to those I found at Malham Cove, I turned my attention to the bottom of the hill and the level footpath alongside the lake. This proved to be considerably more successful, though the habitats were *not* calcareous grasslands but varieties of grazed wetlands.

The bottom of the hill was simply damp, sporting **Common Cotton-grass**, *Eriophorum angustifolium*, some very short specimens of **Meadowsweet**, **Marsh Thistle** and **Sweet Vernal Grass**.

To the east of the Tarn there is an area of alkaline fen. This was a true treasure that appeared to be nevertheless grazed. Here I found two species of orchid: **Early Marsh Orchid**, *Dactylorhiza incarnata*, and **Northern Marsh Orchid**, *Dactylorhiza purpurella*, plus the even more exciting **Red Rattle** (also known as **Marsh Lousewort)**, *Pedicularis palustris*, a plant-hemiparasite found in wetlands. The dominant plants were sedges and rushes, of course, but the one that excited me most was the **Bird's-eye Primrose**, *Primula farinosa*, a plant almost entirely restricted in Britain to the north-west of England.

Lowland Dry Acid Grasslands

Lowland dry acid grasslands are distributed all over lowland Britain, with around 20,000 ha in England, 4,300 ha in Scotland and 36,000 ha in Wales.[13] These figures are difficult to validate as a considerable range of hectarage is given in the literature. Part of this measurement issue is that lowland dry acid grassland is almost invariably associated with heaths, the two intertwining to form a patchwork, and with such communities often known as 'Grass Heaths'.[14] Also, lowland dry acid grasslands come in several flavours. There are four main community types, made up of twenty-six sub-communities.

As suggested by the name, they are generally well drained as they occur on sands and gravels. Their height requirement is rather arbitrarily put at up to 300 m, which is where upland communities start. They can be rich in species, ranging from five species per 4 m^2 to twenty-five.[15]

Primary locations are the New Forest, the Dorset Heaths, the famous Brecklands in East Anglia, the Suffolk Sandlings and the Wealden heaths. In Wales they occur mostly on the approaches to upland areas, and in Scotland there are large areas west of both Edinburgh and Glasgow. Parks, cemeteries and, rather surprisingly, some roadsides can also support the flora of lowland dry acid grassland.

There was once much more lowland dry acid grassland, but the overall loss is unknown. However, this is estimated at 90 per cent, so 'most of it by far' seems a reasonable way of describing the situation. The usual suspects appear — agricultural improvement through the application of lime, agricultural abandonment and the planting of trees.

HORSESHOE BOTTOM – THE NEW FOREST, HAMPSHIRE

I have spent a great deal of time in the New Forest, my first visit being sixty-plus years ago. In the early 1960s most of my visits were with a school friend and his parents. They owned a model shop in our town, and we would visit a place near Beaulieu where there was (and still is) an area where model aircraft could be flown without annoying the neighbours, though they may well have frightened the horses – well, ponies, actually. One of these trips gave me my first close encounter with fungi. I found a brown, spherical, papery casing surrounding a mass of fibres and dust (spores). I showed it to my friend's father and asked him what it was. It was a mature puffball. Remembering it very well, I now know its species name: *Lycoperdon nigrescens*. I also (now) know its habitat: lowland dry acid grassland.

The Forest is unusual in that it lacks hedges and fences, save the fences that enclose the major roads (lesser roads are left unfenced) and the tree plantations. Even then, the plantation fences are supposed to be removed once the trees are established. This is to allow in cattle – and also pigs where a common law right to do so exists for those in possession of such.

I have always loved the Forest, and love is engendered in all who find the time to visit. For anyone not familiar with this extraordinary place, it may come as a surprise that I am including it in a book about grassland as, surely, it is mostly woodland. In fact, only a quarter is occupied by broad-leaved natives, with another 15 per cent taken up with plantation trees (spruces, pines and larch, mostly), making a neat 40 per cent. The rest is wet heathland at

Wavy Hair-grass

6 per cent, with dry heathland and grassland making up the rest. Grassland and dry heath are included in a single statistic because they weave themselves together in an endless mosaic, depending on the hydrology and grazing practice in any one area. The fact that these acid grasslands are also characterised as 'dry' provides us with another name for them: 'parched acid grasslands'. They are very striking as the often low rolling hills of the New Forest can change from 'rolling green' to 'rolling brown'.

Sometimes this patchwork is mostly grasses, as is the case at the very grassy Horseshoe Bottom. Altogether, the New Forest is a vast open area amounting to 56,658 ha, which is 219 square miles. Charmingly, both the boundary of the Forest and the land within it are known as the 'perambulation'.

The New Forest has survived partly because it was once a Royal Forest, though it is now a National Park, most of which is still Crown land. It was established by William the Conqueror *c.* 1079, which is not long after he claimed England for himself. A Royal Forest is established for one reason: the pursuit of game, usually deer and Wild Boar. The reason why what would become the New Forest was chosen for this honour is that the land is largely useless for anything else. The soil is notoriously poor and, of course, almost entirely acidic. Some attempts to add lime to parts of the Forest occurred some years ago, but its effect is likely to have been transient.

The cause of this poor soil is the underlying geology, which consists almost entirely of sands and clays, with varying proportions of both. The Forest is heroically wet and muddy owing to the sometimes poor natural drainage and the general lack of artificial drainage except on some of the lawns: that is, areas of grassland grazed by animals used by the commoners. I have always asked people to bring Wellington boots on the fungus forays I used to lead there and despair of those who come in trainers or walking boots that they claim are waterproof. They may well be in Clapham, but not in 25 cm of New Forest mud.

I visited Horseshoe Bottom several times for this book. It is certainly a very lovely spot and with a large car park. It is used mostly by dog walkers, most of whom are well behaved (see p. 38).

I wrote earlier of the close sward found on the chalk downland of Hog Cliff, but it has nothing on Horseshoe Bottom. At Hog Cliff it is around 6 to 10 cm, with many areas that are much taller where the grasslands meet scrub and other edges. It can become taller still if grazing is withdrawn for more than a couple of weeks. Not so at Horseshoe Bottom: here the sward is barely 4 cm high, and often only 2 cm. From anywhere further than a couple of metres away, it looks like an impracticably sloping bowling green.

The reason for this is the grazing regime (if such it can be called), which is down almost entirely to the rather large ponies that permanently graze there.

From the car park, the broad valley side drops down and presents a large area of this short turf. At the bottom is a small stream, then the ground rises again. The far valley side is a mixture of grassland, heath and scrub. The valley runs east-south-east to west-north-west. The main slope down from the car park faces north-north-east.

The area of interest is 1.25 km long and averages 320 m wide, though the more northerly edge is anything but a straight line. The total area is 40 ha, which, even deducting the heath and scrub (about 25 per cent), is very large for its type; 71 per cent of such grassland areas are less than 5 ha.

THE PLANTS OF HORSESHOE BOTTOM

As mentioned, an unusual property of this site, and most comparable sites within the New Forest, is the grazing regime. Horses and ponies bite very close to the soil, and the plants react, if they can, by remaining very small. Typically, they are perhaps a tenth of their normal size by volume. I recorded a couple of dozen plant species in the grassland of Horseshoe Bottom. Very nearly all of them were miniatures, and one might ask whether they were small varieties or were simply forced to remain small because of the close cropping of the ponies.

I found a small area where the turf had been disturbed and removed a truly tiny **Ribwort Plantain**. It was 7 cm in diameter and bore a diminutive flower spike. At home, I planted it in a pot in some garden soil and watched it quickly grow to its normal size of around 20 cm, amounting to nearly *thirty* times its original size by volume. What we see at Horseshoe Bottom is very atypical in appearance as the sward on most other lowland dry acid grassland

Horseshoe Bottom

The short sward of Horseshoe Bottom

Bird's-foot Trefoil

Nail Fungus, *Poronia punctata*

Small corner of Kingcombe Moor

Mystery eggs on Watermint

A Rush

Near Brecon

Hillside near Brecon

A mossy rock

Bog Asphodel

Wareham Common

Floodplain grassland of Wareham Common

A view of part of Wareham Common from the town wall

Roesel's Bush-cricket – male

Lesser Marsh Grasshopper – female

Grey-patched Mining Bee – female

Common Green Colonels – female. A soldier fly

Deep Dale

Part of Deep Dale. Main slope in the distance

Meadow Crane's-bill

Wild Marjoram

Hog Cliff Extension

Langcombe Bottom prior to purchase of the site

The depleted land prior to the purchase of the site

Scentless Mayweed takeover

Hog Cliff Extension

An area used for growing seeds for birds and other animals

Cornwall

A modern cornfield in Cornwall

sites will be taller, though seldom lush owing to the lack of nutrients. Nevertheless, Horseshoe Bottom is most definitely lowland dry acid grassland, and a fine example.

It is well known that *upland* acid grassland has suffered from too much grazing, and the recommendation that they should not be grazed at all is often heard. I discuss this issue on p. 46. Does this apply to lowland grassland? If it does, then Horseshoe Bottom with its heavily grazed sward and other similar New Forest grasslands would seem to be good candidates for better-controlled grazing.

The Hampshire & Isle of Wight Wildlife Trust is a major authority on the subject of the New Forest.[16] In 2019 it issued a brief report on various New Forest problems, a major one being overgrazing. It cited the increase in the population of grazing animals as a factor, noting that the population of grazing cattle and ponies had doubled in the previous twenty years. The author appears to be more concerned about the loss of scrub and new woody growth than about damage to grassland, but nevertheless the report shows that there is overall concern about grazing levels.

Of the plants I found, ten were either indicator species of the community or frequently found there. More are certain to be there, but the grasses in particular are very difficult to identify without their flowers, so no doubt I missed the expected Bristle Bent, *Agrostis curtisii*, and Wavy Hair-grass, *Avenella flexuosa*. Several species in the list I made for this site were more typical of the heathland edges or the conspicuously wet areas.

The indicator species that I recorded were **Heath Speedwell, Heath Bedstraw, Sheep's Sorrel, Tormentil, Red Fescue, Lousewort** and **Cross-leaved Heath**, *Erica tetralix*, the last found only towards the bottom of the slope. In addition, there were **Mouse-ear Hawkweed, Bird's-foot Trefoil** and **Slender Eyebright**, *Euphrasia micrantha*. I was particularly delighted to see the last of these as it is not a common species in England. It is mostly found north of Durham, with populations in parts of Wales, Devon, Cornwall and the New Forest. It displays far more of a dark blue/purple than the commonest species, *Euphrasia officinalis*.

Also found, and very common, were **Self-heal**, **Black Medic**, **Bulbous Buttercup** and the grass **Crested Dog's-tail**, though all very much in miniature. The dominant plant was the almost ubiquitous **Ribwort Plantain**.

More interesting, perhaps, than the plants of the dry grassland were the wetland plants that occurred at the bottom of the slope above the stream, or in wet areas that are presumably above a layer of clay. These were ecologically distinct habitats but bordering or entwined within the acid grassland.

Thus I was pleased to see **Lesser Spearwort**, *Ranunculus flammula*, though it is common enough, and also **Marsh Lousewort**, a generally rare hemiparasitic plant of wet acidic areas, with the New Forest being one of its strongholds. There were also **Marsh Pennywort**, *Hydrocotyle vulgaris*, **Marsh Bedstraw**, *Galium palustre*, and the uncommon **Bog Pimpernel**, *Anagallis tenella*. Bog Pimpernel is a real beauty, with a mass of circular/heart-shaped leaves and large number of five-petalled, cup-like pale pink flowers with darker pink lines along their length. With the exception of Marsh Bedstraw, all these plants are rare or uncommon, and certainly specialised. Finally, at the bottom of the hill, there was some **Marsh Thistle**.

THE FUNGI OF HORSESHOE BOTTOM

I returned for a couple of seasons to take a look at the fungi. As explained, I am very familiar with the fungi of the New Forest and on relatively safe ground. Around 3,000 species have been recorded there, which is about half of the species of macrofungi found in the whole of Britain, though a few of these records are for microfungi. Grassland fungi are almost invariably different from those found in woodlands. The short New Forest grasslands are perfect for fungi as they have no competition for space with the plants, which would otherwise grow too tall to accommodate them.

Many of the grassland fungi in the New Forest as a whole are within the CHEGD grouping (see p. 114), but there are also Parasols (*Macrolepiota* spp.), 'true mushrooms' (*Agaricus* spp.), plus puffballs, Fairy Ring Champignon and numerous others. One I always like to see is *Agaricus porphyrocephalus*. It is a rare species, though almost certainly overlooked, but fairly frequent in the New Forest. Like many of the fungi, it is often seen on the grassy roadsides. Sadly, I did not see any at Horseshoe Bottom.

I found around two dozen species on my visits, the most conspicuous of which were waxcaps, and there is no doubt it was a waxcap grassland. My plant surveys took place in the summer, but for fungi the autumn is usually the best. On my first arrival to look for fungi here I could see nothing from the car park, but after a few steps into the grassland I began to see them everywhere. The first thing I noticed was how small the fruiting bodies (mushrooms) were, compared with what I usually see elsewhere. They were evidently following the plants around them by keeping their heads down, though it had been an over-wet spring and summer, which had rather compromised many fungi.

The dominant species were the **Meadow Waxcap** and the **Parrot Waxcap**, *Gliophorus psittacinus*, the former in many, many rings. It is a dull but attractive orange colour. The second of these has to be seen to be believed. Sitting amid the grass, it first appears as a shiny and extremely slimy, brilliant emerald sphere. It then opens out into its natural mushroom-shape, gradually losing its green coloration, which is largely replaced by yellow, oranges and reds. There were hundreds of them.

Less frequent were small, brilliant red **Scarlet Waxcaps**, *Hygrocybe coccinea*, the oranges and lemons of the **Honey Waxcap**, *H. reidii*, the bright yellow of the slimy **Golden Waxcap**, *H. chlorophana*, and the white of the **Snowy Waxcap**, *Cuphophyllus virgineus*. All these species are common and highly conspicuous, yet few people notice them.

Considerably less common were four more waxcaps: the **Oily Waxcap**, *Hygrocybe quieta*, the **Glutinous Waxcap**, *H. glutinipes*, the **Hourglass Waxcap**, *H. constrictospora*, and the **Slimy Waxcap**, *Gliophorus irrigatus*. The first three are a mix of yellows and oranges, the last is grey-brown all over and as slimy as the Parrot Waxcap. These ten species alone make it an area of regional importance, though more may be found on further visits. The so-called 'Pinkgills' were there in force, with three species found – the **Star**, **Silky** and **Blue Edge Pinkgill**, respectively *Entoloma conferendum*, *E. sericeum* and *E. serrulatum*.

Inevitably, as they appear in most grasslands, there were two or three of the very common species of small, slender, brownish toadstools that make up the genus *Paneolus*, dubbed 'Mottlegills' from the unevenly mature patches of black spores on the gills. Taking me back sixty years, there was also a puffball; this time it was the **Grassland Puffball**, *Lycoperdon lividum*.

As I was leaving, I spotted two young men who were neither dog walkers nor naturalists. They too were looking for fungi. I spoke to them, and they told me (as though it was anything other than obvious) that they were searching for the hallucinogenic **Liberty Cap**, *Psilocybe semilanceata*. They did not seem to have been at all successful.

This species displays an unusual feeding regime in that it colonises the cortical tissue of Perennial Ryegrass and a couple of other grasses.[17] The cortical tissue occurs just under the epidermis of the grass roots and is critical for nutrient storage and transport. This is clearly an unusual form of parasitism, but the plants show no signs of distress, and one must wonder if it is an unusual mycorrhizal relationship. Incidentally, some sedges have shown the same or similar association. I did find a few Liberty Caps later and merely noted their presence. Honestly.

One species that I looked out for, but did not see, was an unusual and rare species that grows on pony droppings. It is the Nail Fungus, *Poronia punctata*. This is one of the rarest of all the European fungi; indeed it has often been considered the rarest of all, though it is believed to have once been common throughout Britain.[18] There are now very few other locations where it occurs, with the New Forest considered to be its last major refuge.

It appears as a raised, pale, lead-grey disc about 4 mm in diameter with several visible pores, hence its specific epithet. If removed from its substratum (its substratum holds no fears for your author), its true form is revealed: from the side view it looks like a 1.5 cm tapering funnel, vaguely the shape of an upholstery tack. I presume that the spores are formed towards the top of the funnel and are 'puffed out' through the pores by the percussion of falling raindrops.

Quite why it is so rare is uncertain. It always grows on the droppings of horses and ponies and, much less so, cattle and a few other animals. Horses and ponies are not rare, so why is the fungus so rare? Worming medicines (anthelmintics) have been suggested as the culprits, and indeed there is some research that suggests at least some of them can kill fungi. These medicines have also been shown to be very damaging to any insects that reside in the droppings. In the New Forest, there is minimal and careful use of anthelmintics.

The oddest thing about the rarity of the Nail Fungus is that I see it every two or three years in the Forest, sometimes in truly vast numbers. Fifteen years ago I visited the grassland north of the A35. Here the land is very flat; indeed some of it shows signs of having been used for Second World War airfields. It amounts to many hundreds of hectares, with a great deal of similar land nearby. It was a particularly wet late October, and very nearly every pony dropping was host to an average of five or so fruiting bodies. Allowing for the general practice of ponies to use latrine areas, there may be an average of four droppings in every square metre. This amounts to 200,000 fruiting bodies per hectare, an extraordinary number. As I wrote earlier, even rare species are common *somewhere*.

Purple Moor-Grass and Rush Pastures

These complex communities are exceptionally full of life, providing home for ground-nesting birds and a vast number of invertebrates. They can occur in small, solitary patches, parts or all of a field and coastal plains. They are often seen on gentle slopes. They can on be acid, neutral or calcareous soil, though acidic soils are favoured. The last of these will be peaty and of very low fertility. The primary considerations are that the soil should be wet but not flooded.

Except after a period of grazing or a cut, they consist of tall, generally water-loving or water-tolerant plants, with those indicated in their NVC community names dominant. In addition, mosses and liverworts are also to be found in these pastures. Pastures they are, but they are sometimes cut for hay or bedding.

Sounding precisely like motorways, Purple Moor-grass and Rush Pastures are described in the NVC designations as M22, M23, M24, M25 and M26, with 'M' standing for 'Mire'. Within these communities there are twenty-three sub-communities, clearly indicating the aforementioned complexity.

The true UK extent of these pastures has proved difficult to determine but is generally put at 56,000 ha. Northern Ireland and Wales possess most of these. There are perhaps 2,000 ha in Scotland and 8,000 in England, with most of these in the south-west, particularly Devon. Those in Devon are known as 'culm pastures'.[19] In England there are a few more concentrations in the north-west, East Anglia and the south coast, but elsewhere they are thinly scattered. Many have been lost to agricultural improvement, with only 8 per cent of those in 1900 still in existence – the advances in drainage technology and need for more agricultural land being the primary reasons.

KINGCOMBE MOOR

Idylls are not easy places to find. Those that are anywhere near conurbations will sport a hot-dog stand and car park, and, by definition, are idylls no more. 'Fallen idylls', perhaps. By contrast, Kingcombe Moor, which is found two fields south of Lady's Mead and two fields north-west of Coase Mead, is accessed via a now substantial wooden bridge across the small and very lovely River Hooke.

Stepping onto the Moor, one finds oneself in a narrow strip of short riverside grass that opens out a little to the left, to form a small area of lawn beside the meandering bank of the river. Family picnics have been held there, and I have often taken people there at some point during one of my fungus forays, even though it is too wet for most fungi – I just enjoy showing people this oasis of peace.

The 0.5 ha area of pasture that is the subject of this chapter begins where the tiny lawn stops and continues north-west and ends where the land rises by some 20 m until it reaches the level of the road that runs between Lord's and Lady's Mead. Its average width is a mere 32 m. Such small areas of pasture are relatively common in lowland Britain, being areas that are impossible or too expensive to drain. As is the case here, they frequently form patches within or neighbouring other grasslands.

The definition of 'Rush Pasture' is broad, with most by far containing Purple Moor-grass. Kingcombe Moor does not possess this grass, despite a patch of the plant occurring only 400 m away. This lack is rather damning when one considers the title of this

Purple Moor-grass

chapter. However, the NVC comes to the rescue in the community designation: 'M23a Soft Rush/Sharp-flowered Rush-Marsh Bedstraw rush pasture'. The overall NVC description of M23 is exceptionally long, running to 7,000 words over eight dense pages, plus a two-page table of species potentially found there that notes their frequency of appearance. The long description of M23 is due to its varied nature, with nearly each instance containing different combinations of plants.

As one would hope, rushes dominate, with **Sharp-flowered Rush**, *Juncus acutiflorus*, and **Soft Rush** the most common, with **Hard Rush** also present. The grasses are **Sweet Vernal Grass, Red Fescue, Yorkshire Fog** and **Rough Meadow Grass**, *Poa trivialis*, and there are three sedges: **Lesser Pond-sedge**, *Carex* *acutiformis*, **Glaucous Sedge** and **Common Sedge**, *C. nigra*.

The flowers are **Meadow Buttercup, Creeping Buttercup, Ragged Robin, Greater Bird's-foot Trefoil**, *Lotus pedunculatus*, **Lesser Stitchwort, Meadowsweet, Common Dock, Cuckoo Flower, Water Mint**, *Mentha aquatica*, **Marsh Bedstraw, Meadow Thistle**, *Cirsium dissectum*, **Marsh Ragwort**, *Senecio aquaticus*, and **Marsh Marigold**, *Caltha palustris*.

Most of the plants grow taller than usual (Water Mint, for example) to keep up with the competition, or they clamber or straggle over tall plants such as Marsh Bedstraw. Combined with the colourful flowers evident from the list, Rush Pasture can be a very striking sight.

Kingcombe Moor has been kept as a pasture, and one often encounters cattle there, consuming the younger shoots of grasses and rushes that appear early in the year. They do not rely on this thin gruel, having permanent access to the pasture grasses of the slope. They can make a mess of the rush pasture, but it always recovers. The only time I do see it struggle is in rare, very dry summers, when the soil dries out dramatically and the vegetation becomes brown and trampled.

A short stroll through the Rush Pasture late in summer is an extraordinarily aromatic adventure, with Meadowsweet and Water Mint vying for one's attention. Except during drought conditions, this walk will defeat ordinary shoes and even walking boots: this is 'welly' country.

Such a habitat has a very lively invertebrate community. Damsel and Dragon Flies are common. The surrounding woodland and grass pasture, also rich in plant species, enable the interactions between habitats that prove so productive.

My contribution (if so it can be called) to the recording of invertebrates here was to find an orange-coloured patch on the underside of a Water Mint leaf. Thinking it to be a rust fungus (most are bright orange), I took it home for identification. However, through my loupe I saw that the patch was a cluster of eggs – each less than 0.5 mm in diameter, with network-like ridges. Canvassing any number of specialists has failed to find out what they were, compounded by my failure to incubate them successfully. Their photograph is on Plate 26.

Upland Acid Grasslands

Upland acid grassland is the commonest of all the semi-natural grasslands in Britain, with figures quoted either side of 1,500,000 ha – many times that of semi-natural lowland dry acid grasslands. It is also the grandest from a panoramic point of view. Its biology, however, is the least interesting.

Most readers will guess where they may occur: Dartmoor and Exmoor in the south-west of England, the uplands of northern England, the Mourne and Antrim mountains of Northern Ireland and much of upland Wales and Scotland. In other words, much of the land that is above 250–300 m, reasonably well drained and acidic.

Upland acid grassland is very much an outlier in this book as it is not considered a 'priority habitat', and, critically, in most instances it comprises a degraded state of more interesting communities – chiefly various types of mire (mostly blanket bog) and heathlands. Such habitats are often associated with peat.

This book is not an unthinking champion of grasslands; it is biodiversity and the abundance thereof that it seeks to defend. I have included upland acid grassland here because there is so very much of it, making it difficult to ignore, and some such grasslands, notably those on thin soils and well drained slopes, *are* of interest. Also, they come with a belated warning that unforeseen (or imaginatively disregarded) consequences can await even the most apparently benign efforts of mankind.

Although some upland acid grasslands have long been established, most of those we now see have come into existence in the last eighty years. This is due to three main factors. Two are matters of grazing practices – the dramatic increase in upland sheep grazing and the dramatic loss of upland cattle grazing. The third is the deliberate establishment of grasslands by heavy sheep grazing of heathland or the burning of heathlands, with subsequent regrowth of heath inhibited by grazing pressure in the resultant grasses. With mires, it was draining, burning and grazing that ensured the loss of very many such valued communities. Grazing intensity was exacerbated by sheep being kept on the upland grassland all year round, with heathland and mire having little recovery time.

Since the early 1940s the practice of grazing cattle in the uplands has declined precipitously, in part because of subsidies and government directives. Cattle are able to consume plants that sheep cannot, certain grasses – Mat-grass, *Nardus stricta*, and Purple Moor-grass – being the most notable by far (see below). With cattle withdrawn, these grasses proliferated uncontrollably and frequently overwhelmed other plants.

These issues became something of a *cause célèbre* in the mid-2010s, with newspaper articles criticising the high density of sheep grazing. Some of the language was emotive, with sheep being described as 'woolly maggots', 'white plague' and other even more colourful terms.[20] More recently, extreme views have been expressed: that the very existence of sheep in Britain should be a thing of the past.[21]

Three particular plants have made a land-grab induced for the most part by changes to grazing regimes. They are Purple Moor-grass, which takes over heathland and blanket bog, Mat-grass, which takes over heathland and established upland grassland, and Bracken, which takes over everything.

This is a complex subject with precisely no easy answers to the problems involved. A 'no sheep policy' that I saw four years ago in a part of Snowdonia has seemingly been successful. But this was only *so far*, and one must wonder what the natural climax vegetation will be, assuming it has not already been reached. If it is a climax community now, then we must celebrate; if it is not, then it is anyone's guess.

The obvious answer is to return to the management system before intensive sheep grazing did so much damage. Bring back blanket bogs; bring back heathland. This, however, is extremely difficult – the horse has already bolted.

The on-the-ground players in this game are the winning plants, so I tell their stories next.

PURPLE MOOR-GRASS

Purple Moor-grass, often referred to simply as 'Molinia', is splendid in its specialist communities. Several respected NVC communities effectively demand its presence: for example, M24 Purple Moor-grass–Meadow Thistle fen-meadow and M26 Purple Moor-grass–Marsh Hawk's-beard mire.

It is an attractive grass up to 1.2 m tall, with stiff, erect stems, and narrow upright panicles that are flushed with the purple that gives the plant its common name. It is never valued, however, for any agricultural merits as it has none. H. Marshall Ward, writing in 1901, tells us that it is 'useless as forage, but used locally for broom'.[22] The great C. E. Hubbard, in his *Grasses* of 1954, states in his description of Purple Moor-grass that it is 'usually abundant and frequently dominating large areas, often to the exclusion of other flowering plants', nicely encapsulating a problem that has overwhelmed much of our acid uplands. It also indicates that new problems are seldom as new as we think.

Purple Moor-grass forms dense tussocks, providing it with the *potential* of claiming large areas of land – a process aided by pollution from atmospheric nitrogen compounds that cause rapid growth. The main victims are blanket bogs, a species-rich group of communities that have been colonised by this grass to local extinction. Some 600,000 ha of upland Britain are now believed to be dominated by what can be characterised as a 'grass-in-the-wrong-place'. Areas in hectares are difficult to imagine, but it is four times that of Greater London and 10 per cent of the British uplands.[23]

It is extremely difficult to remove this grass, generally involving the reduction of burning, and also the blocking of drainage as it cannot tolerate high soil water-levels. Successful field studies have been performed, but with so great an area under its thrall the problem is quite intractable. Many ecologists throw up their hands in despair. An article in *The Applied Ecologist* was entitled, 'How Do You Solve a Problem like Molinia?'[24] How indeed?

MAT-GRASS

Mat-grass is an exceptionally long-lived and slow-growing grass, with six to eight years to get started and another eleven to fifteen to achieve maximum complexity, the generative phase. It then lives a further twenty years before becoming senescent and dying five to seven years later. It survives perfectly well in nutrient-poor acid grassland. Cattle will eat it, though not preferentially, but sheep will avoid it. With Mat-grass, it is chiefly upland heath and established grasslands that suffer.[25]

BRACKEN

One more plant species has caused problems for both lowland and upland areas. It is Bracken, *Pteridium aquilinum*. It covers 1.6 per cent of Britain's land area, mostly in the wetter west, with uplands bearing a disproportionate load. This area is slightly more than that covered by all of Britain's buildings.

Bracken spreads via underground stems (rhizomes) and produces a dense canopy when in leaf, followed by a dense layer of litter when it dies back, thus excluding other plants. If that is not enough, it suppresses wannabe neighbours by producing plant toxins. No agricultural animals will eat the stuff because it is poisonous, though they might do so *in extremis*. Cattle are good at trampling it and were once able to control it with their hooves, but upland cattle farming is now a rare practice.

However, Bracken was once collected in large quantities for the bedding of cattle, with two beneficial effects – this, and the clearance of Bracken. This practice has not entirely died out, with some farms continuing the tradition.[26] It is certainly sensible if the manpower is available, as no straw or other bedding needs to be brought in. Fame and fortune await anyone inventing a financially profitable use for Bracken, though it was once used in glassmaking.

There are no reliable methods of removing it that do not involve multiple applications. Cutting and rolling, for example, need to be done two, three or even four times a year for several years, and rolling is difficult on steep slopes. There are no approved herbicides. On the positive side, no plant is an island: Bracken too has its associated organisms.

Bracken provides excellent cover for birds, mammals and reptiles. Several birds also use it for nesting: Whinchats, Ring Ouzels and Merlins. The Nightjar is one of the uncommon birds that use it for cover. Although not a birder to any extent, I once watched a Nightjar fly overhead in Sweden. I will always remember the strange flight path it followed.

Bracken does not always take over grasslands, and where it is well behaved as a small patch in a field, or as an understory to neighbouring wood, it can substantially add to the biodiversity of the grassland itself. For example, twenty-seven invertebrates live *only* with Bracken or are frequent visitors, and Bracken accommodates several more that use it only occasionally.

For the last word on Bracken, I hand you to Guy Shrubsole, author of *The Lost Rainforests of Britain*. He writes about the possibility, advisability even, of planting native species of trees in areas that only support Bracken. A dense first planting would overwhelm the Bracken for several years, and we would benefit from new native woodlands. Bracken, believe it or not, is considered to be a woodland plant, so it would no doubt re-establish itself on wood edges and within the wood once the canopy becomes more open. The best of both worlds, perhaps.

THE BRECON BEACONS (BANNAU BRYCHEINIOG)

In my research of upland grasslands I visited several places but write about just one, a steep hillside not far from Brecon in South Wales. I will leave it nameless, as I am not sure it bears a name. Although a hillside, the differences between it and Hog Cliff are stark indeed. Its craggy, boulder-strewn nature contrasts dramatically with the evocative curves of The Chalk, and the impervious shales and sandstone and some overlying peat had, it seemed, kept the landscape permanently wet. The grasses, although grazed, were tall and dense; rushes and sedges were all around. A wild landscape, not a tame one.

My total species count for the plants was thirty-five. I was pleased enough with this achievement as I had not expected to find even that small number. I was less delighted with the weather, which was cool and wet, even though it was the second week of July.

Starting from the roadside, I took a steep sheep track up the hillside to reach nearly 500 m above sea level and 150 m above the road.

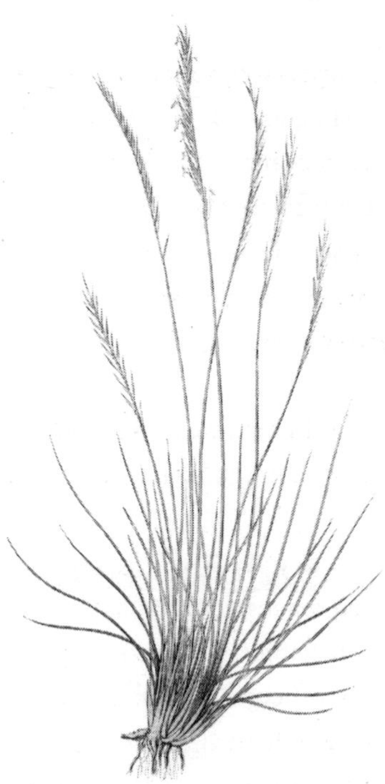

Mat-grass

Exposed rocks formed a major component of the landscape, with flowering plants and ferns growing around their edges and in cracks, and with mosses and lichens growing on their surfaces. Each thus adorned rock, when viewed close up, looked like a garden in miniature.

As with nearly all the grasslands mentioned in this book, the land and communities varied a great deal, providing a complex mosaic of grasses, rushes, mossy blanket bog, small trees, heathland and scrub, the last two of these represented in the form of **Common Heather**, *Calluna vulgaris*, and **Bilberry**, *Vaccinium myrtillus*.

The rushes were **Hard Rush**, *Juncus inflexus*, **Soft Rush** and **Toad Rush**, *J. bufonius*. All three are extremely common; however, Toad Rush is seemingly despised by naturalists and by gardeners with over-wet soils. It is, in fact, a charming little plant and a native species that has been in Britain for millennia, not a troublesome latecomer. It is common along damp path-sides (which is where I found it) and, unusually for a rush, an annual plant. The path also supplied a slightly trodden **Hard Fern**, *Blechnum spicant*. Another member of the Poales was the pretty **Common Cotton-grass**, a species of sedge, and indicative of a patch of blanket bog.

Of the eighteen wild flowers found, a handful were interesting. The buttercup species **Lesser Spearwort** is common throughout most of both upland and lowland Britain, though largely absent where the soil is too dry. It earns its common name from its distinctly spear-shaped leaves. The prettiest of the plants found was **Bog Asphodel**, *Narthecium ossifragum*. The scientific name comes from *narthex* ('rod'), reflecting perhaps the straight up-and-down flower stem, in turn reflecting its status as a monocotyledonous plant that was formerly in the Lily Family. The specific name means 'bone-breaker', owing to its ill-deserved reputation for weakening the bones of sheep that eat it. Its flowers are very striking, with six narrow yellow petals and six corresponding brilliant orange anthers on filaments ornamented with woolly yellow hairs.

Two other plants caught my attention on that day, both of them on the roadside, and thus it is questionable whether or not they should be included, especially as I could not reliably identify one of them was because I was travelling at 40 mph at the time. This high-speed identification was nevertheless clearly a species of Lady's Mantle. The specimens were abundant and with large leaves, so I am guessing the common garden species *Alchemilla mollis*. The other was the **Heath Spotted Orchid**, *Dactylorhiza maculata,* which grew in considerable numbers on a broad area of short grass in front of one of the roadside car parks.

One headline plant that is known to grow in the Brecon area is the Globeflower, *Trollius europaeus*, a conspicuously close relative of the buttercups. It flowers from May to June, so there was little hope of spotting it. I was disappointed to fail in my attempt as it has a story to tell.

Trollius perhaps derives from 'troll', a word that, among others, means 'to capture' – which is what it seems to do. It is tall, at 30–60 cm, with unusually compact flower heads with no petals, despite appearances to the contrary. In fact, what look like petals are ten yellow, petal-like sepals. It is a sizeable flower at 2.5–3 cm in diameter.

The flowers never open but allow certain small fly species to squeeze in between the sepals and effectively be captured, for a while. These are mostly small anthomyiids in the genus *Chiastocheta*, and are the plant's primary pollinators.[27] Once inside, both males and females will feed and rest. Mating takes place, and the female lays her eggs on a spiral arrangement of carpels in the centre. The resultant larvae feed on the seeds which would have developed by the time they hatch from eggs. One might imagine that the seeds would quickly be consumed, leaving insufficient for the larvae and none to enable the plant to grow elsewhere. Fortunately, the larvae are highly aggressive towards one another, lethally fighting it out between themselves, leaving few survivors and enough seeds left for dispersal. I do not know any more details, but the males *must* leave the flower to visit others, while the females need not go anywhere. Overall, such complex arrangements are the tightrope walks that most commensal pairs of organisms must take.

With all their troubles, upland acid grasslands are nevertheless places of grand beauty. The plants I found in my visit were few in number, but there will be many more that I missed or which occur nearby.

Water Meadows

It can be surprising to learn how very wet Britain once was. Oliver Rackham estimated that 25 per cent of Britain was once wetland of one sort or another, an extraordinary amount of intractable land.[28] During the post-glacial period, early settlers could only survive on hillsides and hilltops, or in the fens on 'islands' of slightly higher ground. Vast areas of low-lying land now drained were once fenlands, and many valley bottoms were uninhabitable prior to the construction of river embankments.

According to a 2024 government report, Britain has lost approximately 90 per cent of its wetlands.[29] The overall percentage of wetland is now 5 per cent, though not all are within my catholic definition of grassland. As far back as 1971 there was a move to protect wetlands worldwide with the establishment of the Ramsar Convention, so called because the meeting took place in the city of that name in Iran, a few years prior to the fall of the Shah.

Mankind has been very active over the millennia in draining wetlands to make them suitable for farming. Ditches sometimes as deep as 2 m are common, and very many fields have unsuspected drainage pipes hidden beneath their surface. Rackham notes that our cereal crops are derived from dry-adapted plants and compares this with China, where cultivation of the most decidedly wet-adapted rice was mastered. If there is a UK exception, it is to be found in watercress beds.

The main losses have been through agricultural improvement and urban and industrial development. It has long been known that such activities have been excessive, and every time Britain suffers heavy rain we remember (or should remember) that natural flood buffers of permanent vegetation have been removed by man. I believe that a little sense has been introduced when a lowland wetland is proposed for some form of urban development but not, I suggest, quite enough, and only late in the day.

One advantage that wetlands have is the support they receive from people and organisations interested in birds, and the more general public, always ready to support a lapwing over a liverwort, provides further support in turn. 'Birders' tend to be more vocal than, for example, anyone else, in their criticisms of habitat loss or mismanagement and in their support for restoration projects. One such project was the restoration of the Lower Derwent Valley reserve in Yorkshire, and it is telling that the headline species for this area were all birds. Even though this shows an obsession with 'feathery' over 'green', it is both understandable and to be welcomed. Few interested parties are likely to care what drove the people who do this good work; what matters is just that it is done.

Water meadows are just one of many wetland grassland types, an artificial and now abandoned type where the grasslands were flooded early in the year to raise the temperature of the soil and encourage the early growth of grass. Those south-east of my village are pretty enough but have had inorganic fertilisers applied and are thus species-poor. Wareham Common, however, is both wetter and better.

WAREHAM COMMON – DORSET

On occasions, and for several years, I would find myself driving alongside a piece of land to the north of Wareham in Dorset. The grassland looked to be rich in species, with, I thought, the potential to support fungi. Eventually I decided to take a look but found no fungi in what transpired to be a very wet grassland

Marsh Foxtail

of near-towering rushes, sedge and grasses. It was a floodplain. Though disappointed by the lack of fungi, I was pleased to see many plants there that were unfamiliar, to me at least – and at the time. Many years later I thought it might be an excellent candidate for this book. I visited the site four times in my research and found something new every time, one of the great joys of such explorations.

Wareham Common is a truly splendid site, containing a variety of community types, nearly all of them grasslands of one variety or another. In addition to the floodplains that are all neutral wet grasslands, there are dry neutral grasslands (meadow) and lowland acid grasslands. Part of the area I studied (and could not resist including) is a narrow strip of scrub and heavily grazed plants on lowland acid grassland, though unusual in that it conspicuously, if only occasionally, floods. The total area of the SSSI is a little over 80 ha.

At 35 ha, the part of Wareham Common of interest for this book still looks rather grand in its own way. But it was ruthlessly, if inevitably, divided into two sections by the bypass that was built in 1973. I only made a detailed study of the 15 ha area between the bypass to the north and the splendid Saxon town wall (built to exclude presumptuous Vikings) to the south.

This area provides one of the oddest approaches to any nature reserve that I have encountered: a walk northwards from the car park atop the western wall. Where the western wall turns east to form the northern wall, all of Wareham Common comes into view from a first-class vantage point. There is even a bench. A slightly tricky walk down the wall and through a gate will bring you to the southern edge of this part of the Common. The river is close at this point.

Wareham is well supplied with rivers: a little too well on occasions. The one to the south of the town is the Frome, the very same river that flows through the valley one mile to the south-west of Hog Cliff, 28 km to the west. To the north, and the one that runs through Wareham Common, is the Piddle. The name of this river deserves an explanation. There are a few possibilities, but it is usually thought to be a polite derivation rather than a vulgar one, originating in the word *pydel*, for a marsh or fen. By contrast, and as an irresistible aside, Shitterton, a mere seven miles away, has no such get out of jail card, its name being a reference to the aromatic open sewer that once graced its high street. For once in their lives, those residents who take no pride in the name drop their 'h'.

As noted, Wareham Common wetlands are more extensive than the relatively small area I looked at. Indeed, Wareham is surrounded by similar habitats, such as those at Priory Meadows to the south of the town and a continuation of the floodplain to the east. The species-rich areas to the north of the Common are all characterised by being very *low* lowland wetlands indeed, with the heights above sea level ranging from zero to 1 m, with the meadows managing a couple of metres.

Poole Harbour is almost immediately to the east of Wareham, and tidal influences inevitably affect the rivers and the land around them. On a visit during the summer of 2024 I saw obvious evidence of serious flooding in the form of thousands of small and dead freshwater snails stranded on (now) dry land. I was told by a local that this area had been a lake just a few weeks previously. The flooding seemed to have done little damage (snails aside), and no doubt it has been flooded many times over the years. However, it has been a problem for grazing animals and deer. In the same year, my wife took the train through the lowlands to the west of Wareham when they were flooded further upstream, and she saw large herds of deer stranded on small islands of exposed grass.

As with very nearly every location described in this book, Wareham Common contains more than one habitat. The Frome brings base-rich (calcareous) waters from the chalk hills, while the catchment area is naturally acidic from the sands and clays of the Bagshot Beds. This has produced a great deal of variation in soil conditions, themselves moderated by variations in local hydrologies. This has enabled the site to develop those different community types. The floodplains themselves are classified as 'wet neutral meadows'.

THE PLANTS OF WAREHAM COMMON

My selected patch just to the north of the town wall was very wet, but with a dryish path running east–west. I was pleased with the three dozen or so species I found. Many were common enough, but others were wetland specialists. The usual suspects on wetlands were there, chiefly **Water Mint**, **Brooklime**, *Veronica beccabunga*, **Marsh Horsetail**, *Equisetum palustre*, **Greater Water Dock**, *Rumex hydrolapathum*, **Reed Canary Grass**, *Phalaris arundinacea*, **Yellow Flag Iris**, *Iris pseudacorus*, and **Cuckoo Flower**, also known as Lady's Smock, with **Hemlock Water-dropwort,** *Oenanthe crocata*, dominating the edge of the path. This last plant is deadly poisonous and extremely common in wet areas of southern and western Britain. I was delighted to find a substantial gall on one of them. It formed on the 'rays' that supported the floret umbels. Unfortunately, no amount of research has revealed the name of the organism that caused its manufacture. Other Water-dropworts, particularly **Tubular Water-dropwort**, *O. fistulosa*, are mentioned as being present in Wareham Common's SSSI citation.

In addition, there were also a couple of sedges, two rushes and the astonishing relative of Bullrushes, the **Branched Bur-reed**, *Sparganium erectum*. I found a few less common species typical of wetlands: **Amphibious Bistort**, *Persicaria amphibia*, **Blue Water Speedwell**, *Veronica anagallis-aquatica*, **Fen Bedstraw**, *Galium uliginosum*, and a **Water Starwort**, *Callitriche* sp., though the last of these is a species complex and sometimes rendered as *Callitriche stagnalis* agg. Amphibious Bistort I considered my best find, as it is relatively rare.

Two more I found that I must mention are **Marsh Marigold** and **Crested Dog's-tail**. Neither, in itself, is particularly notable, but together and combined with other indicator species, they suggest the NVC classification of 'MG8 Crested dog's-tail — Marsh-marigold grassland'.

Some uncommon plant species have been recorded by a friend, who found them in the ditches throughout the Common: the sedge, **Floating Club-rush**, *Eleogiton fluitans*, **Whorl-grass**,

Catabrosa aquatica, and **Arrowhead**, *Sagittaria sagittifolia*.[30] All are rare, and the Floating Club-rush is exceedingly rare in England, except in Cumbria, the far south-west and the central south coast. Arrowhead is the most conspicuous and has effectively been given the same name three times. It is quite a beauty, with a very distinctive arrow shape to its above-water leaves. The submerged leaves are vaguely grass-like. Very few British plant species have only three petals, most of them, like the Arrowhead, in the water-plantain family, the Alismataceae. Its petals are white, with a distinct purple spot at their base.

Since this area of water meadow is so rich, I investigated further by asking a local naturalist who had published an annotated and very long illustrated list. The three that stood out were **Common Cudweed**, *Filago vulgaris*, **River Water-dropwort**, *Oenanthe fluviatilis*, and **Subterranean Clover**, *Trifolium subterraneum*. The last of these was on the slightly acidic grass bank alongside the bypass and thus does not really count but is nevertheless too interesting to pass by. The flowers of Subterranean Clover are white, with faint, radiating pink lines. It has acquired its odd name from its odd habit of burying its own seeds in the ground – 'drilling' in agricultural terms. It is missing from most of Britain, and chiefly coastal from Cornwall and eastwards round to King's Lynn, with the highest population centred around the New Forest. Despite its rarity in the wild, it is planted as a fodder crop in some parts of the world, including in Britain, as it is able to tolerate soils of low fertility.

I have belaboured this list of plants a little, but it is good to know that the rarer species are not in fact extinct, just rare!

THE BIRDS OF WAREHAM COMMON

Grasslands alone are sufficiently engaging to fill many lifetimes of study. However, they are also home to larger organisms such as mammals, reptiles and birds, most of which I have neglected unless they impact the grasslands directly – sheep and badgers, for example. All 'higher' animals depend entirely on plants, or on other animals that depend on plants, and plants occur in a particular habitat, so there is clearly a connection. However, I here break the mould of the other chapters, telling a little more about the higher animals – in this case, the birds.

Wareham Common and other nearby areas are among the very few large areas in Britain of permanent grasslands adjacent to an overall estuarine system. As such, Wareham Common is a first-class site for wildfowl that over-winter there and for waders that feed and roost there. Several birds have warranted a mention in the SSSI citation.[31] Even at Wareham Common the birds have declined in species variety and number, following a regrettable countrywide pattern of loss. Two birds mentioned in the SSSI description as being of significance have, sadly, not been recorded there for years: the Black-tailed Godwit and the Dunlin.

The recording of bird species is something I have never attempted, and I have great admiration for those willing to stand in lay-bys in January with binoculars in hand and a tripod-mounted camera bearing a lens that cost as much as a brand-new, medium-range car.

Since birds have the annoying habit of flying around, the area in which they have been recorded on (or above) Wareham Common in fact encompasses most of the adjoining areas, including a part of Wareham itself. One hundred and forty-four species have been recorded from this broad area. This is over a fifth of the species on the British list of 640.

Unlike plants, fungi and, to some extent, invertebrates, all of which are either there or not, birds can be difficult to link to a particular location. Many on the list are 'fly-overs' and easy to discount unless they are of particular interest. Some are known to be migratory, but are they just passing through? The gold standard, however, is when they breed at a particular location. However, this needs to be *observed*, something that is seldom easily accomplished. Some of the observed birds were known to breed nearby and receive the benefit of the doubt. These matters are no doubt familiar to all ornithologists, but anathema to your author, who prefers species that stay in one place.

As with the other 'big lists' in the book, I will provide a condensed version, largely ignoring birds that depend on trees and those that are common more or less everywhere. I have also omitted the Latin names to aid clarity. Most of the records are within the last ten years, with a handful that are historic. The bulk of the included species have a strong habitat-based relationship with the wetlands, so expect a lot of ducks.

Four geese were recorded – **Barnacle Goose**, **Greylag Goose**, **Canada Goose** and **Egyptian Goose**. The Barnacle Goose was seen only once – in the late 1990s, in company with six Canada Geese, a sad story that means it can hardly be described as native to the Common.

The **Egyptian Goose** is a denizen of grasslands, consuming grass and seeds, so clearly connects by habitat to the broader Common. It breeds in this country, with populations along the south coast and a large area around the Thames and East Anglia. The RSPB reports nearly two thousand breeding pairs in the UK, though they have not been seen to breed on the Common.

The **Mute Swan** is common here, with breeding pairs, though it is a long time since the similar but smaller **Bewick's Swan** made an appearance. It is now on several lists, with its UK Birds of Conservation Concern status being red.

Sticking with the Family that contains swans and geese, the Anatidae, it is the turn of the promised ducks, of which there are eight species recorded. They are the **Shelduck**, **Mandarin**,

Shoveler, Gadwall, Mallard, Teal, Goosander and **Coot**. A few of these breed here occasionally, and the Mallard frequently and regularly, with no fewer than seventy-four found on one day.

I have long had a place in my otherwise ornithologically hard heart for the **Lapwing**, a bird that has been seen occasionally on the Common. My connection with it began many years ago, when I would see them congregating in the fields in the area that is now the new town of Poundbury in Dorset. This bird feeds on pasture, wet grasslands and arable land, consuming invertebrates from the soil. It is not because of the building of Poundbury that this sight is no longer there to delight, but because of a change in the sowing times of arable crops in the former fields. The related **Little Ringed Plover** has also been seen on occasions on the Common.

Six riverine/wetland birds have been seen: **Snipe, Spoonbill** (though very rarely), **Heron, Kingfisher, Dipper** and the rare visitor the **Glossy Ibis**. (The last time I saw a Dipper it was between the jaws of a friend's repulsive Siamese cat.)

Four species bear habitat-specific names: the **Meadow Pipit**, which is not known to breed there, despite appearing in large numbers, the **Sedge Warbler**, seen only on migration, the **Reed Warbler** and the **Reed Bunting**. The last two of these are known to breed there. Both Warblers consume insects, spiders and berries, the Reed Bunting living on seeds and invertebrates in the warmer months and the seeds of arable land in the winter.

The Common also houses six of Britain's nine corvid species: the **Jackdaw, Magpie, Jay, Rook, Carrion Crow** and **Raven**; two owls – the **Barn Owl** and **Tawny Owl**; seven gulls plus the **Cormorant**; eleven birds of prey – the **Sparrowhawk, Goshawk, Marsh Harrier, Hen Harrier, Red Kite, Buzzard, Kestrel, Merlin, Hobby, Peregrine Falcon** and, a true fly-in, a single, young **White-tailed Eagle** flying over the West Wall in the late morning of 7 September 2020, with 'Ravens in hot pursuit!', as the lucky recorder tells it.

One more bird: the **Hoopoe**. This was seen in April 2020 at the base of the North West Walls, then disappearing over the houses in Wareham. I would love to see a Hoopoe in Britain as it is one of the most beautiful of all birds and comes with the very best of all the Latin names given to a vertebrate: *Upupa epops*, the name of the Hoopoe hero in Aristophanes' comedy *The Birds*, a play which we must also thank for the term 'Cloud-cuckoo-land'.

Northern Calcareous Grasslands

I hesitated to include another downland, but this site is so exquisite that I could not resist. Anyway, it differs from Hog Cliff in several ways. One is that Hog Cliff is much lower, running from 120 m to 180 m, whereas Deep Dale starts above this height, from 220 m to 310 m. This is reflected in the weather, with the nearby town of Buxton, often known as the highest and coldest of England's market towns, both considerably wetter and much colder than Dorset. Deep Dale is also not on chalk: it is on limestone. Together these factors have resulted in a different community type from the CG2a/b/c found at Hog Cliff: CG2d, the '*Dicranum scoparium* sub-community'. The named species is the Broom Forkmoss and is almost entirely absent from the other three communities. Informally Deep Dale is classed as a 'dry limestone dale', of which there are several others from Derbyshire through to Yorkshire.

DEEP DALE, DERBYSHIRE

I have been to Buxton many times over the years, invariably staying in the very grand Palace Hotel. When I first visited the hotel, it had the feel of Miss Havisham's dining room, though with fresh food, but has since been spruced up, though the gilded whirls and swirls that are too difficult and expensive to restore appear to have been painted over. Along the road a few miles eastwards of the hotel is Deep Dale Nature Reserve.

The primary areas of interest are the very steep slopes. The one I surveyed was a 28° – and a considerable challenge when

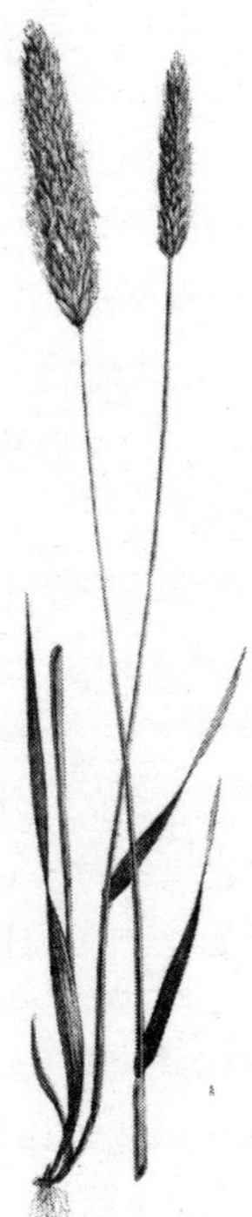

Meadow Foxtail

exploration of anything above the bottom path was required. It did, however, possess stock-made terracettes that had formed sloping tracks. The landscape is one of limestone, with a thin layer of soil on the slopes and deeper superficial deposits on the tops and at the bottoms of the valleys. The valley bottoms were more species-rich than those at Hog Cliff, owing in part to the ploughing the latter has received in the past.

As with most steeply sloped valley sides, the plants are taller and most closely packed at the bottom and progressively thinning at the top. The most noticeable characteristic of this landscape is the preponderance of limestone outcrops. Visually, this was the most impressive place I visited in my research, one of grand beauty and profound peace.

The leafy area of relatively coarse grassland before I reached the path along the valley bottom housed several species. The first was a patch of tall plants that had overwhelmed the surrounding grass: a mass of splendid **Musk Mallow**, *Malva moschata*, **Meadow Crane's-bill**, *Geranium pratense*, along with straggling **Field Rose**, *Rosa arvensis*, and a background of contrasting **Common Ragwort** which it might have been better without but nevertheless added to the colour palate.

Up a nearby bank that supported a straggling hedge were several large patches of an *Alchemilla* species. As mentioned elsewhere, these are notoriously difficult to identify to species, but a best guess – one that took a couple of hours with loupe and book to make – is that it was *A. filicaulis*.

The trackside along the valley bottom had the typical plants one would expect – Bramble, more Ragwort and coarse grasses, with scrub and scrubby woodland to the north-west of the path. One of the most surprising plants in the scrubby woodland was a 'rose tree'. This was a Field Rose with a trunk that was an extraordinary 10 cm in diameter. I also noticed **Raspberry**, *Rubus idaeus*, reflecting the scrubland's acidic nature. The steep limestone slope rose immediately up to the south-east from the narrow path.

The bottom of the slope where rocks were exposed and soil partially bare was more productive, with **Oxeye Daisy** and **Wild Marjoram**, *Origanum vulgare*. The latter is a common and very attractive plant, especially just before the flowers open. It is found in calcareous areas wherever the bedrock is very close to the surface. The ubiquitous **Maidenhair Spleenwort**, *Asplenium trichomanes*, was also present.

The sward that covered the slopes was scattered with **Hazel** and **Hawthorn**. No doubt these are kept under control, though they look as though they are ready for a takeover bid. As I mentioned, the plants were typical of calcareous soils, and most are also to be found at Hog Cliff, including the **Common Rock-rose**.

There were also a handful of pleasant surprises such as the hemiparasitic **Yellow Rattle**. The most attractive plant was **Columbine**, *Aquilegia vulgaris*, a relatively uncommon beauty. A few headline species that I did not see, but which are mentioned in various public descriptions of the site, include **Early Purple Orchid**, **Wild Clary**, **Mountain Pansy**, **Meadow Saxifrage**, the rare **Mossy Saxifrage** and **Dark Red Helleborine**. Respectively, their Latinised names are *Orchis mascula*, *Salvia verbenaca*, *Viola lutea*, *Saxifraga granulata*, *Saxifraga hypnoides* and *Epipactis atrorubens*.[32] The saxifrages are typical of limestone areas, sometimes forming large mats of flowers among the rocks. The Mountain Pansy is a slight outlier here as it is typical of more acid conditions. Therefore I have little doubt that it was recorded on the more acidic top above the calcareous slopes.

These brief stories of the various types of grassland show the huge diversity that lies behind the broad definition of 'semi-natural grasslands'. It is not, of course, a complete list: many, many more examples could have been included. But even these brief glimpses reveal hundreds of species in a variety of landscapes and show that few grasslands stand alone: each exists within a mosaic of interacting communities.

We tend to form a bond with places that we visit and which impress us – almost a sense of ownership. The above grasslands are, in a way, *my* grasslands, though they could be yours too. And, of course, it is a perfectly simple matter to find your own 'pastures new'.

When we develop that sense of ownership, it comes with a sense of responsibility. It may be expressed in as small a gesture as not littering (or picking up others' rubbish), or it may push you to fight for the protection of 'your' grassland against the forces of destruction. In other words, beyond admiring and enjoying grasslands, there is more that can be done: become involved in restoring a grassland, or even create a new one. This is the subject of Part Five.

Part Five

A (HOPEFUL) FUTURE OF GRASSLANDS

Restoration of Grasslands

The great losses we saw in Part One over the last one hundred years continue still, though at a greatly reduced rate – at least partly because there is very little left to lose. Often this is a matter of ignorance of what is at stake, sometimes a matter of *wilful* ignorance – these are 'just patches of grass', after all. Having lost so much, it is now time to look after what is left and begin to create new grasslands that will dazzle the eye and buzz with life.

It is encouraging, then, that attempts are now being made to restore those that have been damaged by poor grazing regimes, the application of inorganic fertiliser and simple abandonment.

Rewilding by private individuals with either land to spare or money to buy it is taking something of a lead in this – though there is the potential for problems if the rewilder feels that planting everything with trees is the right course of action or believes that 'leaving it to nature' produces an exquisite natural landscape. Should you decide to spend your millions on such a project, do make use of the services of a professional who knows what he or she is talking about, and not just someone with bright ideas.

There are endless encouragements through subsidies and grants to improve privately owned land if the owner is prepared to face the paperwork involved and the restrictions that will apply. Government bodies, acting under various directives and their own natural inclination, are restoring grasslands that they have bought outright. Wildlife Trusts and various other charities do the same.

There are even moves to transform arable land on suitable sites into species-rich grasslands, and I have had some small involvement in this on a recent extension of the Hog Cliff National Nature Reserve in my own parish. This project will serve as an example of how a major grassland restoration might be accomplished and we will return to it later in this chapter.

This is not the place to give finely detailed advice on how restorations or reintroductions of long-lost communities might be made; it is just an overview of the methods involved. However, it is an interesting and varied process, and the on-the-ground practicalities are worth relating in general. The possibilities are 'sward enhancement', more general restoration such as weed control and scrub clearance, and the 'blank slate' approach.

SWARD ENHANCEMENT

This is possible and worthwhile on land that is poorer in species than might be hoped, and which is largely free of weeds. The first step is to remove those perennial weeds that might still be there. This should be achieved by wiping or spot treatment. Since perennial weeds are generally taller than the desired plants, herbicides can literally be wiped directly onto them without fear of damaging other plants. This can be achieved with a hand-held, T-shaped tool with a herbicide-saturated rope held by fixings at both ends of the tee. Although this can be useful for small patches and individual weeds, a wheeled, tractor-drawn wiper that uses a long brush is required for anything more. Spot spraying, preferably with targeted herbicides, is sometimes possible where there is little chance of damaging welcome plants. With heavy weed infestations, removal of the dead weeds is necessary to avoid a thatch and the release of nutrients from subsequent rotting. Since there is likely to be a large seedbank in the soil, the regrowth of weeds will need to be addressed over several years. After the first application of weedkiller and removal of the dead material, the soil will need a little preparation.

The two methods of sowing, 'over-sowing' and 'slot-seeding', require different schemes of preparation. For the former, the best way is to graze the land very intensively so that about half of the ground is bare soil. This is the charmingly named 'hoof and tooth' method, with cattle preferred unless the ground is wet, when sheep can be used. A powered harrow or disc set is an alternative, but the soil disturbance can increase fertility and encourage any seedbank of weeds.

For the alternative of 'slot seeding' you will need some serious kit. The land requires less soil preparation, though the weeds must still be dealt with. It must be grazed close, then allowed to grow a little. Shallow grooves about 60 cm apart are cut in the soil and the seeds sown.

For both methods, seeds should be sown in late summer to mid-September. In the first year the grazing of pasture should be very light from late spring to summer. In a meadow the cut should be later than is usual: that is, after mid-July. An eye should be kept on the weeds – they never leave without a struggle.

GENERAL IMPROVEMENT OF AN ESTABLISHED SPECIES-RICH GRASSLAND

Many species-rich grasslands are still species-rich; they are just neglected. Under-grazing, over-grazing, wrong type of stock, lack of weed control and the ingress of scrub: these are the day-to-day concerns of those managing such grasslands.

Grazing animals may be a pleasure to watch, and they are essential for most grasslands. However, it is a great deal of work for those who manage them, with some intervention required nearly every day. On nature reserves, arrangements need to be made with a local farmer to take on the grazing. This can be difficult at the best of times, but when the reserve has difficult access or is small in size it can be nearly impossible. An appropriate grazing regime will be needed if poor grazing has been the problem. Reseeding may be required, but it is not something I have seen a great deal of outside of 'blank-slate' situations.

Scrub is often highly beneficial when adjacent to grasslands but can easily take over a site if left unchecked. It is a permanent management issue, not one reserved for neglected grasslands, so this small section applies generally.

The general principle is to decide on where the scrub should be retained and how large it should be allowed to become. When a cut-back area of shrub has grown to its designated limit, it is cut back again. How often scrub should be cut back is a matter of what you want. If the intention is eradication, then 'as often as it takes' is the only way. If the aim is to cut back the spreading shrubs and the leading edge of tall herbs and grasses, then ten years is often suggested.

On occasions I see work being done to keep scrub under control. This involves cutting the scrub at ground level and burning the brash in the cleared area. It must absolutely not be on any grassy areas, something that must have happened with inexperienced or unthinking teams. With large areas it may be necessary to have it removed from the site, something that potentially has the advantage of retaining any suspected seedbanks of desired plants.

It may be policy, as was the case with Hog Cliff, that some areas of scrub should be returned to grassland. Manual removal and grazing are often mentioned as alternative approaches, but in practice both are used.[1] Recently I saw that a few shrubs had been sprayed with herbicide and left to die. This, at least, prevents regrowth from the roots, removing a major reason for failure, but it has not been employed for larger areas.

The permanent restoration of grassland from scrub is notoriously difficult. It can be a long process, and one often doomed to fail. Nutrient levels will be higher in newly cleared areas, encouraging ruderal plants such as Ragwort, unwanted thistle species and the more vigorous grasses. Ideally, these will be kept in check, with dead material removed to reduce fertility. Nearby plants that produce runners can sometimes re-establish some of the desired grassland plants. There is likely to be an abundance of seeds immediately to hand, but seed dispersal in grasslands is often very poor and they may need to be resown using the methods described below. Seeds and seeding are described shortly.

ARABLE REVERSION – THE BLANK SLATE

If, as in the heavily farmed areas of the Hog Cliff Extension (discussed later), there is nothing remotely worth saving, a blank slate approach is the only possibility. Often a truly blank slate will need to be created by spraying the land with herbicide and ploughing/harrowing etc. and rolling. Unless the area under consideration has a known history of the hoped-for habitat having existed in the past, it cannot truly be described as 'restoration': hence 'arable reversion'.

Whichever grassland type is to be introduced or reintroduced, it must, of course, be feasible for the geology, soil and climate available. There is no point attempting a flood meadow on top of a chalk hill, or an upland hay meadow in Suffolk. These are obvious impossibilities, but the much-repeated list of precise considerations is long. They are the pH, nutrient levels and hydrology of the soil, rainfall, climate, slope and geographical position. If any of these is unsuitable for the project in hand, it is likely to fail expectations. Fortunately, and with a little thought, it is usually a simple matter to decide what is required and whether the proposed site for restoration is appropriate: consider what is in the area already.

DEALING WITH NUTRIENT LEVELS

Again the pH and nutrient levels will still need to be measured in several locations as they need to be appropriate for the grassland type.

Low nutrient levels are almost invariably required, as those that are high invite weeds that will overwhelm the desired wild flowers and grasses. These levels can be reduced, however, though not easily and seldom quickly. The main method is allowing the land to lie fallow for a year, or maybe two, and cutting the vegetation frequently for a year, alternating the cut with the application of herbicides. All of the cut weeds must be removed from the site. Crucially, the weeds must never be allowed to seed. Preparing the soil and planting it for one year with grasses that are removed for hay will also reduce fertility.

Eventually the perennial weeds themselves must be destroyed. The only short cut to this is spraying them with a herbicide, as the most pernicious weeds have substantial and otherwise intractable roots. Some ecologists baulk at so inorganic a method as herbicides, but they are the most efficient method by far on land that contains only, or mostly, weeds. White Clover, which produces very long-lived seeds, can continue to be a problem whatever one does. For those who are unconvinced, the heavy alternative is to plough every three weeks or so, and perhaps leave the field in furrows over winter.

Another method of nutrient reduction is 'topsoil stripping'. This requires heavy equipment, someone to take the soil away and someone who wants it. Topsoil is in short supply, so the last of these should be easy enough.

Fortunately, nitrogen levels are usually very low in arable land that has long been under the plough, though there is a spike in levels after it is ploughed. Once the spike abates, they are sometimes *too* low and will take a while to recover to the typical levels of traditional pasture. This may be addressed by the application of organic fertilisers such as dung, though a few 'lean years' may be tolerated until a stable soil ecology has been achieved. A low phosphate level is, ultimately, more important than nitrogen, so this must be checked too.

ESTABLISHING A SWARD

The now clean soil is ready to be seeded with the required plants. After all the activity of the previous year or two, the aim is to create a productive seedbed. A roller is the best way to firm it and should result in what the normally humourless ecologists describe as 'something it is possible to ride a bicycle on'.

SEEDS

Which seeds should be planted? If you use the seed-rich 'green hay' as described below, it is just a matter of finding a nearby grassland of the type you hope for and applying this to your land. The choice of seeds is, effectively, made for you. If this is not possible, then bought-in seeds will be needed. If there is a local grassland of the type you require, then find out what is there. If this is not the case, then some research may be needed.

Survey work may be required and suitable plants chosen for the individual conditions, requiring the various ecologies of the plants to be checked. This is all but impossible, but it is worth making some effort to match plant with land. At the very least, pH and hydrology should be considered. At the Derbyshire Meadow, for example, Bistort only occurs at the wet bottom of the slope, and an arable reversion of such a site would be wasting its time and money if it attempted the introduction of Bistort to the top.

There is information on what once grew where to be found in the local records, or (less precisely) in such books as the *Plant Atlas 2020*, by Peter Stroh et al. A further possibility is to find historical books on individual areas and see what had been found in the area in the past. Such books are usually county-based: in Dorset, for example, the go-to authority is Ronald Good, who wrote *A Geographical Handbook of the Dorset Flora*, published in 1948. He explored much of the county over many years, and the book can make heartbreaking reading for those sensitive to the losses we now know to have occurred since his time. Another is *The Flowering Plants of Wiltshire* (1888), by the Rev. T. A. Preston, and I have little doubt that every county will have such a book, and often more than one.

It is worth mentioning that the Local Government Act of 1972 redrew many county boundaries, placing administrative expedience above the often profound sentiments of those that lived within them. Even today biological species records use the pre-1972 boundaries – 'vice counties', as they are called – so it is sometimes necessary to check precisely where a plant was found. Another issue is the names of plants. While the common names are more or less stable, the scientific names are not. They change when any biological species has been reassigned to a different genus, an older name has been resurrected or for a couple of other reasons. These are invariably annoying and only overcome by checking the lists of synonyms available for any species.

There are several well-established companies that supply seeds for these types of project, and I have seen the resultant plants growing very well together in the project at Poundbury in West Dorset and elsewhere.

Do not take any short cuts by buying something cheap and cheerful from the local garden centre as there is little chance that they will be quite what you are hoping for. The specialist seed suppliers for such projects source carefully, ensuring that the resulting plants are suitable for the area of land. Seeds from abroad, for example, even those with the correct Latin name on the sack, will seldom be suitable. All successful plants adapt to local conditions, with phenological matters such as the flowering time being synchronised with those of pollinating invertebrates crucial to the success of any replanting. Even plants from the same country may not be suitable – there is a great difference between the lowlands of Northumberland and those of southern England.

A final note on the use of seeds – they are expensive, and the recommended seed-rate of 15 to 20 kg per hectare will soon eat up the pennies.

GREEN HAY

This is much cheaper than seeds and, because of the narrow window of time between harvesting and spreading, *always* locally sourced. It is simply hay that is cut just before the normal harvesting time, put on a trailer and spread on the bare soil. There are even hand-held, petrol-driven 'vacuum cleaners' available that can be used to collect the green hay. The narrow window – not much more than two or three hours – is due to the lawn-mowing phenomenon where piles of cut grass heat up rapidly within a few hours. This would kill the seeds.

Seeds can also be collected with a 'brush harvester', where a wide, powered, rotary brush simply brushes the seeds into a hopper. They are very effective.

There are also 'plugs' of young plants. Since no one is likely to buy a million plugs to repopulate their field, they are reserved for small areas, or to introduce the more uncommon plants once the basic sward has been established.

There is considerably more to all of the above, such as when to make the first cut, levels and timings of grazing, continued weed removal, the problem with disappointed stock used to a rich banquet of Italian Ryegrass and White Clover, and so on and on.

RESTORATION AND ARABLE REVERSION: AN EXAMPLE FROM DORSET

In my previous book, *The Observant Walker*, one of the walks, known informally as 'the Horseshoe', closely followed the hedges around what was then part of Manor Farm, now the Hog Cliff Extension (HCE).[2] Much of this walk was through a long, narrow, green 'oasis', with swathes of intensively farmed land either side. The path is to the east of the village and west of Hog Cliff.

I was not to know it at the time, but this arable land and its adjoining permanent grasslands were soon to come up for sale. The permanent grasslands consisted of species-rich strip lynchets, and there are some substantial areas of chalk downland and other grasslands of interest, so, thinking matters might be made worse rather than better, I was a little worried who might buy it and for what.

As it happened, it became another open-the-bottle moment, the bottle being that of the Château Rothschild 1998 that an old friend had given me by mistake. Natural England bought the lot in 2023. And they have a plan.

Much of the surviving species-rich land is on the slopes where the chalk is not overlaid by clay and flint, major parts of them being the 400 m of chalky strip lynchets and the coombe of chalk downland to the south, the steeper areas of which have not seen the plough for millennia.

It is gratifying, and very surprising, that Natural England included those several large arable fields in their purchase that had been under the plough for years; indeed, most of what is now a nature reserve then consisted of intensively farmed land. Most recently, some fields were engaged in the regrettable production of maize for biofuel and were in a poor state. A friend in the village who takes a profound interest in the local natural history told me what he saw in one of the fields just after the area had been secured for the nation: 'It looks like a beach!' Repeated ploughing and run-off from over-exposed soil had left just flint with the occasional area of clay.

The field that constituted this 6 ha 'beach' must seem like a poor investment, but it does have a clear rationale: it joins Hog Cliff to the new extension, providing a wildlife corridor. It also allows energetic people to walk the nearly two miles from the village to the far reaches of Hog Cliff without leaving a nature reserve. I, of course, am delighted with this as forty-five years ago, when it was permanent pasture, I used to walk the linking field, watching and (mostly) listening to the Skylarks hovering anxiously high above. It is also where my wife trod on that pheasant.

At the time of writing, the heavy work of erecting fences, gates, signposts and information boards that comes with every such project is completed and restoration is well under way, with the arable fields mostly and variously planted up and the grazing improved on the strip lynchets and the coombe.

THE PLAN

There are nine of what could very loosely be called 'fields'. They are shown in the map on p. 314. Anonymous as they were, all have been provided with a name linked to the history of each.

The established grasslands that lie directly on the chalk are **Lynchets** and **Bowl** (both strip lynchets) and **Langcombe Hill** (the coombe valley sides) which are being restored through scrub clearance and improved grazing. Duke of Burgundy butterflies

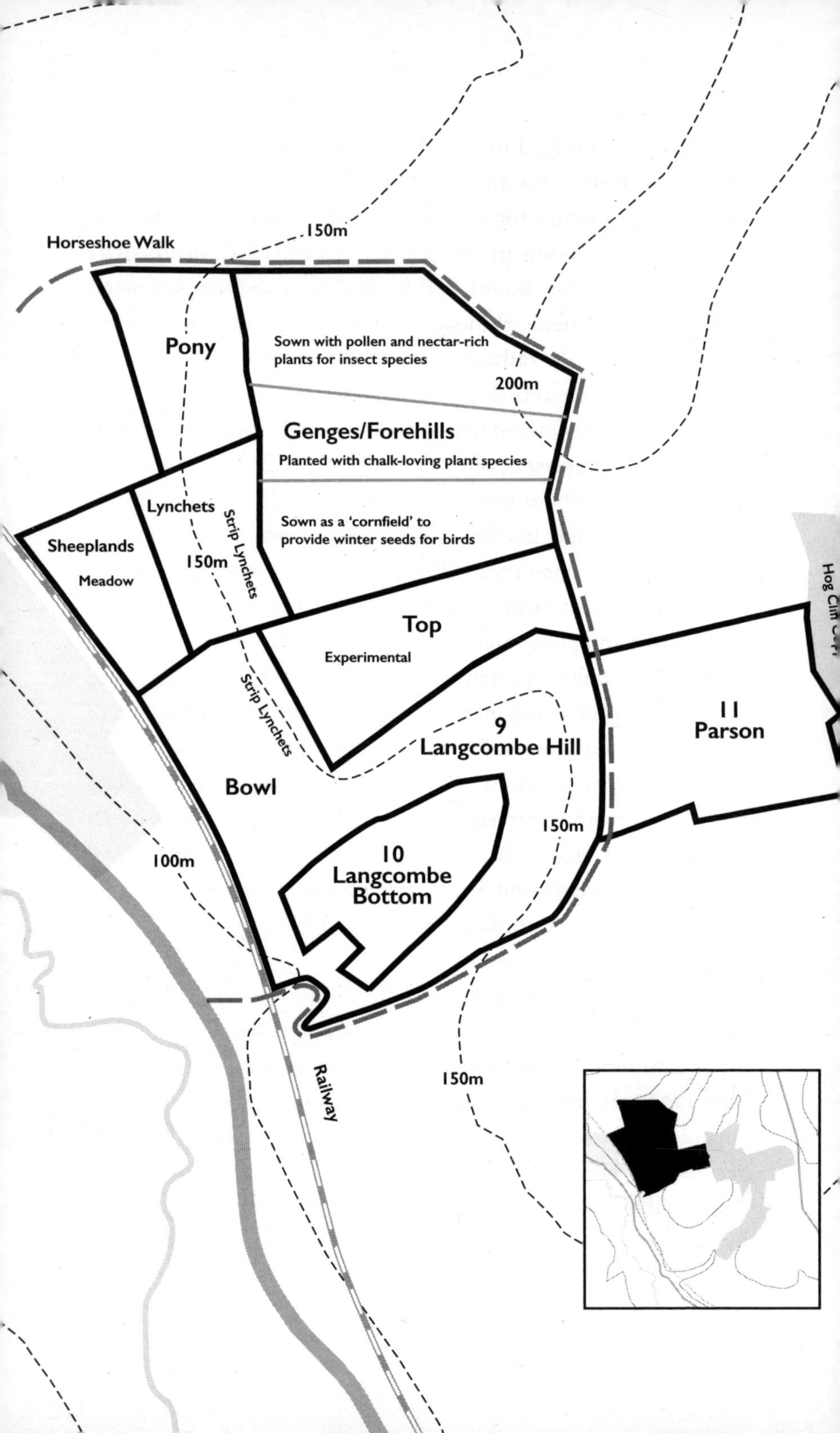

Horseshoe Walk
150m
Pony
Sown with pollen and nectar-rich plants for insect species
200m
Genges/Forehills
Planted with chalk-loving plant species
Lynchets
Sheeplands
Meadow
Strip Lynchets
150m
Sown as a 'cornfield' to provide winter seeds for birds
Top
Experimental
Hog Clm Corr
Strip Lynchets
9
Langcombe Hill
11
Parson
Bowl
150m
10
Langcombe Bottom
100m
Railway
150m

have been encouraged by planting plugs of Cowslips, its larval food plant. **Pony**, also directly on the chalk, was once ploughed but has been pasture for several years. It has been left for more careful sheep grazing in the hope that a richer plant diversity might ensue. This leaves arable reversions of the formerly ploughed hilltop fields, the low-lying field below the coombe, and a small field near the railway line.

These fields are mostly clay-with-flints territory and unsuitable for a chalk downland flora. However, some of them now have a substantial component of chalk in what passes for soil, perhaps from the heavy ploughing and loss of clay due to soil erosion.

The 16 ha field known as **Genges/Forehills** acquired its awkward name when two fields were joined as one, *c.* 1900. The central 40 per cent of this field has been prepared and sown with chalk downland plants and will, in time, be grazed.

All of the fields that required sowing received a commercial mix made up of brush-harvested seeds with an 80:20 ratio of grasses and wild flowers. For this chalky area the mix comprised nine species of grass, with Timothy and two Bent grasses dominating, and nineteen wild flower species. All but one of these occur at Hog Cliff, the odd one out being Wild Carrot, *Daucus carota*. Devil's-bit Scabious seeds were sourced elsewhere, introduced as the foodplant of the Marsh Fritillary, a butterfly that is struggling at Hog Cliff.

The northern strip of Genges/Forehill has been planted for nectar and pollen to attract insect species. The species mix comprises Common Vetch, Sainfoin, Crimson Clover, Alsike Clover, Lucerne, Red Clover, Bird's-Foot Trefoil, Oxeye Daisy, Common Knapweed, Yarrow and Wild Carrot. The first seven are all in the Pea Family, with the first five of these being non-native, all of them used by farmers as fodder and soil improvers.

Together they form an odd mix of natural and agricultural

wild flowers, and I was slightly stunned when I first saw it in its summer glory. Nevertheless, this was never meant to be natural, just useful for insects and those that prey on them. Anyway, the field is lovely to behold and vastly better than what was there before: maize.

The southern strip in this large field is effectively a type of cornfield, but one with a difference. The cornfield mix of Field Poppy, Cornflower, Corn Marigold, Corn Cockle and Corn Chamomile was supplemented with Sunflower, Kale, Linseed, Quinoa and Spring Triticale, a hybrid of wheat and rye. This too was a stunning sight, especially the Sunflowers back-lit against the setting sun.

The point of this extremely odd collection is to provide winter feed for birds, with the plants left uncut in the field. It is, effectively, a vast bird-table. A friend of mine who has been deeply involved in the whole project jokingly mentioned that they are slightly worried about over-wintering rats, but said there is enough food for bird and rat alike. I pointed out that the rats (and birds) will eventually run out of food and thirty thousand hungry rats might descend on the village. We will see.

Top is the field to the south of Genges/Forehills and is left as something of an experiment to see what might appear. Its eastern edge was left fallow for a year or two prior to Natural England's purchase and has been yellow with Common Ragwort ever since. Sheep grazing will clear this to an acceptable level. Topping is likely too. Again, we will see.

Sheeplands is a barely 1 ha field next to the railway line. It has been planted as a meadow, with twenty-nine wild flowers, seven grasses and Glaucous Sedge. It seemed like a foreign country when I followed the path that runs across it early in the dry August of 2025. By this time the vegetation was high and mostly out of flower and in seed, an unfamiliar sight in meadows.

Black medick

The Wild Carrots were going strong and almost everywhere, with one Wild Parsnip for every hundred Wild Carrots, the parsnips being uninvited guests. One of them had yet to open its florets and presented a spray of pink/purple gems. Fabergé would have been astonished at its delicacy. Its photograph is on Plate 2. With all of these projects, the plants themselves will provide seed for the next year and beyond. At Sheeplands, Black Medick, which is usually just a few centimetres tall but here around 90 cm, had produced copious quantities of seed. Both my knowledgeable friend and I wondered if it had grown from seed originating in continental Europe.

The lowest field is **Langcombe Bottom**, held within the curved embrace of Langcombe Hill. At the time of writing its future is undecided, but it has been mooted as some sort of wetland to absorb run-off, this idea no doubt stimulated by the less than attractive sewage works at is western edge.

Unlike all the other fields, **Parson's Hill** is to the east of the footpath, the 'Horseshoe', that encompasses the rest. As noted, it was bought for the purpose of joining the reserve to Hog Cliff, albeit to the woodland known as Parson's Coppice. Bar the intervening footpath, this provides some continuity between the two reserves and may help reduce species loss from isolation.

Reflecting the woodlands to the east and the grasslands to the west, it is to be planted with a pasture mix *and* native trees to form a wood pasture. While I hope there will be some pollarded oaks, the plan is to plant fruit-bearing trees such as Crab Apple, Wild Damson, Bullace and maybe Wild Pear. Before any such planting could occur, Parson's Hill required deer fencing and clearing of weeds. At the time of writing it is a monoculture of Ryegrass, which will be cut and removed to reduce the fertility.

The overall plan is hugely exciting, but how well has it fared? I would say very well, but the desired pastures, downlands and meadow take a long while to settle, with the plants fighting it out among themselves. There have been few upsets, such as the scattering of seeds rather than slot-drilling them, weeds introduced by tractor tyres, a contractor from next door turning his machinery at the top of Genges/Forehills, resulting in a huge patch of the decidedly ruderal Scentless Mayweed that had previously contented itself with growing along the path. Some seeds, notably Devil's-bit Scabious, did not grow well. Ribwort

Plantain grew too well, all too clearly marking out the drilling lines. Grasses, despite being planted in vast numbers, struggled to a surprising degree.

It is, then, early days, but a truly wonderful experiment that I trust will succeed and become a model for other such noble efforts. There has been local involvement with children from the primary school planting trees, and the thoughtful arrangement of pathways and shiny new farm gates has encouraged walkers.

CORNFIELDS

There is no shortage of cornfields in the UK, but of the many thousands that exist very few are the cornfields of old, those that once sported splendid displays of wild plants.

Cornfields are *not* permanent grasslands, though they can be species-rich and arguably semi-natural in that the plants for which they are valued arrived there via no human intent. Nevertheless, I pondered a long time whether or not they should be included in this book. My argument for their inclusion is that they *are* grasslands: ephemeral ones made up entirely of annual plants. They also represent a highly significant historic loss of plant species, with many formerly common plants now languishing on those grim lists that tell us how endangered they are.

With a cornfield or any arable field, one starts anew each year with the plough. It will contain no perennial plants as ploughing destroys them. Grasses other than those sown may be found in traditional cornfields as 'weeds', though they will all be annuals — there was even an annual species of the ubiquitous Sweet Vernal Grass found in such cornfields — Annual Vernal Grass, now virtually extinct. Such fields are seen elsewhere in the world, and I saw a few in Lazio in Italy in 2024. They were blindingly bright with flowers. We need them back.

Some of these plants bear their habitat in their name: Corn Spurrey, Corncockle, Corn Marigold, Corn Buttercup, Corn Gromwell, Corn Chamomile, Broad-fruited Cornsalad and Cornflower. All of these plants and many more are rare, because traditional cornfields are rare.

Traditional cornfields have been declining since the beginning of the agricultural revolution. There had been moderate 'improvement' since the mid-nineteenth century, but it was in the 1940s that the revolution truly began, most notably as a result of the 1947 Agriculture Act, itself due to a determination that Britain become self-sufficient in food.[3] Its implementation was through capital grants, price control and the heavy hand of the Ministry of Agriculture that induced farmers to 'improve' their land and farming practices.

Aided by huge technological advances in agriculture, the plan was highly successful. In 1940 the wheat yield in the UK was 2 tonnes per hectare; now it is 8 tonnes. As a matter of context, *c*. 1400 it was half a tonne per hectare, rising to 1 tonne by 1700.[4] We should always think *very* carefully when we complain about agricultural improvement, but perhaps we could 'sacrifice' some land to the reintroduction of grasslands teeming with life.

Other factors in their loss include a massive decline in mixed farming, resulting in a correspondingly dramatic loss of interaction between arable and pastoral. Smaller farms became no more than a memory and are now only represented by smallholdings.

Approximately 120 wild plant species have been associated with cornfields. Some are common, with the Common Poppy, *Papaver rhoeas*, being (now) the best-known and, it seems, the last to leave the building. Some weed species still appear despite the heroic efforts of farmers – the Wild Oat, *Avena fatua*, which conspicuously towers above the present dwarf varieties of corn,

Cleavers, *Galium aparine*, Blackgrass, *Alopecurus myosuroides*, and several more.

In a remarkable list produced by Plantlife, fifty-four species of cornfield plants that are occasional or rare are described, with their conservation status noted. The list is for plants of interest in Britain and says nothing of their conservation status elsewhere in the world.

The most commonly used system of denoting conservation status, the International Union for Conservation of Nature (IUCN) Red List of Threatened Species, categorises plants into five classes. They are LC (least concern), VU (vulnerable), EN (endangered), CR (critical) or EX (extinct). 'LC' seems to be intentionally loaded in that it suggests there is always something to worry about, even though it represents species for which there is little or (most often) no concern: Stinging Nettles and Common Ragwort, for example.

Nevertheless, there is a statistical rationale behind all of these classifications. For example, among the reasons for being characterised as LC are there being a lower than 10 per cent chance of extinction within the next hundred years and the existence of at least 100,000 individuals. The plant should also not have suffered a population loss of more than 50 per cent over the last ten years or over three generations.

Only two species of arable weeds in the Plantlife list are recorded as LC. These are two of the five fumitories: Purple Ramping-fumitory, *Fumaria purpurea*, and Western Ramping-fumitory, *F. occidentalis*. Most of the fifty-four species listed fell into VU and EN, with twenty-three of each. This leaves five that are classed as CR, which means on the edge of extinction, and one that has fallen off the edge – the pretty, dark pink Corncockle, *Agrostemma githago*. Fortunately, the Corncockle was famously rediscovered in Britain and has made a comeback.

Cornflower

The five critically endangered species are Upright Goosefoot, *Chenopodium urbicum*, Red Hemp-nettle, *Galeopsis ladanum* var. *angustifolia*, Corn Buttercup, *Ranunculus arvensis*, Shepherd's-needle, *Scandix pecten-veneris*, and Corn Cleavers, *Galium tricornutum*. All are rare representatives of common groups – goosefoots, buttercups, umbellifers (the Shepherd's-needle), cleavers and hemp nettles.

An unusual-looking species, Ground Pine, *Ajuga chamaepitys*, has yellow flowers, smells of pine and has leaves that make it look a little like a pine tree seedling. It is a close relative of the leafy and very purple Bugle. The only species in the list that I know well is Henbane, *Hyoscyamus niger*. It is in the Nightshade Family, famously toxic and notorious for producing euphoria in anyone mad enough to eat it. It appears every seven or so years in my vegetable patch. It grew this year (2025), and I have saved the seeds.

How easy would it be to introduce species-rich cornfields? Annual plants are seldom concerned with high fertility, so one could be created in any good-quality arable land. There is no problem with the preparation of the soil, as this would be ploughed and harrowed. From the known soil conditions, geography, climate, historical data and using the list supplied by Plantlife it would be a relatively simple task to determine which plants to grow. The main issue is finding the seeds of the rarer species of plants.

The seeds of rare plants are equally rare, and most will be hard to find, with the old corn varieties perhaps impossible to track down. Being optimistic, I envisage a gentle entrepreneur scouring the countryside for the seeds and starting a nursery.

Some projects are under way to reintroduce species-rich cornfields, not least at the Hog Cliff Extension, and some are part of rewilding schemes. There is a very appealing and well-thought-out traditional cornfield in Somerset: Fivehead Arable Fields.

The Somerset Wildlife Trust proudly notes that it contains 'a wide variety of arable weeds, several of which are now nationally scarce'. They list: 'Broad-leaved Spurge, Spreading Hedge-parsley, Narrow-fruited Cornsalad and Slender Tare, Small Toadflax, Dwarf Spurge, Sharp-leaved Fluellen and Round-leaved Fluellen.'[5] Most of these are sister species to well-known plants, with the more obscure Fluellen species being in the Antirrhinum Family.

I wish Somerset Wildlife Trust well with this project, and hope that others will follow their path.

CODA

This book comes late in the day. The pleas it contains should have been made in 1976, not fifty years later, or perhaps 1946 would have been better, though they would then have fallen on ears not ready to hear them, and understandably so. But while most of our ecologically valuable grasslands are lost to us, agricultural subsidies and agreements now almost completely favour the salvation or restoration of grasslands and other semi-wild communities. Government bodies such as Natural England are vigorous in their protection of grasslands, though very many are still missed through limited funding, lack of understanding or simply through people not noticing them. Efforts to reintroduce species-rich grasslands are largely led by the many rewilding projects. For the fungi, my hope is that the neglected fields that harbour few plants but many fungi will be recognised as areas of great biological interest and protected.

Having overcome the upset I felt forty-five years ago when I first learned of the terrible losses that had occurred and continued to occur, I am now very positive. I hope that you are too, but do mention to someone if a treasured piece of land comes under threat. You might well save it.

Glossary

Aftermath The stubble and subsequent regrowing vegetation that becomes available for grazing in a cut meadow.

Angiosperm Any flowering plant.

Arthropods Animals with chitinous exoskeleton, such as insects, spiders and crustaceans.

Ascomycete A member of the Ascomycota, a Division of the Kingdom Fungi.

Ascus (pl. Asci) A structure within an Ascomycete that produces, contains and ejects the spores.

Autotroph An organism that produces the food it needs using photosynthesis.

Basidomycete A member of the Basidiomycota, a Division of the Kingdom Fungi.

Blanket bog Wet moorland underlaid with peat.

Bryophytes Non-vascular, non-flowering plants consisting of mosses, liverworts and hornworts.

Calcareous Pertaining to limestones.

Chamaephytes Plants that produce their perennating buds from just above ground to 25 cm.

Commensalism A relationship between two organisms in which one receives no benefit or harm and the other benefits.

Diploid Having two chromosomes, one from each parent.

Domain The highest categories in the tree of life: the Bacteria, Archaea and Eucaryotes are all Domains.

Enclosure A physical barrier erected to surround a field.

Facultative Behaviour that is employed opportunistically and not necessarily essential for life.

Floret A single flower in an inflorescence.

Generic name The first part of a Latinised name for an organism.

Glaucous A dull greyish blue/green, often seen in grasses, sedges and rushes.

Hemicryptophyte A plant that produces its perennating buds at ground level.

Hemiparasite A plant that obtains some (but not all) of its nutrients from parasitism and some from photosynthesis.

Herbaceous Relating to any non-woody flowering plant, including grasses.

Heterotrophic Relating to an organism that acquires the food it needs from autotrophs or from organisms that have consumed autotrophs.

Improved grassland Grassland that is cultivated using ploughs and fertiliser.

Inclosure Land that has been removed from common ownership and rights.

Inflorescence A flower head consisting of multiple florets.

Instar One of the stages in the development of an arthropod (such as an insect, spider or crustacean).

Kleptoparasitism One organism stealing food from another.

Ley Grassland sown with grass and other plants for pasture or silage for a short period. It is then resown.

Mesotrophic Of moderate fertility.

Microfungus A fungus with a small but not necessarily microscopic fruiting body. Such fungi are usually associated with plants.

Mutualism Interaction between organisms where both benefit.

Mycorrhiza Fungal threads that connect to the roots of a plant in a mutualistic relationship. Can be prefixed by 'Ecto-' or 'Endo-'.

Mycota Members of the Kingdom Fungi.

Obligate A relationship between organisms that is necessary for one or both of the partners.

Parasitoid A parasite that always kills its host.

Perennating bud Buds that produce new vegetative growth.

Phylogeny How organisms are related on the tree of life.

Priority grasslands Grasslands deemed of high conservation importance, often under the UK Biodiversity Action Plan.

Protozoa A polyphyletic (not closely related) group of single-celled animals or animal-like organisms.

Rhizosphere The volume of soil around the roots of a plant or plants.

Ruderal Descriptive term for a species that colonises disturbed ground, and usually a weed.

s.l. (sensu lato) 'In the broad sense', indicating a name that encompasses a close grouping.

Saprotroph An organism that lives on dead organic matter: typically a fungus.

Semi-natural grassland Grassland that has escaped the plough and fertilisers.

Sheep walk Grassland pastured by sheep.

Specific epithet The second part of a Latinised name for an organism, and generally used as a qualifier for the Generic name.

SSSI Site of Special Scientific Interest.

Sward Turf or area of grass.

Taxonomy The study of the identification, description, naming and classification of organisms.

Therophyte A plant that completes its life cycle in one year, growing seeds for the next year or more.

Wild flower [In the context of this book] A herbaceous plant that is not a grass.

Acknowledgements

As always there are many people and organisations to thank, all of whom have supported me unstintingly and with great generosity.

First on this list is Miles King. He is a grassland specialist and a very good friend. He has taken me on many walks and is always ready to answer my numerous questions, the commonest being, 'What's this then, Miles?' He was also my expert reader for parts of the book that dealt with areas of interest that were relatively new to me. In this role he saved me from numerous and often profound embarrassments.

The second, though of equal standing, is Bryan Edwards. He is the 'knowledgeable friend' who accompanied me on many of the walks I took for this book. In the field, over dinner at my home or via a phone call he has been ever ready to answer my sometimes tiresome questions. 'Knowledgeable' is a vast understatement, as he is held in the highest esteem by all of the many naturalists who know him.

I first met Jim White at Hog Cliff some forty years ago. He was the officer from (what is now) Natural England who recognised the value of this treasured piece of grassland. Much more recently I have become a student on a few of the public grass identification walks he now takes at Kingcombe Meadows. I fancy I am not his best student. Nevertheless, thank you, Jim.

Back in 2019 I went to Grassington to see two very different grassland types. My guide in this instance was Tony Sergeant. It was an extraordinary visit – a beautiful meadow and, by stark contrast, a bleak area of calaminarian grasslands. Tony has also been kind enough to answer my many questions over the years. Also of great assistance with the chapter on Grassington Meadows was Christine Bell from the Upper Wharfedale Field Society. Thank you both.

Thank you, Eddie Bailey, for enlightening me in the messy world of geology, and for leading me by the hand through the even messier world of soil. Eddie is a professional geologist and generous with his knowledge – often too generous.

I have yet to meet Trevor Warrick, but he has nevertheless provided me with numerous records for the birds and plants of Wareham Common. Thank you, Trevor. I owe you lunch.

As you will know if you have read the text of this book, I have two unnamed friends in Derbyshire. Thank you, both, for all your help, most particularly in the form of cake.

My thanks go to the staff of the Dorset Environmental Records Centre (DERC) for supplying the species records for most of the Dorset locations I describe, and for permission to use them in this book. Without their help this book would have been virtually impossible to write. My thanks are due in turn to the dedicated people who recorded what they found and sent their records to DERC.

The Dipterist Forum kindly gave me blanket permission to use their records in this book, a kindness for which I am extremely grateful. As they noted, there is no point in their recording what appears where if no one uses this information.

My friend David Charman has been of enormous help in taking me on walks around the Hog Cliff Extension and supplying a great deal of information about the project. Thank you, David, and also Will Weldon, the exceptionally hands-on site manager.

Sid Hollier is a friend of nearly fifty years. He is also a farmer, and one of the several farmers who have assisted in my understanding of farming practice. Thanks, Sid.

Profound thanks must go to Louisa Dunnigan, my editor at Profile Books. She has steered me through my often self-inflicted travails in the writing of this book. She did this with unwarranted patience, so I owe her a great debt of gratitude.

Thanks are also due to three more editors on the Profile team: Grace Pengelly, Zara Sehr Ashraf and Georgina Difford. They too have performed their duties with skill and uncomplaining patience.

I was delighted to have Matthew Taylor as my copy-editor. I have worked with Matthew before, and his knowledge of correct form and grammar astounds me. His corrections and comments have made me realise how little of what I learned at grammar school has truly stuck.

Thank you Robert Davies, for his fine and all too necessary work of proofreading, and James Alexander for the text design. Ben Murphy has produced a thoughtful and comprehensive index, so thank you, Ben.

To Anna Howarth, who was responsible for guiding the production of this book, Hannah Ross, who has been dealing with publicity, and Rosie Parnham, who deals with the tricky business of marketing, I offer my gratitude.

Gordon Wise has been my agent and friend for nearly twenty years and his help with, and interest in, what I write has encouraged me through the years. Thank you, Gordon.

The grand finale to this litany of gratitude is my wife, Diane, for it is she who suffered most from the writing of this book. She has tolerated the two long years it took me to write it with patience, if not entirely with silence. She also accompanied me on many of my exploratory trips, taking notes as I called out the names of what I discovered. She did, however, refuse to carry the camera tripod. Nevertheless, thank you, dear Diane.

Further Reading

This short list may be helpful should you wish to explore further. It includes books on identification, history, ecology and grassland restoration. Some are out of print, some are expensive and one (the *Plant Atlas*) is a two-volume boxed set weighing in at over 8 kg!

Grasslands is supported by the website: www.grasslands.online. This contains higher-definition versions of many of the photographs in the book plus some additional photographs. There are also discussions on aspects of grasslands, 'cut scenes', and an erratum.

David Blakesley and Peter Buckley, *Grassland Restoration and Management* (London: Pelagic Publishing, 2016)

Martin B. Ellis and J. Pamela Ellis, *Microfungi on Land Plants* (London: Croom Helm, 1997)

David J. Gibson, *Grasses and Grassland Ecology* (Oxford: Oxford University Press, 2008)

H. Godwin, *The History of the British Flora: A Factual Basis for Phytogeography* (Cambridge: Cambridge University Press, 1956)

Ronald Good, *A Geographical Handbook of the Dorset Flora* (Dorchester: Dorset Natural History and Archaeology Society, 1948)

John L. Harper, *Population Biology of Plants* (London: Academic Press, 1977)

Martin Ingrouille, *Historical Ecology of the British Flora* (London: Chapman & Hall, 1998)

Peter Kirby, *Habitat Management for Invertebrates: A Practical Handbook* (Sandy: Royal Society for the Protection of Birds, 2013)

Sophie Lake, Durwyn Liley, Rob Still and Andy Swash, *Britain's Habitats: A Guide to the Wildlife Habitats of Britain and Ireland*, 2nd edn (Princeton, NJ: Princeton University Press, 2020)

Margaret Redfern and Peter Shirley, *British Plant Galls* (Telford: Field Studies Council, 2011)

Emma Rothero, Sophie Lake and David Gowing (principal eds), *Floodplain Meadows: Beauty and Utility. A Technical Handbook* (Milton Keynes: Floodplain Meadows Partnership, 2016)

Clive A. Stace, *New Flora of the British Isles*, 4th edn (Cambridge: Cambridge University Press, 2020)

P. A. Stroh, K. J. Walker, T. A. Humphrey, O. L. Pescott and R. J. Burkmar, *Plant Atlas 2020: Mapping Changes in the Distribution of the British and Irish Flora* (Durham: Botanical Society of Britain and Ireland, 2023)

Peter Stroh, Kevin Walker, Stuart Smith, Richard Jefferson, Clare Pinches and Tim Blackstock, *Grassland Plants of the British and Irish Lowlands* (Durham: Botanical Society of Britain and Ireland, 2019)

A. G. Tansley, *The British Islands and Their Vegetation*, 2 vols (Cambridge: Cambridge University Press, 1939)

Elsa Wood and Jon Dunkelman, *Grassland Fungi: A Field Guide*, 3rd edn (Monmouth: Monmouthshire Meadows Group, 2025)

Notes

Introduction

1 'Rampisham Down: A Wonderful Outcome for Conservation' (Natural England, 2017): https://www.gov.uk/government/news/rampisham-down-a-wonderful-outcome-for-conservation

2 Thomas Laessoe and Jens H. Peterson, *The Fungi of Temperate Europe* (Princeton, NJ: Princeton University Press, 2019).

3 Miles King, personal communication.

4 'Maintain species-rich grassland', https://defrafarming.blog.gov.uk /maintain-species-rich-grassland/

Part One: A Natural History of Grasslands

1 Rhys Charles, 'The Grass Divide', The Bristol Dinosaur Project, 24 September 2019; https://dinoproject.blogs.bristol.ac.uk/2019/09/24/grass-divide/

2 Later translations often (but not always) use such terms as 'vegetation', as the Hebrew is seemingly open to interpretation and the word 'grass' sometimes meant any small flowering plant. Still, I am going with the King James Version, as it is vastly more appealing than the rest.

3 I remind you at this point that, from an ecological perspective, 'improved' means that the existing, species-rich grassland is ploughed and fertilised for crops or pasture.

4 Samuel G. S. Hibdige et al., 'Widespread lateral gene transfer among grasses', *New Phytologist*, 230/6 (June 2021), pp. 2474–86 (not for the faint-hearted).

5 'A Brief History of British Woodlands', Royal Forestry Society; https://rfs.org.uk/wp-content/uploads/2021/05/7.-A-Brief-History-of-British-Woodlands.pdf

6 J. S. Rodwell (ed.), *British Plant Communities*, vol. 3, *Grasslands and Montane Communities* (Cambridge: Cambridge University Press, 1992).

7 David Davies, *The Case of the Labourers in Husbandry Stated and Considered* (London, 1795); Frederick Morton Eden, *The State of the Poor: A History of the Labouring Classes in England, with Parochial Reports*, ed. A. G. L. Rogers (London: Routledge, 1928).

8 R. M. Fuller, 'The changing extent and conservation interest of lowland grasslands in England and Wales: a review of grassland surveys, 1930–1984', *Biological Conservation*, 40/4 (1987), pp. 281–300.

9 'Review of Trends in Grasslands across the UK', prepared for Plantlife International (2023); https://www.plantlife.org.uk/wp-content/uploads/2023/07/Plantlife-report-1-Status-Trends-and-Definitions-of-UK-Grasslands.pdf

10 'Habitat Extent and Condition, Natural Capital, UK: 2022', Office for National Statistics (2022); https://www.ons.gov.uk/economy/environmentalaccounts/bulletins/habitatextentandconditionnaturalcapitaluk/2022

11 Lucy E. Ridding, Stephen C. L. Watson, Adrian C. Newton, Clare S. Rowland, James M. Bullock, 'Ongoing, but slowing, habitat loss in a rural landscape over 85 years', *Landscape Ecology*, 35 (2020), pp. 257–73 (via https://doi.org/10.1007/s10980-019-00944-2 under Creative Commons Attribution 4.0 International License).

12 'Professor Ronald Good', The Good Archive, DERC Dorset Environmental Records Centre (online); https://derc.org.uk/the-good-archive/
13 E. Duffey, M. G. Morris, J. Sheail, L. K. Ward, D. A. Wells and T. C. E. Wells, *Grassland Ecology and Wildlife Management* (London: Chapman and Hall, 1974).
14 Robert Pazúr et al., 'Changes in grassland cover in Europe from 1990 to 2018: trajectories and spatial patterns', *Regional Environmental Change*, 24/51 (27 March 2024).
15 Miles King, 'An Investigation into Policies Affecting Europe's Semi-Natural Grasslands', December 2010; www.efncp.org/download/European-grasslands-report-phase1.pdf. Reproduced by kind permission of the author.
16 'Emissions of air pollutants in the UK – sulphur dioxide (SO2)', DEFRA (2025); https://www.gov.uk/government/statistics/emissions-of-air-pollutants/emissions-of-air-pollutants-in-the-uk-sulphur-dioxide-so2
17 'Ecosyl – for consistently better silage', Forage Additives; https://uk.ecosyl.com/products
18 'Emissions of air pollutants in the UK – sulphur dioxide (SO2)'.
19 'Runaway Maize: Subsidised Soil Destruction', Soil Association (June 2015); https://www.soilassociation.org/media/4671/runaway-maize-june-2015.pdf
20 'Dogs and Nature Conservation', Lincolnshire Wildlife Trust; https://www.lincstrust.org.uk/sites/default/files/2018-03/dogs_and_nature_conservation.pdf
21 Danny A. P. Hooftman, Bryan Edwards and James M. Bullock, 'Reductions in connectivity and habitat quality drive local extinctions in a plant diversity hotspot', *Ecography*, 39/6 (June 2015).
22 P. D. Carey, 'Biodiversity Climate Change Report Card Technical Paper 5: Impacts of Climate Change on Terrestrial Habitats and Vegetation', Bodsey Ecology (2015); https://www.ukri.org/wp-content/uploads/2021/12/101221-NERC-LWEC-InfrastructureReportSource05-ImpactsTerrestrialHabitats.pdf
23 'On the "elevator to extinction": Arctic-Alpine Plants Endangered in Scottish Highlands', University of Stirling (2022); https://www.stir.ac.uk/news/2022/july-2022-news/on-the-elevator-to-extinction-arctic-alpine-plants-endangered-in-scottish-highlands/
24 'Understanding Grass Growth for Beef Rotational Grazing', Agriculture and Horticulture Development Board; https://ahdb.org.uk/knowledge-library/understanding-grass-growth-for-beef-rotational-grazing
25 Janet Mackinnon, 'Horses for nature: equids and extensive grazing in Britain', *ECOS*, 41/2 (2020); https://www.ecos.org.uk/horses-for-nature-equids-and-extensive-grazing-in-britain/
26 Hilary Kehoe, 'Carneddau Ponies – Wildlife Warriors from Snowdonia National Park', PONT; https://www.pontcymru.org/carneddau-ponies-wildlife-warriors-from-snowdonia-national-park/
27 'Impact of Moorland Grazing and Stocking Rates (NEER006)', Natural England (2013); https://publications.naturalengland.org.uk/publication/5976513

Part Two: The Denizens of the Field
1 Clive Stace, *New Flora of the British Isles*, 4th edn (London: C&M Floristics, 2019).
2 https://defrafarming.blog.gov.uk/maintain-species-rich-grassland/
3 A. G. Tansley, *The British Islands and Their Vegetation* (Cambridge: Cambridge University Press, 1939; repr. 1965).
4 John L. Harper, *Population Biology of Plants* (London: Academic Press, 1977).
5 Bodil K. Ehlers, C. F. Damgaard and F. Laroche, 'Intraspecific genetic variation and species coexistence in plant communities', *Biology Letters*, 12/1 (2016).

6 B. Bossuyt, B. de Fré and M. Hoffmann, 'Abundance and flowering success patterns in a short-term grazed grassland: early evidence of facilitation', *Journal of Ecology*, 93/6 (2005), pp. 1104–14.

7 Dora Neina, 'The role of soil pH in plant nutrition and soil remediation', *Applied and Environmental Soil Science* (November 2019).

8 Alfred E. Hartemink and N. J. Barrow, 'Soil pH – nutrient relationships: the diagram', *Plant and Soil*, 486/1–2 (2023), pp. 1–7.

9 Horst Marschner, 'Mechanisms of adaptation of plants to acid soils', *Plant and Soil*, 134 (1991), pp. 1–20.

10 Olivier Husson, 'Redox potential (Eh) and pH as drivers of soil/plant/microorganism systems: a transdisciplinary overview pointing to integrative opportunities for agronomy', *Plant and Soil*, 362/1–2 (2012).

11 Ray R. Weil and Nyle C. Brady, *The Nature and Properties of Soils*, 15th edn (London: Pearson Education, 2017).

12 'The State of the Environment: Soil', Environment Agency (2019): https://assets.publishing.service.gov.uk/media/5cf4cbaf40f0b63affb6aa55/State_of_the_environment_soil_report.pdf; 'Grasslands as a Carbon Store', Plantlife (July 2023); https://www.plantlife.org.uk/wp-content/uploads/2023/08/Grasslands-as-a-Carbon-Store.pdf

13 Jihye Jung, Jun-Seob Kim and Julian Taffner, 'Archaea, tiny helpers of land plants', *Computational and Structural Biotechnology Journal*, 18/11 (September 2020), pp. 2494–500.

14 James J. Hoorman, 'The Role of Soil Bacteria', factsheet, Ohio State University, 2011; https://symbio.co.uk/uploads/PDFs/The%20Role%20of%20Soil%20bacteria.pdf

15 Carmen Ugarte and Ed Zaborski, 'Soil Nematodes in Organic Farming Systems', eOrganic (2009); https://eorganic.org/node/4495

16 Charles Darwin, *The Formation of Vegetable Mould through the Action of Worms, with Observations on Their Habits* (London, 1881).

17 It is vastly more complicated than this as, although they do indeed drop from the gills, to enable them to do so they are first fired from the gill surface at high velocity, using finely tuned 'surface tension catapults'. There is one catapult for every spore, of which there will be billions.

18 Gareth W. Griffith and Kevin Roderick, 'Saprotrophic basidiomycetes in grasslands: distribution and function', British Mycological Society Symposia Series 28 (2008), pp. 277–99.

19 D. J. Read and J. Perez-Moreno, 'Mycorrhizas and nutrient cycling in ecosystems – a journey towards relevance?', *New Phytologist*, 157/3 (2003), pp. 475–92.

20 C. J. Clegg and D. G. Mackean, *Advanced Biology: Principles and Applications*, 2nd edn (London: Hodder Education, 2006).

21 Griffith and Roderick, 'Saprotrophic basidiomycetes in grasslands'.

22 M. J. Richardson, '*Ballocephala verrucospora* sp.nov., parasitising tardigrades', *Transactions of the British Mycological Society*, 55 (October 1970), pp. 307–9.

23 Tandra Fraser, Atul Nayyar and Walid Ellouze, 'Arbuscular mycorrhiza: where nature and industry meet', Chapter 5 of *Advances in Mycorrhizal Science and Technology*, ed. Damase Khasa, Yves Piché and Andrew P. Coughlan (Ottawa: NRC Research Press, 2009), pp. 71–86.

24 Claudia Paz, Maarja Opik, Leticia Bulascochi, Mauro Galetti and Guillermo Bueno, 'Dispersal of arbuscular mycorrhizal fungi: evidence and insights for ecological studies', *Microbial Ecology*, 81/2 (2021).

25 I reiterate: what counts as a Kingdom, Division, Class etc., where groupings are placed within these categories, or even if these concepts have real meaning, is a matter of taxonomic opinion.

26 Stefan Hempel, Carsten Renker and François Buscot, 'Differences in the species composition of arbuscular mycorrhizal fungi in spore, root and soil communities in a grassland ecosystem', *Environmental Microbiology*, 9/8 (2007).

27 Martin B. Ellis and Pamela J. Ellis, *Microfungi on Land Plants: An Identification Handbook*, new enlarged edition (London: Croom Helm, 1985).

28 J König et al., 'Hide and seek: infection rates and alkaloid concentrations of *Epichloë festucae* var. *lolii* in *Lolium perenne* along a land-use gradient in Germany', *Grass and Forage Science*, 73/2 (2017).

29 Gianfranco Cervellin, Ugo Longobardi and Giuseppe Lippi, 'One holy man, one eponym, three distinct diseases. St Anthony's fire revisited', *Acta bio-medica: Atenei Parmensis*, 92/1 (2020).

30 John Feehan and Roland McHugh, 'The Curragh of Kildare as a hygrocybe grassland', *The Irish Naturalist's Journal*, 24/1 (1992), pp. 13–17.

31 Gareth W. Griffith, J. L. Bratton and G. L. Easton, 'Charismatic megafungi, the conservation of waxcap grasslands', *British Wildlife*, 15/3 (2004), pp. 31–43; G. W. Griffith, G. L. Easton and A. Jones, 'Ecology and diversity of waxcap (Hygrocybe spp.) fungi', *Botanical Journal of Scotland*, 54/1 (2002).

32 Griffith, Easton and Jones, 'Ecology and diversity of waxcap (Hygrocybe spp.) fungi'.

33 D. Jean Lodge et al., 'Molecular phylogeny, morphology, pigment chemistry and ecology in Hygrophoraceae (Agaricales)', *Fungal Diversity*, 64/1 (2013).

34 J. Ramsbottom, 'Rate of growth of fungus rings', *Nature*, 117/2935 (30 January 1926); Peter J. Edwards, 'The growth of fairy rings of *Agaricus arvensis* and their effect upon grassland vegetation and soil', *New Phytologist*, 110/3 (April 2006), pp. 377–81.

35 Yoshie Terashima, Toshimitsu Fukiharu and Azusa Fujie, 'Morphology and comparative ecology of the fairy ring fungi, *Vascellum curtisii* and *Bovista dermoxantha*, on turf of bentgrass, bluegrass, and Zoysiagrass', *Mycoscience*, 45/4 (January 2004), pp. 251–60.

36 Maurizio Zotti et al., 'One ring to rule them all: an ecosystem engineer fungus fosters plant and microbial diversity in a Mediterranean grassland', *New Phytologist*, 227/3 (May 2020).

37 Teresa Marí et al., 'Fairy rings harbor distinct soil fungal communities and high fungal diversity in a montane grassland', *Fungal Ecology*, 47/3 (October 2020), p. 100962.

38 Peter Chandler, *Fungus Gnats (Diptera: Mycetophilidae, Mycetophilinae)*, RES Handbooks for the Identification of British Insects, 9 (Egham: CABI, 2022).

39 'Schedule 8' is the highest level of protection under the Wildlife and Countryside Act, 1981.

40 Thomas I. Wilkes, 'The influence of a soil amendment on the abundance and interaction of arbuscular mycorrhizal fungi with arable soils and host winter wheat', *Access Microbiology*, 6/1 (2024).

41 Samiran Banerjee et al., 'Biotic homogenization, lower soil fungal diversity and fewer rare taxa in arable soils across Europe', *Nature Communications*, 15/1 (January 2024).

42 This is accomplished using a remarkable technique sometimes called 'shotgun sequencing', where everything from, say, a soil sample is put in a DNA sequencer and the results are fed into a computer, which compares bits of DNA with those of known species, or at least species groups such as Genera or Families.

Part Three: One Patch of Grass

1   Our Chalk Grassland; https://www.southdowns.gov.uk/wildlife-habitats/habitats/chalk-grassland/
2   Fiona Fleming, 'Upper Frome and Sydling Valleys, West Dorset, Dorset Aerial Investigation and Mapping Project', Cornwall Archaeological Project; https://doi.org/10.5284/1120965
3   Christopher Taylor, *The Making of the English Landscape: Dorset* (Bridport: Dovecote Press, 2004).
4   Fleming, 'Upper Frome and Sydling Valleys, West Dorset, Dorset Aerial Investigation and Mapping Project'.
5   Don T. Aldiss, Andrew R. Farrant and Peter M. Hopson, 'Geological mapping of the Late Cretaceous Chalk Group of southern England: a specialised application of landform interpretation', *Proceedings of the Geologists' Association*, 123/5 (September 2012), pp. 728–41.
6   William Henry Huxley, *Nature in Downland* (London: Longman, 1900).
7   Aldiss, Farrant and Hopson, 'Geological mapping of the Late Cretaceous Chalk Group of southern England'.
8   The BGS Lexicon of Named Rock Units; https://webapps.bgs.ac.uk/lexicon/
9   John Wright, *The Spotter's Guide to the Countryside* (London: Profile, 2021).
10 William Cobbett, *Rural Rides* (London, 1826).
11 W. H. Hudson, *A Shepherd's Life* (London, 1910).
12 Daniel Defoe, *A Tour through the Whole Island of Great Britain* (London, 1724).
13 Beth Burritt, 'Ingestion of Toxic Plants by Livestock' (2013); https://www.academia.edu/77718108/Ingestion_of_Toxic_Plants_by_Livestock
14 Tansley, *The British Islands and Their Vegetation*.
15 Botanical Society of the British Isles, 'Plant Crib: Euphrasia'; https://bsbi.org/wp-content/uploads/dlm_uploads/Euphrasia_Crib_3.pdf
16 Wiltshire Core Strategy: Assessment under the Habitats Regulations, Wiltshire Council, 2013.
17 'Calcareous Grassland', https://www.britishbryologicalsociety.org.uk/learning/habitats/calcareous-grassland/
18 John Wright, *River Cottage Handbook: Mushrooms* (London: Bloomsbury, 2007).
19 Huan Zhang et al., 'Moss–pathogen interactions: a review of the current status and future opportunities', *Frontiers in Genetics* (February 2025).
20 Robert Wolton, 'Life in a hedge', *British Wildlife*, 26/5 (June 2015), pp. 306–16.
21 C. J. Smith, *Ecology of the English Chalk* (London: Academic Press, 1980).
22 A. J. Pontin, 'The numbers and distribution of subterranean aphids and their exploitation by the ant *Lasius flavus* (Fabr.)', *Ecological Entomology*, 3/3 (August 1978), pp. 203–7.
23 A. J. Pontin, 'Population stabilization and competition between the ants *Lasius flavus* and *L. niger*', *Journal of Animal Ecology*, 30 (30 April 1961), pp. 47–54; https://www.antwiki.org/wiki/Lasius_flavus
24 Tim J. King, 'The persistence of *Lasius flavus* ant-hills and their influence on biodiversity in 2 grasslands', *British Journal of Entomology and Natural History*, 3/3 (2020), pp. 215–21.
25 Antje Ehrle, 'Yellow-meadow ant (*Lasius flavus*) mound development determines soil properties and growth responses of different plant functional types', *European Journal of Soil Biology* (July 2017).
26 Timothy J. King, 'Ant-hill heterogeneity and grassland management', *Ecological Solutions and Evidence*, 2/1 (January 2021).
27 T. Parmentier et al., 'Chemical and behavioural strategies along the spectrum of host specificity in ant-associated silverfish', *BMC Zoology*, 7/1 (2022), p. 23.

28 Julio Arroyo et al., 'The mite (Acari: Oribatida, Mesostigmata) assemblages associated with *Lasius flavus* (Hymenoptera: Formicidae) nests and surrounding soil in an Irish grassland', *Biology and Environment: Proceedings of the Royal Irish Academy*, 115 (2015), pp. 17–28.
29 Franklin H. Rocha, Jean-Paul Lachaud and Gabriela Pérez-Lachaud, 'Myrmecophilous organisms associated with colonies of the ponerine ant *Neoponera villosa* (Hymenoptera: Formicidae) nesting in Aechmea bracteata bromeliads: a biodiversity hotspot', *Myremecological News*, 30 (2020), pp. 73–92.
30 UK Beetles https://www.ukbeetles.co.uk/claviger-spp
31 Smith, *Ecology of the English Chalk*.
32 Konrad Fiedler and Christine Saam, 'Ants benefit from attending facultatively myrmecophilous Lycaenidae caterpillars: evidence from a survival study', *Oecologica*, 104 (1995), pp. 316–22.
33 Leonardo Dapporto and Roger L.H. Dennis-Macfie, 'The generalist–specialist continuum: testing predictions for distribution and trends in British butterflies', *Biological Conservation*, 157 (2013), pp. 229–36.
34 https://www.nhm.ac.uk/discover/tiniest-moths-in-the-world.html
35 Andrew A. Forbes et al., 'Quantifying the unquantifiable: why Hymenoptera, not Coleoptera, is the most speciose animal order', *BMC Ecology*, 18/1 (2018).
36 Dave Hubble, *Leaf Beetles*, Naturalist's Handbooks 34 (London: Pelagic Publishing, 2017).
37 https://dipterists.org.uk/
38 https://bugmanjones.com/tag/ogcodes-pallipes/ 29 July 2016; Christian Kehlmaier, Stanislav Korenko and Radek Michalko, 'Ogcodes fumatus (Diptera: Acroceridae) reared from Philodromus cespitum (Araneae: Philodromidae), and first evidence of Wolbachia Alphaproteobacteria in Acroceridae', *Annales Zoologici*, 62/2 (2012), pp. 281–6.
39 Graham E. Rotheray, *Colour Guide to Hoverfly Larvae (Diptera, Syrphidae) in Britain and Europe* (Sheffield: Derek Whiteley, 1993).
40 Paramveer Singh et al., 'Larval feeding capacity and pollination efficiency of the aphidophagous syrphids, Eupeodes frequens (Matsmura) and Episyrphus balteatus (De Geer) (Diptera: Syrphidae) on the cabbage aphid (Brevicoryne brassicae L.) (Homoptera: Aphididae) on mustard crop', *Egyptian Journal of Biological Pest Control*, 30/1 (2020).
41 Patrick Lhomme and Heather M. Hines, 'Ecology and evolution of cuckoo bumble bees', *Annals of the Entomological Society of America*, 112(3) (October 2018).
42 Lars-Åke Janzon, 'Description of the egg and larva of Euphranta connexa (Fabricius) (Diptera: Tephritidae) and of the egg of its parasitoid Scambus brevicornis (Gravenhorst) (Hymenoptera: Ichneumonoidea)', *Insect Systematics and Evolution*, 13/3 (1982), p. 313.
43 Hans Hagen Goetzke, Jonathan G. Pattrick and Walter Federie, 'Froghoppers jump from smooth plant surfaces by piercing them with sharp spines', *Proceedings of the National Academy of Sciences*, 116/8 (February 2019).
44 S. Harris and D. W. Yalden, *Mammals of the British Isles: Handbook*, 4th edn (Gloucester: The Mammal Society, 2008).

Part Four: Pastures New
1 George Peterken, *Meadows* (London: Bloomsbury, 2013).
2 Gervase Markham, *The English Husbandman* (London, 1635).
3 'Make Field-Dried Hay or Haylage'; https://defrafarming.blog.gov.uk/make-field-dried-hay-or-haylage/
4 'Grazing for Wild Plants and Diversity: Flora Locale'; www.wildmeadows.org.uk
5 Jim White, 'The farm that time forgot', *Dorset Life* (June 2017).

6   For 'blow-ins' see Peterken, *Meadows*, p. 31.
7   John L. Harper, *Population Biology of Plants* (London: Academic Press, 1977).
8   BGS Geology Viewer.
9   UK Biodiversity Action Plan Priority Habitat Descriptions: Upland Hay Meadows, 2016; https://jncc.gov.uk/our-work/uk-bap-priority-habitats/
10 Ruth E. Starr-Keddle, 'Evaluating the success of upland hay meadow restoration in the North Pennines, United Kingdom, using green hay transfer', *Ecological Solutions and Evidence*, 3/1 (February 2022).
11 Grassington Hospital Grounds North Yorkshire; https://www.planning.data.gov.uk/entity/14501401
12 Joint Nature Conservation Committee (JNCC), Craven Limestone Complex. Designated Special Area of Conservation (SAC); https://sac.jncc.gov.uk/site/UK0014776
13 Sophie Lake et al., *Britain's Habitats: A Guide to the Wildlife Habitats of Britain and Ireland* (Princeton, NJ, and Oxford: Princeton University Press, 2015).
14 Brian Hicks and Kieron J. Doick, 'Lowland Acid Grassland: Creation and Management in Land Regeneration', Forest Research 2000; https://cdn.forestresearch.gov.uk/2022/02/lru_bpg16.pdf
15 Ibid.
16 Debbie Tann, 'Under Pressure: Is the New Forest Losing Its Wildness?', Hampshire & Isle of Wight Wildlife Trust (2019), https://www.hiwwt.org.uk/blog/debbie-tann/under-pressure-new-forest-losing-its-wildness
17 Susan M. Keay and Averil E. Brown, 'Colonization by *Psilocybe semilanceata* of roots of grassland flora', *Mycological Research*, 94/1 (1990), pp. 49–56.
18 Jonathan Cox and Richard Reeves, *A Review of the Loss of Commonable Grazing Land in the New Forest* (Eastleigh: Hampshire & Isle of Wight Wildlife Trust, 2000).
19 'UK Biodiversity Action Plan Priority Habitat Descriptions: Purple Moor Grass and Rush Pastures' (2016); https://data.jncc.gov.uk/data/6fe22f18-fff7-4974-b333-03b0ad819b88/UKBAP-BAPHabitats-43-PurpleMoorGrass.pdf
20 George Monbiot, 'Sheepwrecked', *Spectator* (30 May 2013).
21 'Call to remove sheep from the UK draws industry body anger', *The Scottish Farmer* (17 March 2023).
22 H. Marshall Ward, *Grasses* (Cambridge: Cambridge University Press, 1901).
23 (L.) Moench et al., 'Molinia caerulea', *Journal of Ecology*, 89/1 (2001), pp. 126–44.
24 'How do you solve a problem like Molinia?', *The Applied Ecologist* (March 2022).
25 Donald F. Perkins, 'Ecology of Nardus stricta', *Journal of Ecology*, 56/3 (1968), pp. 633–46.
26 Scythe Cymru, 'In Praise of Bracken'; https://www.scythecymru.co.uk/scything-guide/in-praise-of-bracken/
27 Botanical Society of Britain & Ireland, Species account: *Trollius europaeus*; https://bsbi.org/wp-content/uploads/dlm_uploads/Trollius_europaeus_species_account.pdf; Tomasz Suchan et al., 'Asymmetrical nature of the *Trollius–Chiastocheta* interaction: insights into the evolution of nursery pollination systems', *Ecology and Evolution*, 5/21 (2015).
28 Oliver Rackham, *The History of the Countryside* (London: J. M. Dent, 1986).
29 'Freshwater habitat restoration', UK Parliament Post (17 January 2024); https://post.parliament.uk/research-briefings/post-pn-0709/
30 Wareham Meadows, SSSI description of site, Natural England.
31 Ibid.
32 Andrew Kearsey and Elizabeth Cooke, 'Deep Dale Plantlife Nature Reserve, Sheldon, Derbyshire', Botanical Socety of Britain and Ireland; https://bsbi.org/events/deep-dale-plantlife-nature-reserve-sheldon

Part Five: A (Hopeful) Future of Grasslands

1   Pauline Oliver, 'The Restoration of Scrub Invaded Chalk Grassland: A Comparison of Scrub Clearance Techniques (Manual Clearance and Livestock Browsing)', PhD thesis, University of Bedfordshire, 2004.

2   This area of Manor Farm has an identity crisis in that it is now a nature reserve looking for a new name. 'Glebe Farm' was what it was sold as, but it is now informally and unromantically known as the 'Hog Cliff Extension'. It is likely to be encompassed within the 'Hog Cliff National Nature Reserve'.

3   Robert A. Robinson and William J. Sutherland, 'Post-war changes in arable farming and biodiversity in Great Britain', *Journal of Applied Ecology*, 39/1 (2002), pp. 157–76.

4   'Wheat: Yield 2023', Our World in Data; https://ourworldindata.org/grapher/wheat-yields

5   'Fivehead Arable Fields', Somerset Wildlife Trust; https://www.somersetwildlife.org/nature-reserves/fivehead-arable-fields

Picture Credits

INTEGRATED IMAGES

Kind permission to use the images on pp. 4, 60, 63, 145, 149, 155, 169, 317, 322 has been granted by Lizzie Harper (copyright © Lizzie Harper)

Page 413: Hog Cliff Plan drawn by James Alexander based on a drawing by the author

All other integrated drawings come from *A Natural History of British Grasses*, E. J. Lowe (John C. Nimmo, London, 1891, third edition)

PLATES

All images are the copyright of the author (copyright © John Wright), except for:

An Arcella amoeba; Rotifer and ciliates (copyright © Eddie Bailey)

The very local Chalk Milkwort; Mating Common Blue butterflies; Cistus Forester Moth; Marsh Fritillary; Wood Tiger Moth; Female Wilke's Mining Bee; Red-tailed Mason Bee; Waisted Bee-grabber fly; Machimus atricapillus, a robber fly; Floodplain grassland of Wareham Common; Roesel's Bush-cricket – male; Lesser Marsh Grasshopper – female; Grey-patched Mining Bee – female; Common Green Colonels – female. A soldier fly (copyright © Bryan Edwards)

A modern cornfield in Cornwall (copyright © Alamy)

Index

British Geological Survey 141
British Mycological Society 100, 125
British Wildlife 177
Bromeliaceae 58
Bronze Age 22, 137
Brooklime (*Veronica beccabunga*) 290
Broom Forkmoss (*Dicranum scoparium*)
    296
Broomrape Family (Orobanchaceae)
    154, 230, 231, 238
Brown Argus (*Aricia agestis*) 187
Brown Puffball (*Bovista nigrescens*) 170
Brown Rat (*Rattus norvegicus*) 208
Brownedge Bonnet (*Mycena
    olivaceomarginata*) 168
bryophytes (mosses, liverworts and
    hornworts) 36, 163–5, 226–7, 254,
    326
Bugle (*Ajuga reptans*) 233, 243, 322
Bulbous Buttercup (*Ranunculus
    bulbosus*) 151, 158, 232, 257, 266
bumblebees (*Bombus*) 199, 200–202, 235
Burnet Companion (*Euclidia glyphica*)
    191
butterflies (Papilionoidea) 6, 88, 108,
    152, 161, 177, 186–90, 235–7, 243,
    313, 315
Buzzard (*Buteo buteo*) 214, 294

Cabbage Family (Brassicaceae) 98, 160
calaminarian grasslands 219, 250–53
    near Grassington 250–53, *251*, *253*
calcareous (chalk and harder
    limestones) grassland (CG) 41, 76,
    79, 97, 159, 221, 271, 289, 326
    Hog Cliff and 141, 146–7, 148, 151,
        152, 156–9, 163, 165, 166, 167, 191
    lowland calcareous grasslands 25,
        221
    Malham Cove and Malham Tarn
        255–9
    northern calcareous grasslands
        296–300, *297*
    number of sites, drop in 30, 32, *32*
    upland calcareous grasslands 25,
        254–9, *257*
    waxcaps and 113–14

Camel Hill, Dorset 162, 209
Canada Goose (*Branta canadensis*) 293
Cardueae 157
Carex sp. 64, 157, 248, 273–4
Carnation Sedge (*Carex panicea*) 248
Carrion Crow (*Corvus corone*) 294
cattle 24, 39, 40, 44, 47, 49–53, 72, 95,
    114, 135, 137, 178, 189, 190, 221, 237,
    238, 261, 265, 269, 274, 277, 279–80,
    305
'Celtic' fields 22
Cepaea 203
Chalk, The 135–7, 139–55, 157, 281
    grasses and sedges of 146–7
    plants of 144–5, *145*
    wild flowers of 147–56, *149*, *155*
chalk downland 24, 25, 34, 37, 38, 46,
    232
    distribution of plants in 69, 72
    fungi communities and 117
    grazing animals and 53
    Hog Cliff and 1, 133–58, 161, 162,
        163, 165–6, 170, 178, 181–2, 188,
        202, 210, 213, 219, 254, 263
    lichens and 109–10
    mosses and 114
    rabbits and 52, 109, 210
    Salisbury Plain and 27
    restoration and arable reversion and
        312, 313, *314*, 315
    upland calcareous grassland and 254
Chalkhill Blue (*Polyommatus coridon*)
    187–90
Chalk Milkwort (*Polygala calcarea*) 152
Chamaemyiidae 196
Chamaemyia aridella (aphid fly) 196
chamaephytes 74, 155–6, 326
Cheat Grass (*Bromus tectorum*) 17
CHEGD (Clavarioids, Hygrocybe,
    Entoloma, Geoglossoids and
    Dermoloma) 114–15, 267
Chiastocheta 284
chickweeds (*Stellaria* spp.) 176
Choke (*Epichloë*) 8, 91, 105–7, 234
Christopher, John: *The Death of Grass*
    15–16
Chromista 84, 176
cicada (*Evacanthus interruptus*) 205